Summary of Contents

The Flash Anthology

Cool Effects & Practical ActionScript

by Steven Grosvenor

The Flash Anthology: Cool Effects & Practical ActionScript

by Steven Grosvenor

Copyright © 2004 SitePoint Pty. Ltd.

Editor: Georgina Laidlaw

Managing Editor: Simon Mackie

Technical Director: Kevin Yank

Cover Design: Julian Carroll

Printing History:

First Edition: July 2004

Expert Reviewer: Oscar Trelles

Technical Editor: Matt Machell

Index Editor: Bill Johncocks

Published by SitePoint Pty. Ltd.

424 Smith Street Collingwood
VIC Australia 3066.

Web: www.sitepoint.com
Email: business@sitepoint.com

ISBN 0–9579218–7–X
Printed and bound in the United States of America

About The Author

Steven Grosvenor is Senior Systems Architect for a Managed Internet Security company in the United Kingdom, and cofounder of phireworx.com, a Fireworks resource site.

Steven is a contributing author of *Fireworks MX Magic* (New Riders), *Special Edition Using Fireworks MX* (Que), and *Fireworks MX Fundamentals* (New Riders). He has also authored numerous articles on the Macromedia Developer/Designer Center, and a variety of magazine pieces.

Endeavoring to juggle a hectic home life and work schedule, while somehow keeping on top of the latest advances in technology, he nevertheless finds time to maintain *Go Flash, Go!*: SitePoint's Flash Blog.

About The Expert Reviewer

Oscar Trelles is an interaction designer based in New York and an active member of the Flash community. An independent consultant, he has a particular interest in projects that allow scope for innovation and improvement of the user experience, as well as the practice of scalable Flash and Web development. Oscar runs a blog at http://www.oscartrelles.com/, where visitors discuss, among other things, Flash development.

About The Technical Editor

A man of many talents, Matt Machell has been a Web designer, technical editor, writer, and jewelry picker. He is currently contracting in the higher education sector, producing Websites for research centers. He likes music with loud guitars and games with obscure rules. He lives in Birmingham, UK, with his girlfriend, Frances, and a horde of spider plants.

About The Technical Director

As Technical Director for SitePoint, Kevin Yank oversees all of its technical publications—books, articles, newsletters and blogs. He has written over 50 articles for SitePoint on technologies including PHP, XML, ASP.NET, Java, JavaScript and CSS, but is perhaps best known for his book, *Build Your Own Database Driven Website Using PHP & MySQL*, also from SitePoint. Kevin now lives in Melbourne, Australia. In his spare time he enjoys flying light aircraft and learning the fine art of improvised acting. Go you big red fire engine!

About SitePoint

SitePoint specializes in publishing fun, practical and easy-to-understand content for Web Professionals. Visit http://www.sitepoint.com/ to access our books, newsletters, articles, and community forums.

Table of Contents

Preface

Gone are the days when you could satisfy your clients with the creation of simple Flash effects using the timeline. Things have changed... a lot! Basic animated tweens aren't enough any longer—people expect more now, from scalable and reusable scripted animation, to external data interaction.

The problem for most fledgling developers is that, although they may know what they want to do, they don't know how to do it. Perhaps they see the ActionScript Reference Panel and Actions Panel and think, "Whoa, I'm not going near that!" This is where Flash turns most people off. New users tend to either keep to the fringes and miss out on the real power, or they leave the application alone completely. But, it needn't be that way. The use of ActionScript to create effects needn't be an overwhelming experience. In fact, from animation to video, Action-Script can help you achieve your wildest Flash goals. The process *can* be easy, provided the code's broken into manageable, bite-sized chunks.

Flash is about exploration. As you move through the examples in this book, you'll find new applications for each area we explore. With a little imagination and some more ActionScript, you'll have everything you need to create engaging, compelling effects. There's simply no need to shy away from scripted projects. Whether you're a developer or a designer, Flash has something for all levels of ability.

As I walk you though the world of scripted effects and techniques, you'll see exactly what's involved in creating each of the examples offered here. We'll pull apart the code and discuss modifications and ideas you can use to extend each of the effects we consider. These examples aren't dead-end effects created for their own sake. Each one has a variety of potential applications and deserves a place in your Flash arsenal. Soon, you'll be creating first class projects, surprised by how quickly your skills develop as you explore new possibilities and push the boundaries of your knowledge. So, buckle up and get ready to ride the Flash Anthology roller coaster!

Who Should Read This Book?

This book is aimed at beginning to intermediate Flash developers and designers who want to expand their understanding of Flash. The examples are formulated to give you a more comprehensive grasp of Flash's capabilities, encouraging you to employ scripted techniques to create scalable, impressive effects in real-world situations.

If you understand JavaScript, you should find ActionScript a natural step. If you're not familiar with either technology, don't worry! You'll soon pick up the ActionScript syntax and logic as we analyze each example.

After reading a few chapters of this book, you'll probably be comfortable enough to start creating your own modifications to the techniques we discuss. By the end of the book, you'll realize just how many different possibilities there are for Flash in your Web projects. I hope you'll be inspired to apply and experiment with the technology as you continue to develop your skills.

What's in This Book?

There's no need to read the chapters in this book in the order in which they're presented—feel free to dip into whichever interest you. Of course, you can just as easily follow the book from start to finish for a well-rounded picture of Flash and its capabilities.

Chapter 1: *Flash Essentials*
> If you're new to Flash, this chapter will give you a solid grounding in the program's interface, as well as a fundamental understanding of the Action-Script dot notation. Tips and techniques for working with ActionScript and the timeline are also included. Finally, I'll walk you through a few organizational guidelines.

Chapter 2: *Navigation Systems*
> We jump straight into some nifty examples in Chapter 2, which focuses on navigation effects. We start by asking, "What makes an effective navigation system?" We review the planning of common navigation methods, then move on to examples of horizontal, vertical, gadget-based, and advanced systems. If you've ever wanted to build compelling Flash navigation, look no further than this chapter.

Chapter 3: *Animation Effects*
> The question of whether to use timeline-based or scripted animation is one every Flash developer asks at some point. We'll explore the principles behind these effects and attempt to put the timeline vs. script debate to rest once and for all. The basic building blocks provided in this chapter will have you creating stylish animations in no time!

Chapter 4: *Text Effects*

Text effects are part of every top Flash designer's repertoire. A thoughtfully conceived and carefully applied text effect can bring life and interest to an otherwise bland interface. This chapter explores these effects in full, discussing when and how they should be applied, and providing a variety of examples to help you build everything from simple animations, to advanced, three-dimensional text productions.

Chapter 5: *Sound Effects*

One of the most underemployed, yet effective additions to a project is sound. Appropriate sound effects can enhance the impact of movement, provide feedback to users interaction, and build atmosphere. In this chapter, we analyze when sound should be used, how to choose the right sound clip for the job, and how clips can be imported and exported easily. We explore volume and panning, then build a mini sound player, random track sequencer, and much more.

Chapter 6: *Video*

If you think video should be used only in DVD and similar presentations, think again! Here, you'll discover tips and techniques for video importing and exporting, for capturing and compression, and for being creative with video in Flash. You don't have to use full-frame video; we prove this point by harnessing the power of Flash's built-in components to produce effective and subtle video effects. If you always wanted to use video in your projects, but never knew how or when, you need look no further than this chapter for information and inspiration.

Chapter 7: *Flash Forms*

Flash isn't just about fancy animation and clever navigation—it also gives you the power to create some pretty amazing form-based applications. Flash allows you to achieve everything that can be done with HTML-based forms… and then some! In this chapter, we cover form function and data validation, and explore various methods for handling the data received through the forms we build. From there, we create several complete applications, using a variety of built-in components and validation techniques to produce functional, snazzy, and robust Flash forms.

Chapter 8: *External Data*

As a Flash developer, you'll often need to use dynamic data in your projects. There are many facets to working with external data, and this chapter covers several common examples. We'll import data from an external text file in an application that resembles Post-It Notes, interface with SQL Server 2000 through a Blog reading utility, and discuss the storage of user preferences using a Local Shared Object. Whatever your data manipulation requirements, you'll acquire the building blocks you need to get the job done!

Chapter 9: *Debugging*

If your application is misbehaving and you don't know why, or you simply would like to watch your program as it progresses through complex function calls, this is the chapter for you. You'll learn to analyze what happens when good applications go bad, develop an understanding of simple, syntax-based bugs, and examine those nasty event-based problems that are so difficult to track. I'll explain the details of debugging Flash applications using the Debugger Panel and the `Error` class. We also review the `trace` function used to ensure that functions do what they're supposed to. If you have problems with Flash projects and aren't sure why, a read through this material will help you resolve them.

Chapter 10: *Miscellaneous Effects*

This chapter sounds like a mixed bag, and it certainly is! Chapter 10 covers everything that can't be pigeon-holed within the other chapters. You'll find some fantastic examples involving CSS, graphing with commercial components, and search engine optimization.

The Book's Website

Located at http://www.sitepoint.com/books/flashant1/, the Website that supports this book will give you access to the following facilities:

The Code Archive

As you progress through this book, you'll note a number of references to the code archive. This is a downloadable ZIP archive that contains all of the finished examples and source files presented in this book. Simply click the Code Archive link on the book's Website to download it.

The archive contains one folder for each chapter of the book, with both the source `.fla` files as well as the compiled `.swf` files (for quickly previewing the various effects). Wherever possible, the example files have been saved in Flash MX format for the benefit of readers who may not yet have Flash MX 2004. Of course, many of the later examples use features specific to the new version, and will therefore require Flash MX 2004 to open.

Updates and Errata

No book is error-free, and attentive readers will no doubt spot at least one or two mistakes in this one. The Errata page on the book's Website will provide the latest information about known typographical and code errors, and will offer necessary updates for new releases of Flash.

The SitePoint Forums

If you'd like to communicate with me or anyone else on the SitePoint publishing team about this book, you should join SitePoint's online community[2]. The Flash and ActionScript forum[3], in particular, offers an abundance of information above and beyond the material in this book.

In fact, you should join that community even if you *don't* want to talk to us. There are a lot of fun and experienced Web designers and developers hanging out there. It's a good way to learn new stuff, get questions answered in a hurry, and just have a good time.

The SitePoint Newsletters

In addition to books like this one, SitePoint publishes free email newsletters including *The SitePoint Tribune* and *The SitePoint Tech Times*. Reading them will keep you up to date on the latest news, product releases, trends, tips, and techniques for all aspects of Web development. If nothing else, you'll get useful Flash articles and tips. If you're interested in learning about other technologies, you'll find them especially valuable. Sign up for one or more of SitePoint's newsletters at http://www.sitepoint.com/newsletter/.

Your Feedback

If you can't find your answer through the forums, or if you wish to contact us for any other reason, the best place to write is <books@sitepoint.com>. We have an email support system set up to track your inquiries. If our support staff members can't answer your question, they'll send it straight to me. Suggestions

---

[2] http://www.sitepointforums.com/
[3] http://www.sitepoint.com/forums/forumdisplay.php?f=150

for improvements as well as notices of any mistakes you may find are especially welcome.

Acknowledgements

I'd like to thank the following people, in no particular order, for their help during the development of this book.

A big thank you to Oscar Trelles for his refreshing outlook and alternative viewpoints; to Matt Machell for his input and last minute alterations; to Georgina Laidlaw for correcting my caffeine-induced grammatical and spelling mistakes; to Simon Mackie for steering the ship in the right direction at all times over the past few months; and to SitePoint for investing the time in helping me to develop this book. Thanks also to the many other people who have helped during the development of the book—you know who you are!

1

Flash Essentials

Life without Flash would be uninteresting and mundane. Flash sites are to static HTML sites what a family-size, deep-crust pizza with all the toppings is to a piece of toast. Many of today's big-impact sites are either full-blown Rich Internet Applications (RIAs) or a prudent blend of HTML and Flash. This careful melding of technologies, coupled with seamless integration, means the difference between an online experience that's striking, and one that's utterly forgettable.

Sites that use Flash as the sole medium for conveying their message, and sites that use several mini-Flash applications to punctuate static HTML, have a common underlying theme: they all harness the power of Flash to create lightweight vector- (or coordinate-) based interfaces, applications, and animations. Flash has become a powerful tool for the communication of ideas, its capabilities having inspired a large and passionate following of dedicated users.

Why Use Flash?

The new user can approach Flash from many different angles. Designers may well be impressed by Flash's capabilities in the realms of interface design, aesthetics, and functionality. If you have a strong coding background, mathematical experimentation and the opportunity to learn new coding techniques may pique your interest. Regardless of which direction you approach it from, the technology offers something to every budding Flash developer.

Flash's inherent ability to create super-compact, vector-based animations, coupled with a powerful scripting language (ActionScript), allows users to develop complex effects, transitions, and interfaces with relative ease—something that would take many more hours, or be completely impossible, using traditional HTML and DHTML coding methods.

Flash has enjoyed several incarnations since the early days before Macromedia acquired the now ubiquitous plug-in and authoring tool, and development continues today with the recent release of Flash MX 2004 Professional. The passing years have seen the use of Flash technology shift from black art to mainstream Web development practice, as each new version of the software provides users with additional capabilities, from animation, sound, and interactivity, to application server access and video inclusion.

If a complete Flash newbie were to purchase the latest copy of Flash and install it, he or she would likely be overwhelmed by the plethora of panels, drop-down menus, and user options available. Yet, after some experimentation, and a little time spent reading the manual and online tutorials, things would start to make sense. If you're in this boat—if this is the first book you've purchased since your recent acquisition of Flash—congratulations! You're in good company. If, on the other hand, you know your way around the application and its interface, and know what you want to do but are not exactly sure how to do it, then you, too, have come to the right place. Throughout this book, I'll attempt to present methods and procedures that address the questions that are most commonly posed in online forums and newsgroups. Sure, there are thousands of examples I could show you, but the solutions I've included here are the pick of the crop. Once you understand how the examples in this book fit together, you'll be able to apply them to many different instances and situations, and use them as building blocks for other Flash applications you may create.

Flash's power springs from its dynamism and versatility. There are so many things you can do with it, from creating simple animations for inclusion in your Web applications, to building robust SQL and XML data-feeding super-applications. It can be difficult to identify a single point at which to start or stop. You could decide to create a low-bandwidth animated headline for your Website; you might choose to build the whole of your Website as a Flash application or series of Flash applications. The choice is entirely up to you. This book provides real-world examples and leading-edge techniques involving different aspects of Flash. After each example, modifications will be presented that will allow you to extend that example to suit your particular needs.

I'll assume you're using Flash MX or later, and that you have some understanding of the software. This book won't walk you through the interface and tell you what it can do; instead, I expect you have a grip on the basics, and that you're itching to start using the program to its full potential. Some of the examples in this book are specific to Flash MX 2004, demonstrating powerful techniques for getting the most out of that version in the shortest time, but the majority apply to Flash MX and above.

It's time to buckle up and turn on the ignition. Let's see what Flash has to offer!

What's New In Flash MX 2004?

Flash MX 2004 is a step above previous versions. Not only does it offer a plethora of enhancements and new features, but the software comes in two "flavours": Flash MX 2004 and Flash MX Professional 2004. Your needs will determine which version is right for you. Flash MX 2004 is the ideal instrument for developing multimedia content, or adding video, audio, graphics, or data to your projects. Flash MX 2004 Professional, on the other hand, contains additional features such as forms-based programming (much like Microsoft Visual Studio), data connectors for binding XML and Web Services to your projects, and project management tools.

If you intend to create projects that contain anything more than a modicum of ActionScript, you require connection to external data sources, or want to harness the power of advanced components, then I would strongly advise you to buy Flash MX Professional 2004. The day will come—probably sooner than you expect—when you'll need the extra horsepower it delivers. Don't get caught short!

Flash MX 2004 Features at a Glance

Let's take a look at the major improvements and new features offered by the 2004 releases. Those features marked (PRO) are available in the professional edition only.

ActionScript 2.0
A major object-oriented improvement to the ActionScript model, ActionScript 2.0 allows for strong typing and inheritance in accordance with the ECMA specifications. Don't worry if these terms are new to you—we'll discuss them in detail later.

Performance

The new version of the Flash Player has been substantially overhauled to increase playback speeds and responsiveness.

Error Reporting

The error reports generated when a Flash movie is previewed internally have been much improved in this release of the software. The reports provide more descriptive information, which makes it easier to fix show-stopping errors. See Chapter 9 for more information.

Security Model

The Flash Player security model has been improved significantly, and now provides even tighter security for your applications.

Importing

Flash developers can now import several new formats, including Adobe PDF and Adobe Illustrator 10. Flash MX 2004 also includes a Video Import Wizard to make importing video formats easier. See Chapter 6 for details on this functionality.

Spell Checking

A fantastic new feature, spell check allows you to search text within your movies for typographical errors.

Help Panel

The Help Panel includes context-based help as well as a full ActionScript reference that updates at the click of a button with the latest content from Macromedia.

New Templates

A list of new templates designed to aid the rapid development of Flash applications is available with the 2004 release of Flash. The templates include:

- ❏ Advertising

- ❏ Form Applications (PRO)

- ❏ Mobile Devices

- ❏ Photo Slideshows

- ❏ Presentations

❏ Quiz

❏ Slide Presentations (PRO)

❏ Video (PRO)

To access the templates, select File > New, and click the Templates tab.

Timeline Effects

Timeline Effects allow you quickly to create editable common effects such as exploding text, blurred animation, and opacity transitions. Due to the extended API of Flash in the 2004 editions, many third-party software vendors now create these effects for use in Flash. An excellent range of third-party Timeline Effects is available from Macromedia's online store[1], and includes Distort FX, Pixel FX, and Text FX, developed by Red Giant Software[2]. These allow you to create some mind-bending visuals from within Flash.

Behaviors

Behaviors allow you to quickly add basic ActionScript commands to your movies. They can form building blocks for your code, or you can simply use them to add interactivity without getting your hands dirty with ActionScript.

To access the Behaviors Panel, select Window > Development Panels > Behaviors.

Advanced Components (PRO)

Flash MX 2004 Professional includes a new series of components that facilitate the development of complex applications.

Flash Form Presentation (PRO)

Flash Form Presentation reflects a new development system much like that of Microsoft Visual Studio. It allows for the rapid creation of, for example, contact and registration forms. See Chapter 7 for more.

Flash Slide Presentation (PRO)

Creating slide-based applications has never been easier, thanks to the inclusion of built-in navigation to help users move through the slides.

---

[1] http://www.macromedia.com/software/flash/extensions/
[2] http://www.redgiantsoftware.com/

Data Binding and Data Connection Objects (PRO)

Flash MX 2004 Professional introduces built-in data connectors to external data sources such as Web services and XML. With the introduction of Data Binding, components such as ComboBoxes can be populated with external data relatively easily.

Source Control (PRO)

You can now easily leverage source control in your Flash projects by integrating Flash with Microsoft Visual SourceSafe. This ensures you don't overwrite work by other team members on critical projects via the 'Check-In/Check-Out' methodology.

Comparing Vectors and Bitmaps

During the early days of Web design, bandwidth was always an issue—the greater the page content, and the larger the number of images, the longer the wait for the page to render in the browser. Long download times proved to be a big turn-off for many surfers. However, as the Web evolves and high-speed connections become more commonplace in homes and workplaces, less emphasis is placed on creating super-tight pages with ultra-skinny images. Of course, it's still best practice to write concise code, and make sure your images are as small as possible, in order to keep download times to a minimum. With Flash's vector-based graphics system, you can consistently generate Web-optimized images and create low bandwidth applications. The beauty of creating images within Flash is that when you zoom into the movie, you don't experience the loss of clarity or the pixellation that occurs with traditional bitmaps. This produces a crisper look and feel, as shown in Figure 1.1.

Figure 1.1. Compare bitmap and vector image file formats.

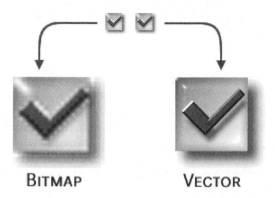

You can import traditional bitmaps into Flash, but these will obviously increase the size of the final movie. For example, if you compared a vector-based interface created within Flash to an interface built from multiple bitmaps and HTML, the Flash-developed interface file size would be dramatically lower, and the download speed significantly faster, than the bitmap-and-HTML version of the page.

Interactivity Unlimited

Flash uses an object-oriented programming language called ActionScript, which shares many themes and functions with JavaScript. As JavaScript is familiar to many Web designers, understanding the ActionScript syntax can be relatively easy. In fact, this is the case even for those without a programming background. Subsequent chapters provide a full explanation of how the application fits together, as well as the reasoning behind ActionScript code.

Designing interactive effects in Flash stumps many developers. They might have an idea of what they want to do, but they don't know how to do it, what can be scripted, or which effects require normal timeline interaction and tweening. The major advantage of creating scripted effects is that merely altering a few variables or the way a function is referenced can have a dramatic impact upon the final movie. Creating effects with traditional methods means altering the timeline, keyframes, and tweening, and can be quite daunting—especially when you're working with a large number of frames and layers. The techniques outlined in this book will involve scripted effects unless otherwise noted.

When a new user casts their eye over several lines of ActionScript, the typical response is a glazing over of the eyes. The sight of virtually any programming language can scare beginners away, but it's important to remember that Action-Script isn't difficult to understand; its learning curve is comparatively gentle. Events are triggered in three ways: buttons within the interface are clicked, certain conditions are met, or the playhead of the timeline reaches a certain frame.

While ActionScript can get very complicated, there are many ways to create quick, pleasing effects with minimal effort. Every line of ActionScript you create will help you understand further the intricacies of the language and how it can be modified to suit your needs. Every line you write will give you more confidence to undertake increasingly complex and rewarding projects.

With this in mind, let's move on to explore ActionScript's common terminology, the programming interface, and how it all fits together to create the effects you desire.

ActionScript Uncovered

ActionScript is an Object-Oriented Programming (OOP) language that interacts with a movie's objects and controls the movie's playhead. ActionScript is ECMA-262-compliant, which means it conforms to the international standard for JavaScript.

While we will examine many aspects of ActionScript, it's beyond the scope of this publication to cover every built-in function and object. The books listed below cover most of the extended functionality of JavaScript and ActionScript, and are invaluable references that should be a part of any Flash developer's library.

❑ *ActionScript: The Definitive Guide* (2nd Edition, O'Reilly)

❑ *Professional JavaScript* (2nd Edition, SAMS)

Throughout this book, I'll explain why we're using particular pieces of code; where appropriate, I'll also show how similar functions can be carried out by timeline manipulation, and why it's best practice to script them in most circumstances.

Here's a simple example that illustrates the benefits of ActionScripting and indicates how easy it is to manipulate parts of the ActionScript to alter the final outcome.

To animate an object's movement from point A to point B, you could create a movie clip of the object you want to move, create two key frames on the timeline, and tween between them to produce the movement. While this is a legitimate method for creating animation, you can instead script this process in a few lines of simple code.

Assume we have a movie clip named myMC. Adding the following ActionScript code to the main timeline moves the movie clip to the right if the horizontal position (_x) is less than 500:

```
myMC.onEnterFrame = function ()
{
  if (this._x < 500)
  {
    this._x++;
  }
};
```

Pretty simple, isn't it?

The good thing about scripting animation and other effects is that the scripts can be stored within your own script library (or a shared library), ready for inclusion in your Flash applications whenever you need them. Changing the scripts to suit your needs, rather than altering nested timelines, has obvious benefits in terms of your own productivity, and in helping you develop a reference library. To change the range of motion in the above example, we could simply alter the numeric value from 500 to some other value.

Let's take a quick look at some of the objectives ActionScript can accomplish, bearing in mind that these are just a few of its many uses. In later chapters, we'll cover many more, including some that may surprise you.

❏ Simple or complex animation effects

❏ Transitional effects

❏ Interactive user interfaces

❏ Menu systems that cannot be produced in any other medium

❏ Experimental mathematical effects

❏ Simple or complex interactive games

☐ Connection to databases or external files via a middle tier (ASP, ColdFusion, PHP, or Macromedia Data Connection Components)

ActionScript Dot Notation

ActionScript uses a special method to reference objects that appear on the stage and are embedded within movie clips and buttons. If you're familiar with JavaScript, you'll be at home with the ActionScript Dot Notation for referencing objects within your Flash movies. According to this notation, `document.layer1.form1.checkbox1.value` refers to the value of a checkbox within a form inside a layer contained in the current document.

If you're not familiar with this method of referencing objects, don't worry—it's as straightforward as falling off a bike. You'll soon pick it up!

There are three special keywords in ActionScript that can be used to address objects on the stage:

`this`   refers to the actual object to which the script is attached (i.e. itself)

`_parent`   refers to the movie clip that *contains* the object to which the script is attached

`_root`   refers to the main Flash movie, which contains the entire hierarchy of objects

In this discussion, let's concentrate on `_root`. Say you create a Flash movie that contains a movie clip called `Cloud`, which in turn contains another movie clip called `Water_Droplet_001`. To find the `alpha` property value (opacity) of the `Water_Droplet_001` clip, you could use the following ActionScript expression:

`_root.Cloud.Water_Droplet_001._alpha`

How does this code work? Have a look at Figure 1.2 below. Notice that the water droplets are contained within the cloud (i.e. they're children of the parent cloud). We reference a single water droplet—for the sake of simplicity, the first water droplet (`water_droplet_001`)—within that cloud. The reason we use the term `_root` before the object is to tell Flash to start looking from the very top of the movie hierarchy within the stage.

Figure 1.2. Understand the impact of the ActionScript dot notation.

Cloud

Water_Droplet_001
Water_Droplet_002
Water_Droplet_003

Cloud

Water_Droplet_001

_root.Cloud.Water_Droplet_001._alpha

Grabbing this value of the _alpha property of the Water_Droplet_001 movie clip, and storing it in a variable named Water_Droplet_001_Alpha, is as simple as this:

```
Water_Droplet_001_Alpha = _root.Cloud.Water_Droplet_001._alpha;
```

Objects placed on the canvas can have many properties controllable both from within, and outside, the objects themselves—all of which adds to the fun of experimentation and learning.

Actions Panel Unraveled

Actions are pieces of ActionScript code that perform specified functions. Functions that are commonly used to create basic actions within Flash include:

getURL	Sends the browser to an HTML page you specify
stop	Stops the playhead of the timeline
play	Starts the playhead of the timeline
gotoAndPlay **gotoAndStop**	Jumps the playhead of the timeline to either a labeled frame or frame number

These core ActionScript functions are among the most common you'll use to navigate to different parts of a movie. You may already have encountered them while dabbling in Flash 5 or later versions of the software. This really is just the tip of the iceberg when it comes to ActionScript. As you'll see later, it offers numerous ways to increase interaction and add special effects to your work.

ActionScript is added to the stage via the **Actions Panel**. If you've ever created a scripted animation, or any effects that use these basic methods, you will have seen the Actions Panel. In this book, it will be the single most important weapon in your arsenal, so let's go through it now to make sure you understand everything this tool places at your disposal. You can access the panel through Window > Development Panels > Actions, or by hitting **F9**.

Figure 1.3. The Actions Panel in Flash MX 2004 is your single most important weapon.

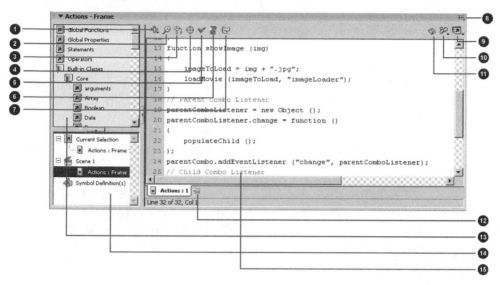

Figure 1.3 shows the Actions Panel with the following components indicated:

1 Add a new item to the script window

2 Find code

3 Find and replace (very useful)

4 Insert target path browser

5 Check syntax

6 Auto-format code (you can change formatting preferences from the Options menu)

7 Show code hint (when at a relevant point)

8 Options menu (useful in configuring code hinting, code colors etc.)

9 View options (line numbers, word wrap, **Esc** shortcut keys)

10 Debug options (see Chapter 9)

11 ActionScript reference

12 Pin active script within Actions Panel

13 Actions toolbox

⑭ Script navigator

⑮ Script pane

Actions Panel Framework

The Actions Panel doesn't offer Expert and Normal modes in Flash MX 2004 or Flash MX 2004 Professional. In earlier versions, the Actions Panel could be run in one of these two modes, toggled to from its Options menu. In Normal mode, actions could be inserted only via the menu system; Expert Mode allowed the developer to enter actions by typing directly into the Actions Panel itself. In the 2004 editions, you can add ActionScript to the Script pane only through direct input, the Actions toolbox, or the + button above the Script pane.

If you're still "finding your feet" when it comes to the Actions Panel, you aren't left completely on your own. Flash's code hinting functionality will attempt to complete your code automatically, or offer you a choice of syntax based on what you've already typed. For example, if you type "Math" within the Actions Panel, you'll be presented with a list of methods that are available for the `Math` class, ordered alphabetically from `abs` to `tan`. You can then either select the method you require from the drop-down menu or continue typing the script yourself.

Optimizing the Actions Panel

One of the important elements of working efficiently within Flash, and decreasing the development time of scripted effects, is an efficient and comfortable working environment. Now, I'm not about to tell you to vacuum your room and polish your desk (although I have to admit that before I sit down to a scripting session, I do sort my papers out and try to clear up my workspace). But remember: a tidy environment reflects a tidy mind, and tidy code is easier to understand when you come back to it at a later date.

Figure 1.4. Get to know the important options within the Actions Panel.

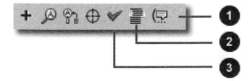

There are three major options available within the Actions Panel that are great time-savers, and will aid you in your quest for coding perfection. The buttons for these are found in Figure 1.4:

1 Show Code Hint: When you type directly into the Actions Panel and Flash suggests syntax to complete your code, you'll note that if you don't accept this suggestion, after a short time it will disappear from the screen. At other times, you may be happily coding away, only to have the ActionScript gremlins run in and steal thoughts from your brain—suddenly, you forget what you were typing! In either event, click this button to have the program display a code hint relative to your current position in the script.

2 Auto Format: After heavy code editing, additions, and deletions, the comments and formatting within your code can get a little out of kilter. A simple click of the Auto Format button will format your code beautifully, based on either preset rules or custom rules you set up, as described in the next section. This is one of the most frequently clicked buttons in my copy of Flash—it's a welcome addition to Flash MX and later versions.

3 Check Syntax: When you're examining the impact of a piece of script on the final movie, the last thing you want to see is an output window full of errors. To check your code for errors without either exporting the movie or viewing it within the internal Flash Player, click on the Check Syntax button (**Ctrl-T**, or **Command-T** on Mac). This will report any errors immediately, which can save a lot of time in the initial development phases.

Configuring Auto Format

Coming back to a piece of code you developed six months earlier can be a pleasant experience if your code is effectively formatted and commented; if not, it can be a veritable nightmare.

The Auto Format button helps keep your code in the best possible condition. While it doesn't comment code for you, it does make code readable—definitely a bonus when you're revisiting libraries of compiled code. To alter the Auto Format options to your liking, select Auto Format Options... from the Options drop-down menu in the corner of the Actions Panel. To keep your code in pristine condition, I suggest you check all the checkboxes, which will produce a similar result to that shown in Figure 1.5.

Figure 1.5. Adjust the Auto Format options to generate cleaner code.

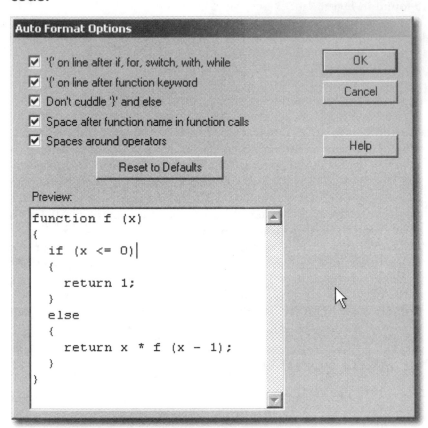

Code Commenting

There comes a time during every project, be it large or small, when you return to a line or chunk of code and think 'Hmm… what does that bit do again?' There's nothing worse than having no idea what your code does, and needing to work through it all again to make alterations or reuse it in another project. Commenting will make your code more readable, easier to navigate, and, if you work as part of a team, more easily transferred or shared via common libraries.

Comments in ActionScript are not executed when a movie is running; in fact, Flash completely ignores them. They're for *your* benefit, used to describe your code or temporarily disable sections of it.

As an example, here's a snippet I include as the first line of every function I write. I save this as a text file in the ActionScript library on my hard drive so that I don't need to retype it each time I use it. It contains a wealth of information that makes it easy for me (or any other developer) to see what the code does, what variables it will accept and/or output, and relevant revision data:

```
//-------------------------------
//Function Name: Name of Your Function
//Function Date: 15/09/2003
//Input:         Input Variables (e.g  Color Variable (String))
//Output:        Output Variables (e.g  Hex Color Reference)
//Revision Date: 28/09/2003: Added Non Numeric Error Checking
//-------------------------------
```

A double slash (//) tells Flash to ignore the remainder of a line of code. In the example above, each line of the comment begins with a double slash. You can also use this trick to temporarily disable a line of code, like so:

```
// var TestVar = _root.parentMovieClip.childMovieClip.value;
```

You can create multiline comments by starting them with /* and ending them with */. Here's what the function description would look like using that style of comment:

```
/*-------------------------------
  Function Name: Name of Your Function
  Function Date: 15/09/2003
  Input:         Input Variables (e.g  Color Variable (String))
  Output:        Output Variables (e.g  Hex Color Reference)
  Revision Date: 28/09/2003: Added Non Numeric Error Checking
  -------------------------------*/
```

This style of comment can be used to "comment out" entire blocks of code, like this:

```
/*
_root.Option_Button.onPress = function ()
{
  getURL ("http://www.google.com");
};
*/
```

Taking a little extra time to comment code will save you and others time in the long run. Once you get into the habit of commenting, you'll wonder how you ever got by without it.

ActionScript Coding Tips

There are a few key points to remember about creating functions and actions within the Actions Panel. These are by no means the be-all and end-all of best coding practices within Flash; they're merely standards that will see you spend more time developing, and less time searching for and squashing bugs.

ActionScript is Case-Sensitive

Just like the JavaScript on which it's based, ActionScript will not work as expected if it's written in the wrong case. But there are some exceptions. For example, consider the following function:

```
function TestTrace () {
  trace ("hello");
}
```

This function is completely error-free, and will output 'hello' to the Output Window when it's called. Now, even though the function name is capitalized (`TestTrace`), you can call the function without the capitalization (`testtrace`), and Flash won't complain:

```
myButon.onRollOver = function ()
{
  testtrace ();
}
```

 In Flash MX, the ActionScript compilation routine is quite forgiving—it's not case-sensitive. ActionScript will be treated as case-sensitive if you include `#strict pragma` as the first line of a script.

Just because ActionScript is forgiving with your own function and variable names, don't expect it to do you the same favors when it comes to built-in names. These mistakes will stop your code from executing and are often the most annoying and difficult to find as you introduce more code into your project. For this reason, the best policy is to always take care to use the correct capitalization.

Externalize ActionScript

Externalizing large blocks of ActionScript is a good way to separate the elements of your project and help keep your code tidy and concise. Imagine, for example, that we have a piece of navigation code that's 50 lines long. We could externalize it by cutting and pasting the code chunk into Notepad (Windows) or BBEdit (Macintosh), and saving it as `navigation.as`. We would then replace the code in the movie with this line:

```
#include "navigation.as"
```

This `.as` file would then be included in the SWF file at compilation time and need not be distributed with it.

 Tip To quickly export your ActionScript into an external file, select Export Script... from the Options menu within the Actions Panel.

Script Pinning

Because you can associate ActionScript actions with almost any element of a Flash movie, you may be working on one script fragment and need to refer to another somewhere else. Clicking the other element will display that other fragment; if you need to return to the fragment you were working on, you could easily lose your place.

To help developers avoid confusion while jumping between multiple script fragments, Macromedia has provided script pinning. Simply click the Pin Script button in the Actions Panel, and Flash will keep the currently displayed script fragment open in a tab along the bottom of the Actions Pane. You can then navigate to another element to view its script without fear of losing your place in the original script—simply click the tab to switch back to the pinned script whenever you need to. You can even pin multiple script fragments when the situation calls for it.

 note Flash MX 2004 introduces an extra pane in the Actions Panel—the script navigator pane. Located just below the Actions toolbox, this new pane allows easy navigation through all the code in a movie.

Lift and Lock

Actions can be added to the timeline within keyframes, or assigned to objects on the stage. Regardless which type of action you're creating, however, it's best practice to create a new layer, give it a meaningful name such as 'ActionScript', and lock the layer before placing your ActionScript in it. This way, you can easily see the objects containing ActionScript and navigate to them without having to open the Movie Explorer.

Naming Conventions

When you write code, create functions, or name layers and folders, there is a set of best practices that you should try to implement. Some of these are common sense; others are not so obvious. None of these conventions is essential, but by following these simple guidelines and other suggestions in this chapter, you should be able to organize your Flash projects successfully.

Do	Do Not
❏ create filenames that relate to the purpose or goals of the Flash project	❏ use acronyms that make little or no sense
❏ create names for functions and variables that indicate their roles in the project	❏ shorten filenames
❏ use underscores to separate words; avoid hyphens	❏ create function, file, or variable names that require a Masters degree in Particle Science to decrypt
❏ be consistent in your application of the naming system you decide to use	❏ use spaces or merge words together

The Timeline, Simplified

In our reality, time can only go forward (though some may argue otherwise!); the same is not true in Flash. The playhead within the timeline can move forward and backward—it can even jump frames. The Flash timeline is integral to creating effects, and all Flash movies use the timeline, even if only for the first frame. The introduction of Timeline Effects in Flash MX 2004 has made it very easy to create rapid animations and transitional effects within your projects. With basic Action-

Script, you can start the playhead, play an animation, and send the playhead back to the beginning of the timeline to play again. And, with only slight modification, you can add an auto-incrementing counter to either conditionally jump to another point on the timeline or return to the start of the timeline. It's simple to create basic effects and build them up into something extraordinary.

Timeline Effects also make it easier to develop complex effects that are transferable to other projects or collaborators. Indeed, this concept of scalability should always be considered at the start of a project. Before you begin, ask yourself, "Will I easily be able to use this effect again in the same movie, or another project, without extensive recoding?" If the answer is no, you need to identify ways to make it scalable.

The easiest path to scalability is to invest a little time in scripting common tasks. If you can animate an object using four lines of ActionScript that represent a re-usable function or snippet, go for it! This approach makes for easier maintenance than a script containing multiple duplicated, nested movie clips in which the variables may clash.

Ask yourself these questions before creating a new effect or starting any project:

1. Will multiple effects occur on the stage at the same time?

2. Will I use the same effect more than once in the movie?

3. Can I script the effect I wish to create?

4. Can I make the effect easily portable between projects?

5. Can I easily add new functionality to the effect?

6. If the clients or I don't like the effect, can I easily tweak it?

You can create complex effects using the timeline—in fact, before the release of Flash 5 and later versions, this was the only way to do so. Even today, most of the animation effects we see rely on timeline tweening between frames to create animation, movement, and opacity fading. The combination of Timeline Effects and ActionScript can be a powerful one, but this approach also has a technical advantage. Effects developed this way are more 'tweakable;' changing a few settings here and there impacts the final product considerably in very little time.

The importance of the timeline should not be underestimated. Every single object, from layers to movie clips, is present within the timeline when it's added to the stage. Take some time to become familiar with the best practice principles for working with the timeline.

Label Me Up

After a weekend or holiday, how long does it take you to come to terms with the Flash projects you left behind? Organization is the key to minimizing this "re-familiarization" time. There's no excuse for sloppy code or disorganized Flash projects. Invest a little extra time at the start of a project, add elements with care, and you'll reap the rewards when you return to it after time away or hand it over to your colleagues.

I advocate the creation of a layer named 'Labels' to hold commentary, conditions, and pointers as to what's happening at each step on the timeline. This process is as simple as selecting a frame from the timeline, and adding a Frame Label within the Property Inspector. Maintaining these rolling labels allows you to see what's happening within your movies—you can even add small notes, for example, to remind yourself that code requires alteration, or graphics need to be swapped out.

 Flash MX 2004 allows you to efficiently alter the frame label type. To change a name, label, or anchor's representation within the timeline, simply click the drop-down box that appears beneath the frame label within the Property Inspector.

Adding a Labels layer keeps this information separate and helps you organize your thoughts regarding timeline planning.

Organize Your Layers

In Flash version 5 and earlier, users had the ability to organize work into distinct layers within the timeline. This facility was extremely helpful for separating out design components within the stage. A little planning and organization of these layers can benefit you both during the initial development process and when re-visiting a project at a later date.

In Flash MX and Flash MX 2004, you can organize these layers into discrete folders. Let me show you how this seemingly small enhancement can improve your workflow.

Let's say you've been working for a while on a project that has many movie clips, buttons, and bitmaps on the stage. You're using many layers, though they're not organized into any particular format, and you're scrolling up and down the timeline window to access them as you go. To make matters worse, the project is growing more complicated, which means more layers and even more scrolling. Fear not—this is all about to change! Figure 1.6 shows how you can create and organize folders into discrete compartments, placing relevant layers within each. When you finish editing a folder, just click the arrow next to it to roll it up and give yourself more space within the timeline. As the projects you undertake become more involved and larger, the improved efficiency you can gain from this approach will become self-evident.

In adding components to a project, I usually start with a standard framework. I have a folder containing two layers—one for ActionScript, the other for labels. I have another folder for Animations, which is then subdivided into relevant sections, and a folder for static imagery. Obviously, you can change this structure to suit your development needs and personal preferences.

Figure 1.6. Organize folders and layers with ease in Flash MX and Flash MX 2004.

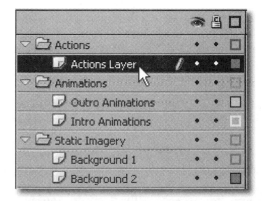

Timeline Effects (New in Flash MX 2004)

New within Flash MX 2004 is a much-anticipated addition to the arsenal of experienced programmers and non-programmers alike: Timeline Effects. These are available from the Insert menu after you've selected an object from the stage. You can access them at: Insert > Timeline Effects > Effect.

There are several effect categories, each containing many possible choices:

- ❏ Blur

- ❏ Expand

- ❏ Explode

- ❏ Fade In

- ❏ Fade Out

- ❏ Fly In

- ❏ Fly Out

- ❏ Grow

- ❏ Shrink

- ❏ Spin Left

- ❏ Spin Right

- ❏ Wipe In

- ❏ Wipe Out

We'll cover these in depth, and see how they can be used to create engaging effects, in Chapter 4.

Traditionally, to fade the opacity of an object from completely transparent to completely opaque, I would access the timeline and tween between two instances of a movie clip, altering the alpha values accordingly. Though functional, this technique can be quite time-consuming and fiddly, especially if you're looking to build an effect with multiple movie clips fading in, in a stepped manner, to produce a blur. The addition of Timeline Effects provides developers a large degree of control over setup parameters. With so many of these at your disposal, it's quick and easy to create compositions for yourself or for presentation to clients.

Figure 1.7 shows that many properties are available within the Fade In command. Straight out of the box, the effect can be applied and previewed within a matter of seconds, shaving considerable time off the old techniques, especially if you're using multiple iterations of the same effect. Combining Timeline Effects often produces unexpected yet pleasing results. The key to creative success is, as always, to experiment until you're happy with the outcome.

Figure 1.7. Edit the Fade In Timeline Effects parameters within Flash MX 2004.

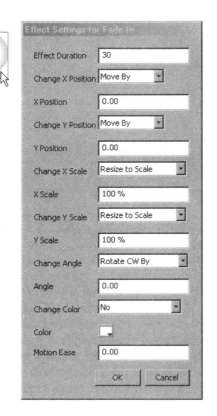

Wrapping Up the Basics

We've covered the basics of ActionScript and the Timeline, and discussed best practices for both. Now it's time to apply these tactics to create stunning effects that are appealing, easily transferable among projects, and fun to explore and expand. In the next few chapters, we'll cover a range of subjects, with examples, suggestions, and explanations of techniques that will prove invaluable in your day-to-day Flash projects.

Reduce Confusion

Avoid creating duplicate links to any page from a given portion of your interface; you may end up perplexing users, who will likely leave the site dissatisfied.

Maximize Your Hierarchy

Plan the structure of your navigation, reducing the number of levels in the hierarchy to a bare minimum without compromising the site's usability. This approach makes even the most distant parts of your site accessible. As content is located further from the top level of your hierarchy, users are less likely to click through to that content.

Don't be too "Out There"

Navigation relies on users' understanding of common concepts. Don't be too swift to discard this common knowledge—it can work in your favor. Force users to search for a navigation system that they don't recognize as an interactive element, and you risk driving them from your site. This doesn't mean, however, that you should be afraid to push the creative envelope. The answer? Try to balance innovative design with practicality. Ask the question, "If I were a visitor, could I use this navigation without undue effort?" If the answer is no, don't discard your system; save it for later or revise it until it is usable.

Keep it Simple

Don't complicate your interface with unnecessary clutter that will confuse users. The more options you present, the longer it will take visitors to assess them and make a selection. Make the purpose or destination of each navigation item self-evident. Make it obvious which parts of the interface are clickable, and which are not. If a design element looks like part of the navigation, then it should act accordingly. If it isn't part of the navigation, remove it or shift the focus of the design away from it. Provide visual or auditory feedback to users so they know, for example, when they've clicked a button. Don't let them click away at your navigation under the misperception that nothing's happening.

Test Usability

The person who develops an application is not a good testing subject. Having designed an interface, you'll be familiar with it, and have a clear idea of what each item in the navigation does. Thus, the route you take may not be indicative of a true user experience. The best people for testing an application are non-biased end-users. If you have a Website, you can easily invite people to join a beta testing program online.

Inviting visitors to become beta testers encourages them to test your application to destruction. You may get the odd rogue comment, but the majority of the feedback could prove invaluable.

Good Team Members Make Bad Testers

Thinking about testing your application on other members of your team? Don't! They are likely to have a mindset similar to yours. While they may be able to spot some obvious issues, they will not provide as objective a review as will your potential customers or clients.

Planning Navigation

Planning is an important step in the navigation design process, yet many developers will launch into designing a navigation system or effects without giving any thought to the goals they want to accomplish. Planning gives you the opportunity to identify and overcome potential problems or constraints, and to address any specific requirements before you even open Flash.

There's more than one way to skin a cat, and it's the planning stage that allows you to identify the best methods for creating effects. This, in turn, increases your efficiency within the design environment when you actually begin construction. With planning, you can dismiss certain methods as too time-consuming and identify problem areas that you may not have noticed otherwise. All in all, a little preparation goes a long way, saving you time, and helping you distill ideas prior to experimentation and development.

Make a Process Flow Chart for Your Navigation

Sketch out on paper, or within a design package, the structure of your navigation, the options available within it (including primary, secondary, and tertiary levels of navigation), and how they'll all fit into your interface.

Keep Track of your Old Ideas

Tip

I have a collection of several hundred Post-It notes that contain preliminary sketches of interfaces and navigation designs I've created in the past. Often, the means to build these systems were not available at the time, but I frequently find myself referring back to those plans as technology advances.

Figure 2.1 is a representation of the flat navigation structure of a Fireworks MX resource site that I run. It's simple, effective, and to the point. As you can see, this design caters perfectly to the number of top level navigation options the site has—none of the categories of information is more than a single click away.

Figure 2.1. This simple flat navigation structure was developed for phireworx.com.

Once you've sketched out the structure of your navigation and developed the pseudocode[2] you'll need for the project, you've done 60% of the work! The steps you've taken to get to this point will help you avoid wasting time. If you dismiss the planning stage, you may discover at a later point that it needs extensive rework because, for example, you forgot you needed an extra level of navigation. Planning is an essential first step—don't skip it!

Figure 2.1 shows a simple navigation system. Move your cursor over any of the icons in the menu and you'll trigger the appearance of a description that slides into place. As you move your cursor away from an icon, the description changes from the highlighted option to a placeholder title. Figure 2.2 represents the process flow diagram for this navigation system.

---

[2]Pseudocode is a tool used by developers to outline the structure of their code in the same way graphic designers sketch out ideas for a design. By simply writing down what you want your code to do, one step at a time, in plain English, you can plan how it will work without having to focus on the details of syntax.

Figure 2.2. This process flow diagram depicts the navigation structure used at phireworx.com.

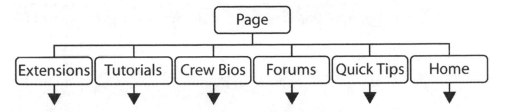

There's no need for a complicated navigation structure on this site. Adding secondary menu items to the primary navigation, however, would require that attention be paid to the rules for effective design discussed previously.

Common Navigation Methods

Choosing a method of navigation is not always easy. Sometimes it is rigidly dictated by a client; at other times, it might be influenced by the layout of the interface, restrictions on screen space, or even the theme of the site. Let's examine several major styles of navigation.

Horizontal Navigation

Horizontal navigation systems are both common and versatile. They come in a variety of different guises, from tabbed interfaces using simple flat buttons (for example, the menu at Amazon.com), to incredibly dynamic scrolling systems such as that of MONO*crafts version 2[1], depicted in Figure 2.3.

---

[1] http://www.yugop.com/ver2/

Figure 2.3. This advanced horizontal navigation is found on V2.0 of the MONO*crafts Website.

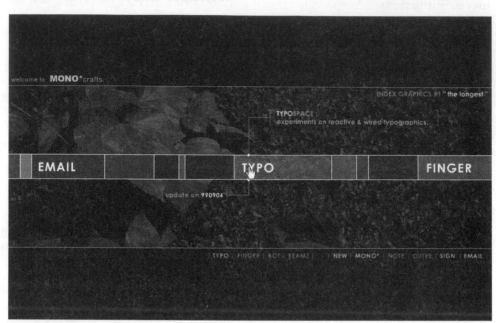

The MONO*crafts navigation system, created with a much earlier version of Flash, is now nearly four years old. It's obvious that a lot of work went into its planning, control code, and execution. One of the most revolutionary systems of its time, the MONO*crafts navigation is extremely well known. It still serves as a benchmark for fitting a large amount of information into a relatively small space. Here are a couple of pointers for creating effective horizontal navigation:

- [ ] If you're designing a navigation system that extends beyond the width of the browser (i.e., a scrolling navigation system), add more time to the project to allow for the development of scrolling code.

- [ ] In designing a scrolling navigation system, don't sacrifice usability for the sake of experimentation; always try to think like an end user.

Vertical Navigation

Vertical navigation has been tried and tested, and, through this process, has become a widely-accepted means of presenting navigation options in a highly usable format. There are many different ways to present menu items via this method, as we'll see later in this chapter when we create a simple yet effective vertical menu. But first, here are some basic tips to bear in mind when employing vertical navigation:

- ❏ Don't create an unnecessarily wide navigation system. Though it might look good, it will only reduce the amount of space available for the rest of the content.

- ❏ Do not place individual navigation elements too far apart, as the user will get click fatigue (not to mention sore fingers).

- ❏ Design for the amount of space you have available. Don't condense your menu into a height of 50 pixels if you don't need to. Instead, attempt to meld the design with the number of items in your navigation.

For an example of effective vertical navigation, see Moluv's Picks[2]. The site provides exposure for Flash sites that are well designed and functional, and push the boundaries of convention. Its navigation design is quite unusual. Move your cursor over the list of sites and a popup box appears, displaying more information about that site (including a highlight of the design, the submit date, the name of the person who submitted the link, etc.). If you're lacking inspiration, or interested to see how others use Flash, I advise you take a look at this site as well as those it links to; you won't be disappointed.

Gadget-based Navigation

Gadget-based systems are among the most difficult to create. They don't fit neatly into the definitions of horizontal or vertical navigation, as they can contain qualities of both. This method encompasses the unconventional, the experimental, and the nonconformist.

Gadget-oriented navigation maximizes the use of available screen space. Though the system might be tucked away in one corner of the screen, upon moving your cursor over or clicking on it, the full menu may well explode into view, fading once you've moved your cursor elsewhere. Of course, this is just one example—the only barriers to what you can create are your imagination, and the usability of the finished menu.

---

[2] http://www.moluv.com

Now that we've discussed the basics, it's time to roll up those sleeves and get our hands dirty! In the next few sections, we'll explore the steps involved in building each type of navigation system. By the end of this discussion, you should have a solid understanding of the requirements and code needed to construct them.

Horizontal Navigation

Let's say you've opted for a horizontal navigation system, seen a few examples you like, and know what you want to create. How do you go about building it? The following examples show you how to achieve great results painlessly.

Simple Horizontal Navigation

The simplest of all navigation systems is based on a flat structure with only a single level, as shown in Figure 2.4. We'll start with the basics, then move into more complex examples that extend and modify this framework.

Figure 2.4. Create this simple navigation structure.

If you're in a hurry, the finished example is `horizontal.fla` in the code archive.

Setting the Scene

To begin, let's build some simple buttons:

1. Open Flash MX or a later version of the software and create a new movie (**Ctrl-N** on PC, or **Command-N** on Mac). Select Modify > Document…, then set the height to 30 pixels and the width to 300 pixels to create a compact navigation area.

2. We will now create four navigation buttons of equal size (30x30 pixels). Select Insert > New Symbol…, enter the name `Option_Button`, and select Button as the Behavior.

3. With the Rectangle Tool (**R**) selected and in position on the Up frame of the button, select a fill color that's light blue with a black stroke. Drag out a 30x30 pixel square[3].

4. Using the Subselection Tool (**A**), select the square, press **Ctrl-C** (**Command-C** on Mac) to copy the object, and move along the timeline to the Over frame. Press **F6** to insert a new keyframe, then select Edit > Paste in Place to paste the square at exactly the same position in the new frame.

5. With the Selection Tool (**V**), select the space inside the rectangle on the Over frame, and change the color to light gray (see Figure 2.5).

6. Repeat step 4 within the Down frame, leaving the color light blue.

7. Select the Hit frame, and press **F6**. This will add another keyframe and automatically copy the contents of the previous frame to the new one. The button will now know when the cursor is above it.

8. Add another layer above the existing one and name it Option_Button_Text. Using the Text Tool (**T**), insert the number 1 as the label for the button within each frame that has keyframes, except the Hit frame, which you can leave blank. Alter the color to suit your tastes.

---

[3]If your mouse work isn't pixel perfect (and really, whose is?), you can size the square precisely by double-clicking it with the Selection Tool and typing the desired dimensions in the Property Inspector.

Figure 2.5. Create the buttons for the simple navigation system.

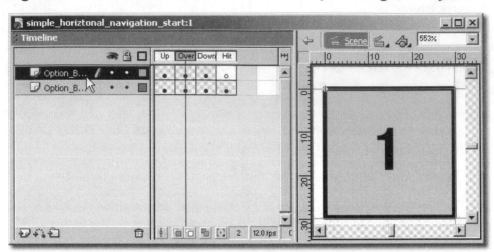

Now that we've created a master copy of the button, we can use it to rapidly create other buttons.

9. Navigate back to the root of the scene, and select Window > Library to open the Library Panel. Create a new folder named 001-Buttons, and move the `Option_Button` button into this folder.

10. Select the `Option_Button` button within the Library Panel, then right click and select Duplicate, naming the copy `Option_Button_2`.

11. Double-click `Option_Button_2` within the Library panel, and alter the text in all the frames to 2.

12. Repeat steps 2 and 3 until you have four buttons, numbered 1 to 4.

We've finished creating the four buttons that will form the basis of our navigation. Now it's time to arrange them appropriately on the stage.

13. Create a new folder named Interface Components on the timeline, and create a new layer called Buttons within this folder.

14. With the Buttons layer selected, drag each button from the Library Panel to the stage, and arrange them left-to-right from "1" to "4," with the last button against the right-hand side of the stage. Select each button instance and assign it the name of its parent symbol, which remains in the Library

Panel. If you preview the movie now, you will see the simple rollover effects on each of the buttons.

Congratulations! You've created a simple navigation system with a logical structure, and followed best practices for keeping your Library Panel and timeline well-ordered. As you'll see in a minute, we can now start adding ActionScript effects to the mix to spice things up!

It was relatively straightforward to create those buttons and simple rollover effects, but they don't actually navigate anywhere! To add links to our buttons, we can simply flip open the Actions Panel and add the following ActionScript to the first frame of the movie:

```
_root.Option_Button.onPress = function ()
{
  getURL ("http://www.google.com/");
};
```

As we saw in Chapter 1, _root refers to the top-level Flash movie. So _root.Option_Button.onPress refers to the onPress event handler of the button named Option_Button in our movie. This is the function that will be called whenever the user clicks on that button. The above sample code uses the getURL function to send the browser to http://www.google.com/ when the button is clicked.

Of course, the buttons' labels—the numbers 1 to 4—don't actually mean anything. As the buttons are too small to display much text, it might be a good idea to make them icons of some sort, like the navigation we saw in Figure 2.1. You may have noticed that the buttons take up only a small portion of the navigation space—there's a huge gap to the left of them. This isn't a mistake; that area will be used to display information. As a user moves the cursor across each button, a description of the content the button links to will appear in that blank space. Let's work on this area next.

To create the illusion of movement, we'll build a large movie clip to contain all the button descriptions. This will shift horizontally to reveal the description for the button over which the cursor is positioned.

15. Create a new movie clip symbol named Information_Area with Insert > New Symbol....

16. If rulers aren't already switched on, select View > Rulers, and add five guides at 0, 200, 400, 600 and 800 pixels. To add guides, left-click and hold down your mouse button in the left-hand ruler, then drag the cursor to the appro-

priate location on the stage. These guides will help you place the text elements accurately within the information area.

17. Add new text elements at the designated locations (x=0, y=-4), (x=200, y=-4), (x=400, y=-4), (x=600, y=-4), and (x=800, y=-4), with the text `Information Area` and `Option 1` to `Option 4`, as shown in Figure 2.6.

18. Return to the main scene and create a new layer called Information Area within the Interface Components folder at the root of the timeline.

19. Drag an instance of the new movie clip from the Library Panel onto the stage. Name the instance `InfoMC`, and place it at (x=20, y=6).

Figure 2.6. Create the `Information_Area` movie clip.

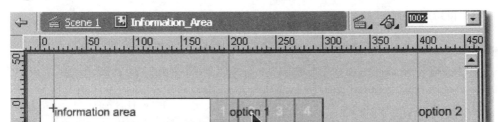

Now that we've created the information area, we'll add control code to have it move in response to user input.

Adding the ActionScript

With the basics out of the way, it's time to get scripting! We need to show information to users as they move the cursor over each of the menu options. We could just flash the information onto the screen in a plain and understated manner, but what would be the fun in that? Instead, we'll construct a sliding information area complete with friction so the information slows down as it moves into place. It's time to get our hands dirty with a little ActionScript.

20. Create a new folder above the existing one located in the root of the timeline, and name it Actions. Within this folder, create a new layer called Actions, and open the Actions Panel by selecting Window > Actions or pressing **F9**.

21. Enter the following code into the Actions Panel, within the first frame of the new Actions layer you just created:

File: **horizontal.fla**   Actions : 1

```
//-----------------------------
//Horizontal Information Area Slider
//Revision Date:  22/04/2004
//-----------------------------
//Global Variables for Sliding Area
_global.speedFactor = 0.3;
_global.InfoStartXPos = InfoMC._x;
_global.InfoXPos = InfoStartXPos;
// Create an array for the positions of the information area
_global.InfoMC_X = new Array (-160, -360, -560, -760);
function InformationSlideTo (number)
{
  InfoXPos = InfoMC_X[number];
}
function InformationSlideBack (number)
{
  InfoXPos = InfoStartXPos;
}
//Code for Buttons
//Option_Button
Option_Button.onRollOver = function ()
{
  InformationSlideTo (0);
};
Option_Button.onRollOut = InformationSlideBack;
Option_Button.onPress = function ()
{
  getURL ("http://www.google.com/");
};
//Option_Button_2
Option_Button_2.onRollOver = function ()
{
  InformationSlideTo (1);
};
Option_Button_2.onRollOut = InformationSlideBack;
Option_Button_2.onPress = function ()
{
  getURL ("http://www.google.com/");
};
//Option_Button_3
Option_Button_3.onRollOver = function ()
{
```

```
    InformationSlideTo (2);
};
Option_Button_3.onRollOut = InformationSlideBack;
Option_Button_3.onPress = function ()
{
  getURL ("http://www.google.com/");
};
//Option_Button_4
Option_Button_4.onRollOver = function ()
{
    InformationSlideTo (3);
};
Option_Button_4.onRollOut = InformationSlideBack;
Option_Button_4.onPress = function ()
{
  getURL ("http://www.google.com/");
};
InfoMC.onEnterFrame = function ()
{
  this._x -= (this._x - InfoXPos) * speedFactor;
};
```

That's quite a chunk of code! It's placed at the root of the movie, where we set the variables and house the main functions that will be triggered by cursor movements. Let's look at what's occurring here.

First, we define some global variables to hold important information that will control the way the animation works:

```
//Global Variables for Sliding Area
_global.speedFactor = 0.3;
_global.InfoStartXPos = InfoMC._x;
_global.InfoXPos = InfoStartXPos;
```

This is a series of variables that is initially set when the movie loads, and includes:

speedFactor   This variable identifies the fraction of the distance between the current and target positions that the InfoMC clip travels per frame. Feel free to adjust this to your taste, but it should be kept between 0 and 1.

InfoStartXPos   We use this to record the starting horizontal position of the InfoMC movie clip (InfoMC._x).

InfoXPos
This identifies the horizontal position to which we want the clip to move. Initially, it is set to `InfoStartXPos`.

We make each of these variables globally accessible by declaring them as properties of the `_global` object. This allows us to access them anywhere in our movie simply by using their names, instead of having to specify where the variables were declared.

We then define another global variable containing an array that holds the desired horizontal position of the `InfoMC` movie clip for each of the four buttons:

```
_global.InfoMC_X = new Array (-160, -360, -560, -760);
```

Next, we define a couple of functions that will tell the `InfoMC` movie clip where to go. The `InformationSlideTo` function is called when the user rolls over one of the option buttons. It sets the `InfoXPos` variable to the value from the `InfoMC_X` array that corresponds to the specified button.

```
function InformationSlideTo (number)
{
  InfoXPos = InfoMC_X[number];
}
```

Similarly, `InformationSlideBack` is called when the cursor leaves the hit area of a button. It sets the target position of the movie clip to its initial position, which we stored in `InfoStartXPos`:

```
function InformationSlideBack (number)
{
  InfoXPos = InfoStartXPos;
}
```

Next, for each of our four buttons, we assign event handlers to respond to the cursor moving over the button (`onRollOver`), leaving the button (`onRollOut`), and clicking the button (`onPress`). This is the code that assigns these event handlers for the first button:

```
Option_Button.onRollOver = function ()
{
  InformationSlideTo (0);
};
Option_Button.onRollOut = InformationSlideBack;
Option_Button.onPress = function ()
{
```

```
  getURL ("http://www.google.com/");
};
```

For the `onRollOver` event handler, we create a new function that calls `InformationSlideTo`, passing the number of the button. For the `onRollOut` event handler, we can simply assign the `InformationSlideBack` function to handle the event directly, since we don't need to pass any special parameters to the function. Finally, the `onPress` event handler is a function that calls the `getURL` function to send the browser to a new URL—in this example, http://www.google.com/.

When a user moves the cursor over the first button (`Option_Button`), `InformationSlideTo` is called with a parameter of `0`. The function uses this parameter to pull a value of `-160` out of the array. This value is set as the x coordinate to which the `InfoMC` movie clip moves. This movement slides the informational text for the first button into view on the stage. Taking the cursor off the button causes a similar series of events to occur, ultimately resulting in the movie clip sliding back to its starting position.

The one missing element here is the code that actually moves the movie clip towards the target location stored in the `InfoXPos` variable. This takes the form of an `onEnterFrame` event handler for the `InfoMC` movie clip. Flash will run this event handler once for every frame of the animation:

```
InfoMC.onEnterFrame = function ()
{
  this._x -= (this._x - InfoXPos) * speedFactor;
};
```

This function calculates the difference between the current horizontal position of the movie clip (`this._x`) and the target position (`InfoXPos`), multiplies that by the `speedFactor` global variable, and then subtracts that value from the clip's horizontal position. This calculation makes the clip start moving relatively quickly. But, gradually, the distance it moves within each frame is reduced, which gives a fluid quality to the motion.

Make the animation smoother

Tip

To increase the smoothness of the animation, increase the frame rate of the movie. As the effect is based on the `onEnterFrame` event handler, this will increase the smoothness and speed of the movie. To alter the frame rate, select Modify > Document... and change the frame rate to 24 fps. To maintain the same speed with an increased frame rate, you'll need to reduce the `speedFactor` variable.

Save your movie, then preview it by selecting Control > Test Movie (**Ctrl-Enter**). You should see the information area sliding smoothly into place as you move the cursor over the option buttons. You have now completed quite a complex scripted animation that is modular, efficient, and—best of all—looks good!

Modifications

Because this effect is scripted, it's easily modified. By editing the global variables, you can quickly alter the speed of the animation or add new effects, such as scripting the opacity to fade in and out. Give it a try!

Conclusion

You have created a simple navigation system that's easy to maintain, easy to modify, and looks good. Navigation doesn't need to be overly complex to be effective; in fact, subtlety is often more appealing. As long as your system conveys the right message and gives users the information they require to move around your site, it will be a success. Try using this example as a starting point to see what other effects you can create.

Silky Fading Opacity Effect

Figure 2.7. The silky fading opacity effect is subtle and effective.

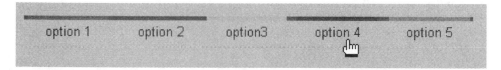

In this example, we'll create a series of navigation items that fade in and out based on user interaction. You could create a similar effect using a series of tweened alpha animations, but it's easier and more scalable to achieve this with script.

Our objective is to create several buttons on the stage and have a subtle background effect fade into view when users roll over them. When the user rolls off the button, the background effect will fade to its original transparency.

The finished effect is called `silky.fla` in the code archive.

Setting the Scene

1. Create a new movie with dimensions of 445x30 pixels, and give it a gray (#CCCCCC) background. Save the file under a name of your choice.

2. Create the folder and layer structure shown in Figure 2.8. This will hold the actions, buttons, movie clips, and background for this navigation system.

Figure 2.8. Create the folder and layer structure for the movie.

3. Open the Library Panel and create two new folders: 001-Buttons and 002-Movie Clips. These will hold all the library items. The stage is now set, organized, and ready for action!

Now, we need to create a series of buttons. The button event handlers will trigger the fading in and out of the scripted opacity effect for each of the movie clips. Each button will sit directly above a movie clip that we wish to fade in and out of view.

4. Start by creating a new button symbol (Insert > New Symbol...), and naming it appropriately (e.g. Button 1). Insert a relevant label and copy content into the Up, Over, Down and Hit states of the button. As you can see in Figure 2.9, I've created a Down state effect for the button. When it's clicked upon, a color-coded chip at the top will extend downwards, and the button label will move down by a couple of pixels. If you do this, make sure the color chip is exactly 80 pixels wide.

Figure 2.9. Create the buttons that will trigger the opacity effect.

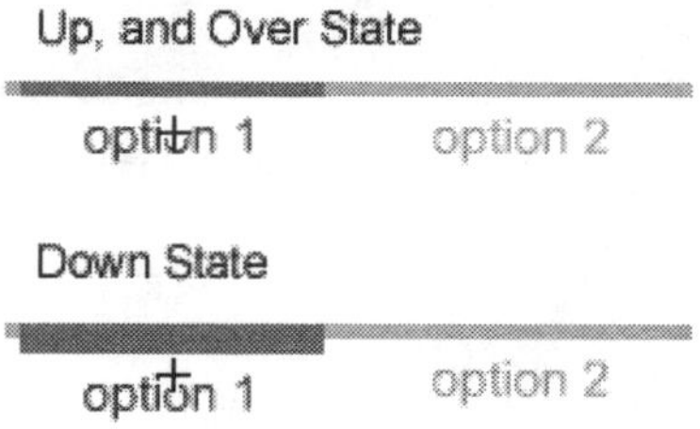

Up, and Over State

option 1   option 2

Down State

option 1   option 2

5. Save your work once you're happy with the button, and open the Library Panel (Window > Library).

6. Duplicate your button in the library four times, and name these new button symbols whatever you like. Now, edit each button's text label and color chip to create five distinct buttons. Move each of the buttons into the 001–Buttons folder you created earlier.

7. With the Main Buttons layer selected in the timeline, drag the buttons from the Library Panel onto the stage. Align them as shown in Figure 2.9 to create a horizontal navigation system. Name these button instances `option1` through `option5` so we can reference them in our ActionScript code. Select each button in turn and type its name into the Instance Name field of the Property Inspector.

8. Now let's create some shaded backgrounds. Create a new movie clip symbol named `Green Shading`. Starting at (0, 0), drag out a new rectangle with either a solid or gradient green fill. If you create a gradient fill, fade the opacity of the end point of the gradient to 0. Your rectangle should be 80 pixels wide and a bit less than 30 pixels high.

9. Within the Library Panel, duplicate this movie clip four times, give each one a distinct color and matching name, and then put them all in the 002-Movie Clips folder of the library.

10. With the Main MCs layer selected in the timeline, drag an instance of each clip onto the stage. Name these instances `green`, `gold`, `red`, and so on to match their colors.

11. Align each of the clips with the appropriate button. It may help to lock the Main Buttons layer within the timeline as you adjust the positions of the clips—otherwsie, the buttons may get in the way.

12. Alter the opacity of each clip via the Property Inspector by choosing the Alpha option from the Color drop-down menu and then selecting a value of 0% (completely transparent).

Adding the ActionScript

Now that we have the framework in place, along with the controlling buttons and movie clips, we are ready to add the actions to see what can be accomplished. We'll need to add the following:

☐ a function to control the 'fading-in' of the movie clips

☐ a function to control the 'fading-out' of the movie clips

☐ onRollOver and onRollOut event handlers for the buttons

13. Open the Actions Panel (Window > Actions). Select the first frame of the Actions layer within the Actions folder on the timeline. Add the following code:

File: **silky.fla**   Actions : 1 (excerpt)

```
function fadeIn (bgClip)
{
  bgClip.onEnterFrame = function ()
  {
    if (this._alpha < 100)
    {
      this._alpha += 20;
    }
  };
}
function fadeOut (bgClip)
{
  bgClip.onEnterFrame = function ()
  {
    if (this._alpha > 0)
    {
      this._alpha -= 20;
    }
```

```
  };
}
```

These two functions fade in and fade out the background movie clips. Each accepts a movie clip as a parameter and works by assigning an `onEnterFrame` event handler to that clip. The event handler is a function that checks the current opacity of the clip (`this._alpha`) and either increases (to fade in) or decreases (to fade out) the value by 20%. As an `onEnterFrame` event handler, this code will be run once for each frame of the animation, causing the background to smoothly fade in our out as its opacity is increased to 100% or decreased to 0%.

Tip

Name your instances!

In order to pass the background clips to these functions so they can be faded in and out, the clips must have names by which they can be referenced.

As a rule of thumb, whenever you drag a symbol to the stage, give it a name if you suspect your ActionScript code will need to access it. It'll save you going back and searching for missing instance names when it comes time to write the code.

With these two workhorse functions in place, we can now assign event handlers to each of our buttons that will call them:

14. For each button on the stage, add the code that controls the opacity of the movie clip beneath it. This will take the form of an `onRollOver` and `onRollOut` event handler for each button:

```
buttonname.onRollOver = function () {
  fadeIn (movieclipname);
};
buttonname.onRollOut = function () {
  fadeOut (movieclipname);
};
```

For example, to make the movie clip named **red** appear when the user moves the cursor over the button named **option4**, you would add the following code to the first frame of the Actions layer:

File: **silky.fla**   Actions : 1 (excerpt)
```
option4.onRollOver = function () {
  fadeIn (red);
};
```

```
option4.onRollOut = function () {
  fadeOut (red);
};
```

15. Save your movie and preview it in Flash by selecting Control > Test Movie.

If everything has gone to plan, when you move the cursor over each button, the opacity of the corresponding movie clip will slowly increase to 100%. The effect fades back to 0% when you move your cursor away.

The beauty of this process is that, by harnessing the power of buttons and movie clips via ActionScript, we have more effects at our disposal. We're using both the `onRollOver` and `onRollOut` event handlers of the buttons to call functions, triggering the ActionScript-driven opacity shift.

This is a subtle effect, but one that can easily be tweaked and modified for applications beyond simple navigation items.

Modifications

The simplest modification is to alter the speed at which the opacity fades in and out. A modified version of the previous effect can be found in `silky-linger.fla`. To alter the opacity shift speed, locate within the `fadeIn` and `fadeOut` functions the lines that increase and decrease the opacity:

```
this._alpha -= 20;
```

```
this._alpha += 20;
```

Change the step amount from 20 to 5, or choose another value that suits your taste. Decreasing it slows down the fade, while increasing it speeds it up.

Taking this a step further, it's quite easy to alter the effect so the fade-in speed is different from the fade-out speed—a delicate change, but one that adds to the overall ambience of the effect. Leave the `fadeIn` speed at 20, but decrease the `fadeOut` to 5 to allow the background to linger after the cursor has moved away.

Conclusion

The subtle navigation system outlined in this example is easy to achieve, and to expand and modify. Try controlling other properties of the movie clip to experiment with the effects we saw in action here.

Properties to play with

A variety of visible properties can be easily modified by ActionScript code. Try them out yourself and see what you come up with!

_alpha	transparency
_height	height in pixels
_width	height in pixels
_rotation	rotation in degrees
_x	horizontal position in pixels
_y	vertical position in pixels
_xscale	horizontal scaling as a percentage
_yscale	vertical scaling as a percentage

Vertical Navigation

A well-planned and properly executed vertical navigation system can be both compelling and intriguing. Although vertical systems have been around since the advent of the user interface, developers employing this type of menu seem to forget the common rules for navigation design, particularly the provision of visual feedback and clear options.

With this in mind, I created the simple system featuring understated movement shown in Figure 2.10.

Figure 2.10. Understated movement is a feature of this vertical navigation system.

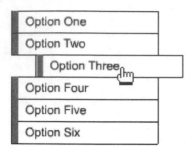

This example is controlled by simple user interaction; as a user moves the cursor over a menu item, it slides slightly to the right and slowly comes to a stop. When the user chooses another menu item, or moves the cursor to another area of the screen, the menu item gently eases back to its original position. It's an uncomplicated, effective system for times when space is at a premium. Let's start the build! To begin, we'll add the relevant design elements to the stage.

If you want to jump straight in and start editing the effect for your own needs, locate `vertical.fla` in the code archive.

Setting the Scene

1. Create a new Flash document that's 550 pixels wide and 400 pixels high. Alter the default frame rate to 24 frames per second (fps).

2. Rename the default layer to Actions and add another layer called Navigation below it.

3. Create a new movie clip symbol named `vNav001` using Insert > New Symbol.... This will act as the base for your interactive menu item. You can add anything you like into the movie clip, but outlined below is the process I used to create the menu in Figure 2.10.

   I created a 146x22 pixel rectangle with a 1-pixel black stroke. I've also added relevant text within the rectangle ('Option One,' 'Option Two,' etc.). A rectangle with a width of 6 pixels, which has a dark gray fill and is aligned with the left hand side of the original rectangle, finishes the effect.

Rather than drawing these elements yourself, you can use File > Import > Import to Stage... to import the elements from navbar.png, which I've included in the code archive, into the symbol. You can then right-click on the imported elements and choose Break Apart to edit them individually.

4. Once you're happy with the look of your menu item, open the Library Panel for the current movie with **Ctrl-L** (**Command-L** on Mac) if necessary and then duplicate the vNav001 symbol five times by right-clicking it and choosing Duplicate, increasing the instance name by one each time. You should now have six movie clip symbols, called vNav001, vNav002, vNav003, vNav004, vNav005, and vNav006, within the Library Panel.

5. Edit the text within each of your clips to reflect the menu option to which the button will link (i.e. 'Option One,' 'Option Two,' and so on).

6. Drag an instance of each of the movie clips into the first frame of the Navigation layer, aligning them at x=5 (the easiest way to do this is to select them all and then type 5 into the X field of the Property Inspector). Make sure you place the clips directly beneath one another so they resemble the layout in Figure 2.10. Name the instances to correspond with their respective symbol names in the Library Panel (i.e., vNav001, vNav002, etc.). Select each instance and type the name into the Instance Name field in the Property Inspector.

You should now have something that resembles the layout we saw in Figure 2.10. Next, let's add the ActionScript that makes the effect come alive.

Adding the ActionScript

7. Select the first frame of the Actions layer and add the following code within the Actions Panel:

File: **vertical.fla**   Actions : 1

```
//Global Variables
_global.speed = 1.3;
_global.stickiness = 8;
_global.baseX = 5;
_global.finalX = 30;
//Movement Functions
function moveOut ()
{
```

```
  this.xStep = 0;
  this.onEnterFrame = function ()
  {
    if (this._x < finalX)
    {
      difference = finalX - this._x;
      this.xStep = (this.xStep + difference * speed) /
          stickiness;
      this._x += this.xStep;
    }
    if (this._x > finalX)
    {
      this._x = finalX;
    }
  };
}
function moveIn ()
{
  this.xStep = 0;
  this.onEnterFrame = function ()
  {
    if (this._x > baseX)
    {
      difference = finalX - this._x;
      this.xStep = (this.xStep + difference * speed) /
          stickiness;
      this._x -= this.xStep;
    }
    if (this._x < baseX)
    {
      this._x = baseX;
    }
  };
}
//Assign event handlers
vNav001.onRollOver = moveOut;
vNav001.onRollOut = moveIn;
vNav002.onRollOver = moveOut;
vNav002.onRollOut = moveIn;
vNav003.onRollOver = moveOut;
vNav003.onRollOut = moveIn;
vNav004.onRollOver = moveOut;
vNav004.onRollOut = moveIn;
vNav005.onRollOver = moveOut;
vNav005.onRollOut = moveIn;
```

```
vNav006.onRollOver = moveOut;
vNav006.onRollOut = moveIn;
```

This code is quite simple; it controls the movement of the movie clips. First, we set global variables for the effect:

```
//Global Variables
_global.speed = 1.3;
_global.stickiness = 8;
_global.baseX = 5;
_global.finalX = 30;
```

Any variable declared as a property of the **_global** object (as these have been) is available anywhere in the movie, which helps keep the rest of the code simple. If we had declared them as ordinary variables, it would have been more complicated to access them later.

Here's what each of these variables does:

speed	Speed of the effect
stickiness	Controls the "drag" on the motion of menu items
baseX	The starting x position of menu items
finalX	The final x position of menu items as they slide out

We have declared two functions: moveOut and moveIn. These slide menu items out when the cursor moves over them, and back in when the cursor moves away, respectively.

If a user moves the cursor over the first movie clip, vNav001, that clip's onRollOver event handler is called. Conversely, when a user moves the cursor away from the movie clip, the onRollOut event handler is triggered. To get the desired effect, we simply assign the moveOut and moveIn functions as the onRollOver and onRollOut event handlers, respectively.

```
vNav001.onRollOver = moveOut;
vNav001.onRollOut = moveIn;
```

Identical lines follow to assign the same event handlers for each of the other menu items.

`moveOut` and `moveIn` basically work the same way, so let me explain `moveOut` and leave you to work out `moveIn` on your own.

We begin by setting a variable called `xStep` in the current movie clip (the menu item to be moved) to zero. As I mentioned in Chapter 1, we refer to the current movie clip as `this`. Because `moveOut` will be running as an event handler for one of our menu item movie clips, the current clip will be that clip. The `xStep` variable will keep track of how many pixels the clip moved in the previous frame. This will factor into our calculation of how much the clip should move in the current frame. Since we may have a number of clips moving at once (e.g., if the user quickly swipes the cursor over the entire menu), we need to keep track of this value for each individual movie clip. That's why this function sets a variable in the current movie clip, rather than using a global variable.

```
function moveOut ()
{
  this.xStep = 0;
```

Next, we want our function to move the movie clip. But rather than make it instantly jump out, we want it to glide smoothly over a number of frames. To cause anything to happen over a series of frames, we need to assign an `onEnterFrame` event handler to make the change(s) required for each individual frame of the animation. In this case, the handler will move the movie clip a number of pixels to the right for each frame until the clip reaches its final position.

Here's how we create and assign an `onEnterFrame` event handler for the current movie clip on the fly:

```
this.onEnterFrame = function ()
{
```

We use two of the previously-defined global variables, `baseX` and `finalX`, to control the movement of the clips. The `onEnterFrame` event handler put in place by `moveOut` will check to see if the x position of the clip is less than `finalX`. If it is, it will move the clip closer to that `finalX` position by a certain number of pixels. That number of pixels is calculated using the distance the clip still has to travel (`difference` in the code below), the number of pixels the clip moved in the previous frame (`this.xStep`), and the other global variables, `speed` and `stickiness`. The code stores this calculated number of pixels in `this.xStep`, then increments the x position (`this._x`) of the movie clip by that stored number:

```
if (this._x < finalX)
{
  difference = finalX - this._x;
```

```
    this.xStep = (this.xStep + difference * speed) / stickiness;
    this._x += this.xStep;
}
```

The `difference` variable decreases as the clip moves toward its final destination, defined by `finalX`. Correspondingly, the `xStep` variable decreases with each frame of the animation, causing the clip to appear to slow down as it slides into position.

Finally, to make sure we don't overshoot our mark (a possibility for particularly high values of `speed` or low values of `stickiness`), the function checks to see if the clip has moved beyond its final position, snapping it back to `finalX` if it has:

```
    if (this._x > finalX)
    {
      this._x = finalX;
    }
  };
}
```

This marks the end of our discussion of the `onEnterFrame` event handler, as well as the `moveOut` function that defines it. As I mentioned before, `moveIn` works almost exactly the same way; the only difference is that it moves the clip toward the left, decreasing its x position and speeding up as it goes.

That's it! Save your document and preview it within Flash. No one said vertical navigation effects had to be boring—in fact, this one's quite intriguing, thanks to the way the navigation items ease in and out. This effect isn't distracting, yet it's unusual enough to make an eye-catching addition to a site. Experiment with the `_global.speed` and `_global.stickiness` values until you're happy with the speed and drag qualities.

In the next example, we'll create a horizontal navigation system that uses similar code to modify the opacity of navigation items.

Gadget-based Navigation

This type of navigation is based on user interaction with an object on the stage. I'm not referring to objects in the ActionScript sense of the word here, I mean a tangible object from the user's perspective—any navigation element that doesn't fit into the "conventional menu" category. These range from mild to wild and come in many different guises.

In the example pictured in Figure 2.11, we've created a circular navigation system that responds to the proximity of the cursor. The navigation's movement slows and a hint is provided when users select a menu option. Because we will control many aspects of the menu's movement, there will be many control loops in the navigation. But don't be put off by the code! Let's go through it together, step by step.

Figure 2.11. This circular navigation system responds to the cursor's proximity.

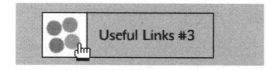

This circular menu system relies heavily on ActionScript and conditional statements: something happens if a condition is met, something else happens if the condition is not met. Building conditional statements within your ActionScript can seem daunting, but it's a necessary evil if we're to create these impressive interfaces and menu systems. And, once you get the hang of it, you'll wonder what all the fuss was about.

In this example, we'll create a single movie clip. This will act as a container for four other movie clips, which will, in turn, hold the buttons that make up the interface. Here's how it will fit together, as illustrated in Figure 2.12:

❑ The main movie clip will act as an invisible container; we'll control its rotation with ActionScript.

❑ The four movie clips nested inside this parent movie clip will eventually need to be controlled with ActionScript as we implement additional effects.

❑ Though they contain no ActionScript, the buttons that sit inside each movie clip are necessary for the additional subtle user interaction effects we'll look at in a moment.

Figure 2.12. Understand the structure of the movie and control points.

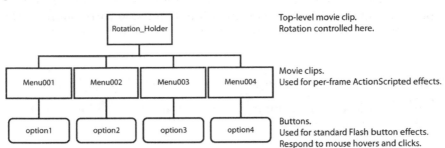

To skip ahead, edit this effect, and modify it for your own needs, locate `gad-get.fla` in the code archive. Otherwise, follow these steps to create the movie from scratch:

Setting the Scene

Let's first create the folder structure and layer organization for this navigation system. The more complex the system, the greater the need for good organization; otherwise, things can get out of control quickly, become messy, and are prone to mistakes. It can only help to have tidy Flash projects, after all!

1. Create a new Flash movie, 250 pixels wide and 65 pixels high, with a frame rate of 24 fps. We use a high frame rate to ensure the effect animates smoothly.

2. Create a new folder on the timeline, called Interface Components, with three layers: Actions, Objects, and Text. Beneath this, create another folder called Background, with a layer named Background Elements. Save the file to a location of your choice.

As we saw in Figure 2.11, the main movie clip with which users will interact contains many nested elements. Now that we've set the scene, we can create the individual navigation elements and start to pull the interface together.

There's no getting around it: the more complex the effect, the more it helps to consider beforehand what will be required to develop it. As we saw previously, it's always a good idea to sketch out the main components of the navigation or effect you want to build, then create the interactions in pseudocode. If you're a little hazy with any areas of ActionScript, it's at this point that you'll be able to identify and research them further. It's best to plan first, rather than get stuck halfway through a project, when changes might not be so easy to make!

Always try to cover all bases when you're sketching interactions, including planning all conditional code and any parameters that may need to be present. Then, when it comes to design time, you'll know exactly what the effect requires, and how long it will take to complete, including extra time for any problem areas that may be a little trickier to code.

Assuming you've done all your planning, let's get started on the individual elements of this navigation.

3. Create a new movie clip (Insert > New Symbol...) and name it `Main Menu`. Leave it blank for now.

4. Create another new movie clip named `Menu-001`. Duplicate this movie clip three times within the Library Panel (Window > Library). Edit the symbol names so they range from `Menu-001` (the original clip) to `Menu-004`.

   If we look at our progress in relation to Figure 2.12, we've just created the movie clips that will hold the buttons—not far to go now!

5. Create a new button symbol named `button1`. In the Up frame, add a 30x30 pixel circle with its top and left edges at (0, 0), and fill it with a color of your choice. Press **F6** to insert another keyframe into the Over frame—this copies the circle you created for the Up frame. Now, alter the color of the circle to give the user visual feedback that something has happened when they interact with the button.

6. Within the Library Panel, duplicate `button1` three times, incrementing the button name so that you finish up with buttons labeled `button1` through `button4`. Edit the Up frame of each of the buttons, assigning them different colors.

7. Within the Library Panel, create the following new folders: 001-Buttons, 002-Menu, and 003-Movie Clips. Move the `Main Menu` movie clip to the 002-Menu folder, and the buttons and movie clips to the 001-Buttons and 003-Movie Clips folders, respectively.

8. Edit each clip (`Menu-001` through `Menu-004`), dragging across and nesting the relevant button (`Button1` through `Button4`) from the Library Panel to the registration point (0,0). That is, drag `Button1` into `Menu-001`, `Button2`

into Menu-002 etc. The easiest way to get the positions right is to type in the coordinates in the Property Inspector.

Make sure you name the instances of the buttons so you can reference them with ActionScript later if necessary (option1, option2, etc.).

9. Edit the Main Menu movie clip symbol and drag an instance of each of the four other clips (Menu-001 to Menu-004) into it, remembering to name each instance as you drag it across. For the sake of simplicity, name the instances Menu001, Menu002, Menu003, and Menu004 so your script is easier to debug later. Arrange them into a diamond pattern, as shown in Figure 2.11, around the center point of the clip.

10. Back in the main scene, with the Objects layer selected, drag an instance of Main Menu from the Library Panel onto the stage. Name the instance Rotation_Holder.

11. With the Text layer selected, add a new dynamic text field (select the Text Tool (T) and choose Dynamic Text from the drop-down menu in the Property Inspector) next to the menu clip, naming the instance option. Also in the Property Inspector for the text object, set the Var value to _root.option-value, and click the Character... button to set the character options to embed font outlines for Uppercase, Lowercase, Numerals, and Punctuation.

You have now created the main rotating movie clip. You've also developed four clips that will be nested within the main clip—we'll look at controlling their properties shortly. Finally, you built the buttons that will give users visual feedback about their interaction with the menu. Now, it's time to add the ActionScript that will bring this creation to life!

Adding the ActionScript

As I mentioned, this navigation is controlled by quite a lot of ActionScript, but if we build it up step by step, you'll be able to gain a clear understanding of the logic behind it all.

12. With the first frame of the Actions layer selected, insert the following code:

File: **gadget.fla**   Actions : 1

```
//Global Variable
_global.Speed = 10;
//Main onEnterFrame event handler for Rotation_Holder
```

```
Rotation_Holder.onEnterFrame = function ()
{
  var stageCentre = Rotation_Holder._x;
  var acceleration = _root._xmouse - stageCentre;
  var braking = 1;
  if (this.hitTest (_root._xmouse, _root._ymouse, true))
  {
    braking = 5;
  }
  var rotation = Speed * acceleration / 100 / braking;
  this._rotation += rotation;
};
//Menu001 Event Handlers
Rotation_Holder.Menu001.option1.onRollOver = function ()
{
  _root.optionvalue = "Useful Links #1";
}
Rotation_Holder.Menu001.option1.onPress = function ()
{
  getURL ("http://www.phireworx.com/", "_blank");
}
//Menu002 Event Handlers
Rotation_Holder.Menu002.option2.onRollOver = function ()
{
  _root.optionvalue = "Useful Links #2";
};
Rotation_Holder.Menu002.option2.onPress = function ()
{
  getURL ("http://www.phireworx.com/", "_blank");
};
//Menu003 Event Handlers
Rotation_Holder.Menu003.option3.onRollOver = function ()
{
  _root.optionvalue = "Useful Links #3";
};
Rotation_Holder.Menu003.option3.onPress = function ()
{
  getURL ("http://www.phireworx.com/", "_blank");
};
//Menu004 Event Handlers
Rotation_Holder.Menu004.option3.onRollOver = function ()
{
  _root.optionvalue = "Useful Links #4";
};
Rotation_Holder.Menu004.option4.onPress = function ()
{
```

```
   getURL ("http://www.phireworx.com/", "_blank");
};
```

That's a fair chunk of code, but it contains nearly identical event handlers for the four rotating movie clips, so there's no need to feel overwhelmed.

First, the script sets up a single global variable that controls how fast the menu rotates:

```
//Global Variable
_global.Speed = 10;
```

The absolute rate of spin will be controlled by the position of the cursor (that's the effect we're aiming for), but this variable also goes into the equation. So for any given cursor position, the menu will spin twice as fast with a `Speed` value of 20 than with a value of 10.

Let's move on to the main `onEnterFrame` event handler for the `Rotation_Holder` movie clip—a sizable chunk of code. We're aiming to have the `Rotation_Holder` movie clip rotate faster as the cursor moves further from it, and to slow down dramatically when the cursor moves over one of the clip's buttons.

So our first job is to determine how far the cursor is from the center of the clip. For simplicity's sake, we'll focus only on the horizontal position of the cursor:

```
var acceleration = _root._xmouse - Rotation_Holder._x;
```

`_root._xmouse` gives us the horizontal position of the cursor, while `Rotation_Holder._x` provides the horizontal position of the clip. This formula will give us a positive value of `acceleration` when the cursor is to the right of the movie clip (higher `_root._xmouse` values), and a negative value when the cursor is to the left of it. This allows us to control not only the speed of rotation, but also the direction! If you're familiar with Pythagoras' Theorem, you may want to add `_root._ymouse` and `Rotation_Holder._y` to the mix to calculate the distance based on the horizontal and vertical coordinates of the cursor[4].

Next, we want to slow the rotation dramatically when the cursor is over one of the menu buttons. To do this, we'll create a variable called `braking` that will have a value of 5 when the cursor is over one of the buttons and 1 otherwise. We could use the`onRollOver` and `onRollOut` event handlers to set this in a global variable,

---

[4]Hint: use `Math.sqrt(…)` to get the square root of a value.

but instead we'll keep everything inside this function and use the `hitTest` method to check if the cursor is over part of the `Rotation_Holder` movie clip:

```
var braking = 1;
if (this.hitTest (_root._xmouse, _root._ymouse, true))
{
   braking = 5;
}
```

As you may be able to infer from this code, `this.hitTest` checks whether a given set of coordinates is over the `Rotation_Holder` movie clip (`this`). As we're interested in the location of the cursor, we pass it the horizontal (`_root._xmouse`) and vertical (`_root._ymouse`) coordinates of the cursor. The third parameter tells `hitTest` whether or not to ignore transparent portions of the movie clip. In this case, we want to note that the cursor is actually over one of the buttons (not the space between them), so we pass a value of `true`.

Now that we've calculated the acceleration and braking variables, we can feed these—along with our global `Speed` variable—into a formula to calculate how many degrees the movie clip should be rotated for the current frame:

```
var rotation = Speed * acceleration / 100 / braking;
```

Interpreting the arithmetic, `Speed` times `acceleration` divided by 100 gives the number of degrees per frame by which the movie will rotate. If `Speed` is set to 10, the clip will rotate one degree per frame for every 10 pixels between the cursor and the center of the movie clip. The exception is when the cursor is over one of the menu buttons, in which case the `braking` variable will divide that rotation speed by five. Feel free to tweak this equation if you'd like the menu to behave differently.

Finally, with the amount of rotation calculated, the event handler finishes by applying that change to the `_rotation` property of the clip:

```
   this._rotation += rotation;
};
```

As in our previous examples, we finish up with event handlers for each of the buttons. Since these buttons are buried inside two levels of movie clips, we can't simply call them by name through our code. The `option1` button, for example, is inside the `Menu001` movie clip, which is inside the `Rotation_Holder` movie clip. So, to access it from the main timeline, we need to refer to it as `Rotation_Holder.Menu001.option1`. The alternative is to declare the event handler for this button in the first frame of Menu001's timeline, where option1 can be referenced directly, but I prefer to keep my code all in one place when possible.

```
Rotation_Holder.Menu001.option1.onRollOver = function ()
{
  _root.optionvalue = "Useful Links #1";
};
Rotation_Holder.Menu001.option1.onPress = function ()
{
  getURL ("http://www.phireworx.com/", "_blank");
};
```

The onRollOver event handler sets the value of the optionvalue variable in the root of the movie. This happens to be the variable we set our dynamic text field to monitor when we were building the interface to the movie, so this value will appear in that text object. The onPress event handler, meanwhile, uses getURL to tell the browser to open http://www.phireworx.com/ in a new window. Similar event handlers are provided for the other three buttons.

Save your Flash movie and preview it within Flash. Congratulations! You've created a funky navigation item that slows down or speeds up relative to the cursor's proximity. The closer the cursor moves to the movie clip, the slower the clip rotates, allowing users to select an option from the navigation. Moving the cursor away from the movie clip increases the rotation speed.

Our work is complete, but we can implement a few subtle modifications to make this effect more interesting.

Modifications

You can easily modify the script to suit your requirements. One such effect involves scripting the opacity of the buttons, and reducing the button opacity to 50% when users moves the cursor over one of the navigation items. Let's look at how this is done.

As we saw in Figure 2.12, nested within the main Rotation_Holder movie clip are four other clips that hold buttons. We nested the objects this way so that we could easily take advantage of the movie clip event handlers to script the properties of the main clip. Let's do that now.

If you'd like a ready-made version of these changes, locate gadget-alpha.fla in the code archive.

We need to fade the movie clip to 50% when the cursor moves over the button, and fade it back to 100% when the cursor moves away. For each of the buttons, we already have `onRollOver` and `onRollOut` event handlers through which we could assign `onEnterFrame` event handlers to perform the fades. Instead, it's simpler to write a single flexible event handler function and assign it as the `onEnterFrame` event handler for each of the four button-holding movie clips.

13. Select the first frame of the Actions layer, and add the following below the existing code:

File: **gadget-alpha.fla**   Actions : 1 (excerpt)

```
function fadeButton ()
{
  if (this.hitTest (_root._xmouse, _root._ymouse, true))
  {
    if (this._alpha > 50)
    {
      this._alpha -= 10;
    }
  }
  else if (this._alpha < 100)
  {
    this._alpha += 10;
  }
}
```

This code ascertains whether or not the user's cursor is over the movie clip and, if it is, reduces the opacity by 10% for each frame of the animation, until it reaches a minimum value of 50% opacity. If the cursor moves out of the movie clip hit area, the opacity increases until it reaches a maximum of 100%.

14. All that's left is to assign this function as the `onEnterFrame` event handler of each of our button movie clips:

File: **gadget-alpha.fla**   Actions : 1 (excerpt)

```
Rotation_Holder.Menu001.onEnterFrame = fadeButton;
Rotation_Holder.Menu002.onEnterFrame = fadeButton;
Rotation_Holder.Menu003.onEnterFrame = fadeButton;
Rotation_Holder.Menu004.onEnterFrame = fadeButton;
```

15. Save the file to a location of your choice, and preview the results in Flash.

This relatively small amount of code takes little time to implement, and won't heavily impact the movie's processing speed. Yet, with these few lines, you've made a considerable enhancement to the appearance of the menu.

Conclusion

Congratulations—you've created a retro, super-cool, compact navigation item that wouldn't look out of place on any Website. The system is different in that it doesn't exactly conform to a standard style, and is reasonably subtle. Navigation systems that are too "in your face" tend to irritate users, while more subtle effects tend to blend into a variety of site structures and work as stand-alone artifacts within your designs.

Subliminal Navigation

Another effect (shown in Figure 2.13) involves the menu buttons behaving elastically in response to user interaction. This effect can be used in either horizontal or vertical formats, scales easily to include as many buttons as you need, and has code that is both concise and easy to understand. Let's get started!

Figure 2.13. Create a subliminal navigation system using simple buttons and ActionScript.

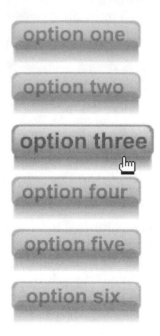

To jump straight in and start editing the effect for your own needs, locate `subliminal.fla` in the code archive.

Setting the Scene

This effect employs an uncomplicated design for the clickable buttons, though of course you can make them more complicated if you wish.

Let's get the groundwork out of the way so we can see how the ActionScript works.

1. Create a new Flash document 500 pixels high and 400 pixels wide. Set the frame rate to 24 fps and click OK.

2. Rename the default layer Actions and add an extra layer below it, called Content.

3. Create a new movie clip named `option1`. Within the movie clip, rename the default layer Text and add another layer below this, named Button.

    We will use this movie clip as a master button that we'll duplicate to create a series of buttons.

4. Select the first frame of the Text layer, and create a new dynamic text field, choosing a font of your choice and a point size of twenty. Having selected the dynamic text field, click Character... within the Property Inspector and chooseSpecify Ranges, Uppercase and Lowercase. Click OK. Enter `Option One` into the text field, or add text of your choice.

5. With the first frame of the Button layer selected, create a suitable button graphic to frame the text. When you're happy with the layout, navigate to the root of the stage.

    In the example shown in Figure 2.13, I have created a 128x44 pixel rounded rectangle with simple gradients to simulate a glassy button. A gray gradient sits behind the effect to create a simple shadow.

6. From the Library Panel, select the `option1` movie clip and duplicate this five times, naming the new movie clips `option2`, `option3`, `option4`, `option5` and `option6`. Edit the text within the dynamic text fields in each movie clip to reflect your menu options, or alternatively, simply label them `option one`, `option two`, `option three`, `option four`, `option five` and `option six`.

7. Drag instances of the clips (`option1` through `option6`) from the Library Panel into the first frame of the Contents layer, naming the instances `option1`, `option2`, `option3`, `option4`, `option5` and `option6`.

8. For each of the button instances on the stage, select Alpha from the Color drop-down list in the Property Inspector and set the value to 70%.

Now that we've added to the stage everything we need to create the effect, we must now insert the ActionScript that will bring it to life.

Adding the ActionScript

To create an interactive elastic effect for the movie clips, we need the help of ActionScript. In this example, we will extend the functionality of all movie clips via a **prototype function**. This technique, which comes from the world of

JavaScript, lets you add a new method to all instances of a built-in class—in this case, MovieClip.

9. Select the first frame of the Actions layer and add the following code within the Actions Panel:

File: **subliminal.fla**   Actions : 1

```
MovieClip.prototype.shiver = function (xScale, yScale,
    strength, weight)
{
  var xScaleStep = 0;
  var yScaleStep = 0;
  this.onEnterFrame = function ()
  {
    xScaleStep = (xScale - this._xscale) * strength +
        xScaleStep * weight;
    yScaleStep = (yScale - this._yscale) * strength +
        yScaleStep * weight;
    this._xscale += xScaleStep;
    this._yscale += yScaleStep;
  };
};
option1.onRollOver = function ()
{
  this.shiver (110, 110, 0.3, 0.8);
  this._alpha = 100;
};
option1.onRollOut = function ()
{
  this.shiver (100, 100, 0.3, 0.8);
  this._alpha = 70;
};
option2.onRollOver = function ()
{
  this.shiver (110, 110, 0.3, 0.8);
  this._alpha = 100;
};
option2.onRollOut = function ()
{
  this.shiver (100, 100, 0.3, 0.8);
  this._alpha = 70;
};
option3.onRollOver = function ()
{
  this.shiver (110, 110, 0.3, 0.8);
  this._alpha = 100;
```

```
};
option3.onRollOut = function ()
{
   this.shiver (100, 100, 0.3, 0.8);
   this._alpha = 70;
};
option4.onRollOver = function ()
{
   this.shiver (110, 110, 0.3, 0.8);
   this._alpha = 100;
};
option4.onRollOut = function ()
{
   this.shiver (100, 100, 0.3, 0.8);
   this._alpha = 70;
};
option5.onRollOver = function ()
{
   this.shiver (110, 110, 0.3, 0.8);
   this._alpha = 100;
};
option5.onRollOut = function ()
{
   this.shiver (100, 100, 0.3, 0.8);
   this._alpha = 70;
};
option6.onRollOver = function ()
{
   this.shiver (110, 110, 0.3, 0.8);
   this._alpha = 100;
};
option6.onRollOut = function ()
{
   this.shiver (100, 100, 0.3, 0.8);
   this._alpha = 70;
};
```

First, we declare our movie clip prototype function (`shiver`), which accepts four parameters.

```
MovieClip.prototype.shiver = function (xScale, yScale,
    strength, weight)
{
```

These parameters are as follows:

xScale	Amount of horizontal scaling to apply to the movie clip
yScale	Amount of vertical scaling to apply to the movie clip
strength	Controls how powerfully the animation will tend toward the specified scaling values
weight	Controls how much the animation will oscillate before settling down to the specified scaling values; use a value between 0 and 1 to produce a realistic wobble

This declaration adds a method called `shiver` to all movie clips in our project. When called on a particular clip, this method uses the `onEnterFrame` event handler of the clip to generate the intended animation. Before it does this, however, it sets up two variables to which the event handler will have access (in addition to the four function parameters): `xScaleStep` and `yScaleStep`. At any given time, these two variables will contain the most recently calculated values that determine how much the horizontal and vertical scales of the clip should change, respectively.

```
var xScaleStep = 0;
var yScaleStep = 0;
```

The `onEnterFrame` event handler calculates how much the scale of the clip should change for each frame of the animation. It does this by calculating the difference between its target scale (`xScale`/`yScale`) and its current scale (`this._xscale`, `this._yscale`), multiplying this figure by the `strength` parameter, and, finally, adding the scaling that occurred in the previous frame (`xScaleStep`/`yScaleStep`) multiplied by the `weight` parameter. It's this second component that causes the scaling to "overshoot the mark" and oscillate back and forth until it settles down to the target values.

```
this.onEnterFrame = function ()
{
  xScaleStep = (xScale - this._xscale) * strength +
      xScaleStep * weight;
  yScaleStep = (yScale - this._yscale) * strength +
      yScaleStep * weight;
  this._xscale += xScaleStep;
  this._yscale += yScaleStep;
};
};
```

The `shiver` method is called for each movie clip in response to the `onRollOver` and `onRollOut` events:

```
option1.onRollOver = function ()
{
  this.shiver (110, 110, 0.3, 0.8);
  this._alpha = 100;
};
option1.onRollOut = function ()
{
  this.shiver (100, 100, 0.3, 0.8);
  this._alpha = 70;
};
```

When users move the cursor over the clip, the `onRollOver` event handler is executed, triggering the `shiver` method. The `xScale` and `yScale` parameters are set to 110%, and the `_alpha` property of the movie clip is set to 100.

Conversely, when the cursor is moved away from the movie clip, the `onRollOut` event handler is executed, resetting the `_xscale` and `_yscale` properties for the clip to 100%, and setting the `_alpha` property for the movie clip to 70%.

Save and preview your work. When you move your cursor over the buttons, they spring into life. Move your cursor away, and they shrink back to their original size in a pleasing, bouncy way.

Modifications

Because this effect is controlled via ActionScript, quickly changing some of the parameters that are passed to the `shiver` method can markedly alter its display.

Lowering the value of the `weight` parameter in the `onRollOver` event from `0.8` to `0.1` produces a smooth scaling effect to the maximum horizontal and vertical scale values of 100%.

File: **subliminal-smooth.fla**   Actions : 1 (excerpt)
```
option1.onRollOver = function()
{
  this.shiver (110, 110, 0.3, 0.1);
  this._alpha = 100;
};
```

If we leave the `onRollOut` event handler code as per the previous example, when we move the cursor away from the movie clip, we see the same pleasant elastic effect. To edit the effect for your own needs, or to play with the parameters further, locate `subliminal-smooth.fla` from the code archive.

I'll leave it to you to modify the other parameters and see how they affect the final outcome, but don't be afraid to play—even a couple of simple changes can produce some weird and wonderful effects!

Advanced Navigation

There are many navigation designs that fit into this category, some of them plain but complex, others extremely intricate. In this section, I'll show you how to create navigation systems that are complex and intricate, but easy to understand and completely scalable. I don't want to write pages on techniques that you're never going to use, but I trust that, when you get to the end of this chapter, you'll have lots of ideas for projects that use the methods we've explored. Don't forget to sketch them down on paper or Post-It notes!

Tabbed Interface Extraordinaire

The tabbed interface has stood the test of time; it's easily recognized and includes tangible qualities of the real world. I've seen good and bad implementations of this method of navigation control; the system we're about to create represents a consolidation of the good points. This discussion includes some nifty tricks, and will show you how much work can go into creating a navigation structure like the one shown in Figure 2.14.

Figure 2.14. Building an advanced tabbed navigation system can require a lot of work.

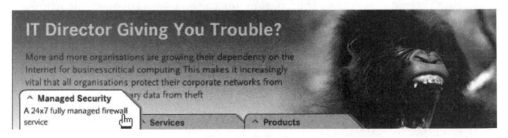

To the final project, or use it as a starting point for another project, find the `tabs.fla` file in the code archive.

It would be easy to create a static tabbed interface that changes color when the cursor moves over one of the tabs, but that's not the primary objective of this example. Instead, we want to introduce dynamic movement and interactivity into the design, to produce a final effect that's sleek, smooth, and pleasing to the eye. During development, we'll also convert the tabbed navigation into a component that we can reuse with ease.

Setting the Scene

Let's start by organizing the layers and folders within the main timeline, to help us keep the individual components separate.

1. Create a new movie that's 600 pixels wide and 150 pixels high. This forms the foundation of the navigation and content areas of our application.

2. Create within the main timeline the folder and layer structure outlined in Figure 2.15.

Figure 2.15. Set up the folder and layer structure for the navigation.

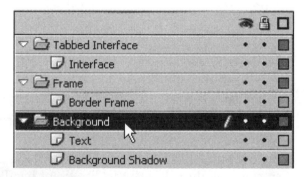

3. Open the Library Panel and set up the following folders for the navigation elements:

    ☐ 001-Buttons

    ☐ 002-Movie Clips

    ☐ 003-Images

☐ 004-Components

4. In the Border Frame layer within the Frame folder, create a rectangle with a 1-point black stroke that stretches to the edges of the stage. This will act as a bounding box for the design.

5. Select the Text layer within the Background folder and add a header and space for introductory text as shown in Figure 2.14.

Creating the Tabs

The structure of the tabs is relatively simple, yet it's important that we plan out the effect before we create it. This will help us avoid problems later on. Figure 2.16 shows how the framework of each tabbed element fits together:

Figure 2.16. Plan the placement of elements of the advanced tabbed navigation.

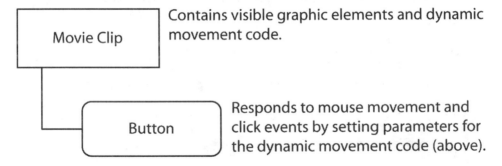

Movie Clip — Contains visible graphic elements and dynamic movement code.

Button — Responds to mouse movement and click events by setting parameters for the dynamic movement code (above).

The top-level container movie clip will include all the visible elements of the tab, plus a trigger button that will sit above all the other layers. The event handlers of this button set the direction of the tab's motion—either up or down—and its color. The main movie clip will be used to control the scripted easing motion.

6. Create a new movie clip, named Tab, and create the following layers from top to bottom:

☐ Trigger

☐ Text

□ Panel_Border

□ Coloring_Clip

□ Panel_Inner

□ Background

7. Create a new button symbol, named `Trigger Button`, and insert into the Hit frame a 150x150 pixel square centered in the symbol. This button will do most of the work to set the direction of movement and color of the tabs, as mentioned above.

8. Drag an instance of the `Tab` movie clip into the Interface layer within the Tabbed Interface folder in the main timeline. Name this instance `menu1`.

9. Double-click to edit the movie clip in place, select the Trigger layer, and drag an instance of the Trigger Button symbol into this layer at coordinates (0, 0). Name the instance `TriggerButton`. Lock and hide this layer, so we can move on to create the interface that will sit below this trigger button.

10. Select the Panel_Border layer, and create within it a shape that's slightly smaller than the trigger button by a couple of pixels both vertically and horizontally. This will act as the outline for the tab, as shown in Figure 2.17.

Figure 2.17. Create the interface for the navigation tab.

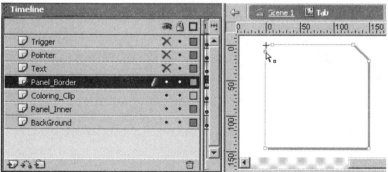

The right tool for the job

Tip

I created the interface for the tab using Fireworks MX 2004. I created a rounded rectangle object, then used the Knife Tool to chop off one of the corners. I copied the object from the canvas and pasted it into Flash. Fireworks is a very handy tool for the rapid creation of vector objects to use in your Flash projects.

11. Copy the object you've just created and, having selected the Background layer, use the Paste In Place command (Edit > Paste In Place) to position it directly beneath the main copy. Darken the stroke color of the object—this will create a subtle shadow effect for the tab—and nudge the selection down and to the right by two pixels.

12. Select the Text layer and add two dynamic text fields: one for the header of the tab, and one for the additional information that will appear when the cursor moves over the tab. Edit the text fields to contain the initial text `Header` and `Body` so you can recognize their purposes quickly. Click the Character button within the Property Inspector and choose to embed font outlines for All Characters or Basic Latin. Set the Var value of the header text element to `header`, and the body text element to `text`.

We will populate these text elements dynamically a little later, but we add them now so we don't forget. If everything has gone to plan, you should see something similar to the display in Figure 2.18. If not, take a peek at the `tabs.fla` source file in the code archive.

Figure 2.18. The final tabbed navigation interface provides scope for extra movement later.

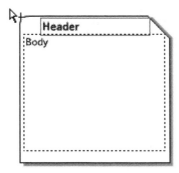

When we finally use this symbol, we'll see only the top third of the tab, which will slide in and out of view in response to user interaction. We've made the symbol this shape to allow us scope for extra movement should we need it later.

Converting to a Component

Each of the tabs in our interface will have its own characteristics, such as the contents of the dynamic text fields. Until now, we've handled this by duplicating a symbol as many times as necessary, then making the required changes. Flash provides a better alternative in the form of **components**.

If we convert what we have at the moment into a component, we can create all the tabs with a single symbol and assign instances of it individual colors, movement characteristics, and more. These characteristics are defined within the Component Definition dialog, which is available through the Library Panel. The Component Definition dialog allows you to assign values to variables; these can later be accessed by instances of the component on the stage.

Let's convert our tab symbol to a component before we add the control code for the movie clip. This way, we'll gain an understanding of how everything fits together and what each of the variables contributes to the effect:

13. Select the **Tab** movie clip in the Library Panel. Right-click on it, and select Component Definition....

14. Click the + button at the top of the Parameters list to add rows to the list, then edit the entries to create the list shown in Figure 2.19. Fill in the other options in this dialog, as shown, and click OK.

Figure 2.19. Convert the tab to a component.

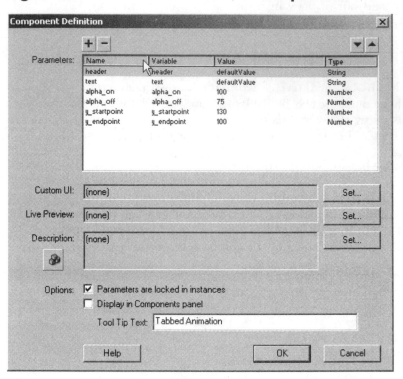

Each of these parameters provides a variable for instances of the symbol that we can easily configure from the Property Inspector. Table 2.1 explains the purpose for each of the parameters we've defined.

Table 2.1. Explanation of Component Parameters

Parameter/Variable	Value	Description
header	Defined at instance creation time	Text for the header area of the tab
text	Defined at instance creation time	Text for the body area of the tab
alpha_on	100	Opacity value when user moves cursor over tab
alpha_off	75	Opacity value when user moves cursor away from tab
y_startpoint	130	Vertical starting position of the tab
y_endpoint	100	Vertical position at end of movement

There are quite a few parameters here, and, as we'll see in a moment, they all play a part in the interactivity of the tab.

Lock parameters to instances

When creating components that will be used multiple times within a single Flash movie, make sure that the Parameters are Locked in Instances option within the Component Definition dialog is checked. Otherwise, your component will behave unexpectedly when used multiple times on the stage.

Adding the Movement Code

Now that we've defined all the parameters for the component, we can edit it, and insert the control code to make the effect come alive.

15. Move the Tab component in the Library Panel to the 004-Components folder. The menu1 instance of Tab in the Interface layer of your movie has been updated to behave like a component. Position it at (11, 140); this will be the initial position of the tab when the movie begins playing.

    Observant readers may have noticed that we set the y_startpoint parameter of the component to 130 in the previous section, but that we've given the tab a vertical starting point of 140 here. This was done deliberately, so that the top of the tab will glide smoothly into view when the movie starts.

16. Select the component instance if it isn't already selected. Notice the new Parameters Panel, which appears by default in the Property Inspector. Use it to change the values of the header and text parameters to provide a title and descriptive text for the tab.

    As the dynamic text fields within the component have been set to display the header and text variables, and because these two parameters are configured to create header and text variables respectively, simply setting their values is all it takes to set the text that appears in the tab. The change won't be visible as you work, but, if you preview the movie in Flash, you'll see the text appear as it should in the tab.

17. With the component instance selected, right-click and select Edit. Add a new layer to the top of the timeline (above Trigger) and name it Actions. With the first frame of this new layer selected, hit **F9** to open the Actions Panel and type in the following code:

File: **tabs.fla**   Tab : Actions : 1 (excerpt)

```
var direction = 0;
this.onEnterFrame = function ()
{
  if (direction == 1)
  {
    this._y += (y_endpoint - this._y) / 2;
    if (this._alpha <= alpha_on)
    {
      this._alpha += 2;
    }
  }
  else
  {
    this._y += (y_startpoint - this._y) / 10;
    if (this._alpha >= alpha_off)
    {
      this._alpha -= 2;
    }
  }
};
```

Let's discuss what's happening here. We've created a variable named direction that we'll use to track whether the tab is "popped up" for display or not. The onEnterFrame event handler for the component uses that variable to control the tab's vertical position (this._y) and opacity (this._alpha). When the tab is popped up, it is moved upwards by half the distance between its current position and the target position (as specified by y_endpoint) and its opacity is increased to the target value (alpha_on) at a rate of 2% per frame. When the tab is released, it returns to its starting position (y_startpoint) and opacity (alpha_off), covering one tenth the remaining distance and losing 2% opacity per frame.

Now that we've added the control code for the movie clip, we need to add to the button the trigger code that will kick off all this animation:

18. Still inside the Tab component, add the following to the existing code for the first frame of the Actions layer:

File: **tabs.fla**   Tab : Actions : 1 (excerpt)

```
TriggerButton.onRollOver = function ()
{
  direction = 1;
  swapDepths (_root.topTab);
  _root.topTab = this._parent;
};
TriggerButton.onRollOut = function ()
{
  direction = 0;
};
```

Remember that TriggerButton is the invisible button in the Trigger layer that covers the entire tab. When the cursor is detected hovering over the button, the onRollOver event handler sets direction to 1, causing the onEnterFrame event handler for the movie clip to pop it up. The tab moves back to its resting position when the cursor is moved away, as the onRollOut event handler sets direction back to 0.

Since the tabs in our interface will overlap slightly, after it has set direction, the onRollOver handler needs to raise this tab above the others. You can't see this effect yet, as we haven't added any more instances of the component to the stage. But, when we do, the selected tab will be brought to the front.

Doing this isn't as complex as it sounds, thanks to a nifty movie clip method called swapDepths, which swaps the current movie clip with another in the stacking order. We must simply record a reference to the clip at the top of the stack in a variable called topTab, which is stored in the main movie's timeline.

19. Navigate back to the main timeline and add a layer named Actions within the Tabbed Interface folder. Open the Actions Panel and add the following code:

File: **tabs.fla**   Actions : 1

```
// Tracks which tab is on top
var topTab = menu3;
```

menu3 is the instance name we'll assign to our third (and initially topmost) tab, once we create it.

Look back at `TriggerButton`'s `onRollOver` event handler. We use `swapDepths` with this new variable (referenced as `_root.topTab` within our component) to move the current tab to the top of the stack. Then, we set the variable to the current movie clip[5], so that the next tab we activate will be able to swap places with it. Clever, isn't it?

Adding Multiple Tabs to the Stage

Now that we've completed all the work within the component, and inserted the control code, we can add more instances of the component to the stage, creating a true "tabby" experience.

20. Drag two more instances of the **Tab** component from the Library Panel onto the stage. Place them within the Interface layer so they overlap slightly.

21. Name the additional tabs `menu2` and `menu3`, taking special care to make sure `menu3` is at the top of the stacking order as indicated by our `topTab` variable.

22. From within the Property Inspector, alter the `header` and `text` parameters to contain suitable content for each tab.

23. Save the file to a location of your choice, and preview it.

Voila—your work is complete! You've produced a tabbed navigation component to be proud of! Try experimenting with the code to see what happens, but bear

---

[5]The especially attentive may wonder why we reference the current movie clip as `this._parent` instead of just `this` (or even just `_parent`). This has to do with scope of button event handlers declared within movie clips like this. In such handlers, the scope is the movie clip; that's why we can reference variables in the movie clip (like `direction`) by name and call movie clip methods (like `swapDepths`) directly. But, perhaps unexpectedly, the `this` keyword points to the button—not the movie clip! We can't use `_parent` either, as that will give us the parent of the movie clip. `this._parent` does the trick, however, since the parent of the button is the movie clip.

in mind that, when you change a component's code, you'll affect the code for every instance of that component on the stage.

Modifications

With just a little work, we can modify the component to increase its functionality and make it even more slick. One such modification involves adding a "coloring layer," the color of which we can control via the trigger button. By linking the color of this layer to parameters in our Tab component, we can have each tab display a different color when the cursor moves over it. First, we need to modify the component definition, adding the extra parameters.

To jump straight to the finished product, grab the file called tabs-color.fla from the code archive.

24. From the Library Panel, select the Tab component, right click, and select Component Definition.... Add the parameters shown in Table 2.2:

Table 2.2. Add Parameters to the Component Definition

Parameter/Variable	Value	Type
clip_color_over	#FFFFFF	Color
clip_color_out	#99CC00	Color

Here, we define the default colors of the coloring movie clip we'll add in a moment. The clip will be white when the cursor hovers over it and light green when the cursor moves away. To take advantage of the values we've defined, we need to add some additional code to the component.

25. Select an instance of the tab from the stage, right-click, and select Edit. Add the following to the top of the code in the first frame of the Actions layer.

File: **tabs-color.fla**   Tab : Actions : 1 (excerpt)

```
var tabColor = new Color(Colorizer);
tabColor.setRGB(clip_color_out);
```

Setting the color of a movie clip in ActionScript is different from setting properties such as position or opacity. Rather than directly setting a property value, we must instead create a new Color object. In the code above, we created such an object for a clip called Colorizer that we'll add to our tab component moment-arily. We store the object in a variable called tabColor and use its setRGB method to set the color of the clip to the value specified by the component's `clip_color_out` parameter.

Next, we alter the trigger button's `onRollOver` and `onRollOut` event handlers to change the clip's color on cue:

26. Change `TriggerButton`'s `onRollOver` and `onRollOut` event handlers as shown here:

File: **tabs-color.fla**   Tab : Actions : 1 (excerpt)

```
TriggerButton.onRollOver = function ()
{
  direction = 1;
  swapDepths (_root.topTab);
  _root.topTab = this._parent;
  tabColor.setRGB(clip_color_over);
};
TriggerButton.onRollOut = function ()
{
  direction = 0;
  tabColor.setRGB(clip_color_out);
};
```

All that's left is to actually create the `Colorizer` movie clip, the color of which our new code additions will control:

27. Navigate to the Panel_Border layer within the `Tab` component, copy the existing shape, and paste it in place (Edit > Paste in Place) into the Coloring_Clip layer. Set the fill color to white (if it isn't already), and convert this to a new movie clip called `Colorizer`, with a matching instance name of `Colorizer`.

28. Save the Flash movie and preview it.

Now that we've created the `Colorizer` movie clip, the effect will fall into place—the color of the clip will change in accordance with the component parameters you've defined.

As we've just seen, it's easy to modify the parameters, add new parameters, and introduce new functionality. So, don't be afraid to try out new techniques—it's the only way to improve your skills!

Creating components for items like this means they can easily be transferred to different projects without your having to create multiple movie clips or alter the code for each instance of a clip.

Conclusion

Phew! That was quite a ride through the realm of navigation. We saw some solid, real-world examples of usable navigation systems, outlined in a way that will allow you to reuse and build on the code in future. The techniques we discussed in this chapter will help you create compelling navigation effects, and might even inspire you to produce something extra-special for a particular project.

When you're building a navigation system and things don't go as planned, or you produce an effect that isn't quite right, don't throw it away! Save those experiments to a folder that you can come back to later—you never know when you may need them as a starting point for another project. When the time comes, you can take those designs and expand them in countless different directions, saving incremental versions as you work. If you take one message from this chapter, let it be, "Don't be afraid to experiment." After all, without experimentation, we wouldn't be able to formulate new methods of design and functionality!

3

Animation Effects

The fads of Internet design may come and go, but one thing that will never change is that the more dynamic you make your Flash creations, the more engaging they are to the user. This dynamism can be counterproductive under certain circumstances, especially when multiple effects battle for the user's attention, or the effects are too garish. Identifying the key to effective animation is like the search for the Holy Grail. What some users think is a cool effect, others find patently uninteresting—and vice versa. Never lose sight of the importance of striking a balance between the interface and the animations you're attempting to produce.

Flash has always had as its nucleus animation and motion. This is, after all, what Flash was originally created for—the animation of objects over time. As new versions are released and the technology evolves, so do the capabilities of Flash's scripting language. What we could once achieve only with keyframes and tweening can now be accomplished in a few lines of ActionScript. Some developers find this reality difficult to grasp, but as we saw in Chapter 2, once you understand the basics, you can build on them with new experiments.

With very few exceptions, what can be done with keyframe tweening can also be achieved through ActionScript. But, what are the advantages of scripting? The answer's simple: portability, scalability, and manageability. You can affect an animation dramatically by tweaking an equation or a few variables in its Action-Script. This process is much easier than laboriously editing motion tweens, which can sometimes appear in their hundreds in large animated effects.

This doesn't mean that motion tweening is dead, however—not by a long shot. If you create simple motion tweens (for example, an effect that shows an object increasing in size), then script the effect multiple times and experiment with it via ActionScript, you can create some pretty amazing effects with a minimum of effort.

With Flash MX 2004, and the introduction of Timeline Effects, creating these motion tween building blocks takes even less work than it did before, as we'll see in the coming chapter. I'll give you the information you need to develop both classic effects you can be proud of and exciting new animations. You'll also learn the techniques involved in creating innovative Timeline Effects. It's virtually all ActionScript from here on, so have your calculator and pencil ready!

Animation Principles

If you are reading this book, then I can be pretty sure you have a copy of Flash MX or later. You probably purchased Flash because of the animation capabilities that lie at its heart. In the most basic form of Flash animation, we can smoothly transition an object's location or shape from point/shape A to point/shape B by altering the properties of that object at keyframes within the timeline. This used to be a cumbersome process in previous versions of Flash, but it's more accessible now. With a solid understanding of ActionScript and the dynamics of motion you can rapidly create animation effects that would have taken many hours to create with previous versions.

Tip

Hit the books!

What did you do with your old Physics and Math textbooks when you left school? Did you throw them away? Shame on you if you did—they can be an invaluable source of inspiration for creating mathematical and motion-related scripted animations in Flash. I'm a bit of a hoarder, which probably explains why I've still got mine!

There are many uses for Flash in creating animation. Perhaps you want to create a straightforward animation that moves an object from point A to point B. Maybe you're itching to build a more complex animation with a "real world" feel, easing objects into position or having them exhibit elastic characteristics. Both simple and advanced animations are possible in Flash via different methods: by hand, using complex keyframes and motion tweening, or with the help of ActionScript.

While the ActionScript method of animation may initially appear difficult, once you become comfortable with its methodologies for movement and learn the nuances of its quick, effective methods, you'll soon be creating increasingly complex animations and building on your existing knowledge. If this is your first experience with ActionScript, you'll soon be surprised how easy it is to create scripted animation. This should inspire you to explore your own ideas and experiments, and take ActionScript to the limit.

Animation Overload

The ability to easily include animation techniques and effects within Flash movies is usually the reason people use this technology for animation development. However, inexperienced users may succumb to "animation rage," as they become a little *too* carried away with the power Flash puts at their fingertips. Over-the-top animation effects are the result—effects that, upon careless replication within the same movie, succeed only in creating an unpleasant experience, to say the very least!

It's easy to become trigger-happy and animate every element of your display, but this approach is a recipe for disaster. The effect that you set out to create will soon be lost, overwhelmed by all the others that surround it.

The key to an effective animation lies in maintaining a balance between the message you're trying to convey and what's happening on the screen. Even tipping the balance slightly can ruin your effect, so adopt the following guidelines as rules of thumb for creating successful animations:

Tame the Animation
  "Because you can" is not a good enough reason to animate something. Users tend to identify excessive animation as the mark of the amateur—though your site will certainly make an impression, it won't be a good one!

Err on the Side of Subtlety
  Effects that are exaggerated or garish will annoy users, especially if the animation is part of the main interface or navigation. Strive to create effects that are pleasing to the eye, not intrusive.

Consider the User
  Try to distance yourself from any effect you create; imagine you're a user viewing it for the first time. If you think it's "too much," then it probably is. If you don't like it, your users won't, either. Of course, you can't please all of the people all of the time, so try to strike a happy medium at which most visitors will be satisfied.

Tip

Stand back!

When previewing your movie, try standing several feet from the monitor. Believe it or not, this gives you a clear sense of the animation's movement across the screen. If you're too lazy to walk to the other side of the room, try squinting so that the screen blurs a little. You'll be able to detect the movement on the screen without the distracting details, which will help you identify whether the movie is over-animated.

Be Conservative with Animations

Yes, you can create cool animations with ActionScript, but you shouldn't include them all in one page, interface, or effect. You may lose focus by adding too many other animations to your design. Try to sprinkle animations through your designs, rather than deluging the user with an animation storm.

To Tween or Not to Tween?

A few years ago, Flash developers had no choice. To create animated effects in Flash, we used keyframes and motion or shape tweening. Now, we have the luxury of choice; we can script the motion, or create it via the traditional route. Both methods deliver benefits, as we'll see shortly, when we compare scripted animation with traditional tweening methods.

One point worth noting, however, is that with motion scripting, the entire movie need not be any longer than a single frame. The ActionScript, not the timeline, controls the animation, allowing for well-organized movies with uncomplicated structures.

Let's take a look at a simple animation technique with which you might already be familiar: linear motion. The most basic effect that you can create is movement from one point to another and, indeed, this may have been one of the effects you tried when you first opened Flash. Let's revisit it now.

Timeline Animation Example

It's easy to create this effect on the timeline. Let's walk through the steps involved.

1. Draw a simple shape (like a circle) on the stage and convert it to a movie clip symbol named `Timeline_Animation`. Position the symbol instance on the stage at (0, 0).

2. Select frame 10 within the main timeline, right-click, and select Insert Key-Frame (**F6**). Notice that the movie clip instance is copied into the new key-frame.

3. Select the instance of the movie clip in frame 10, and move it to (100, 100).

4. Select frame 1, right-click, and select Create Motion Tween.

Preview your movie. You've created a simple animation that moves your clip from one point to another. This is a simple animation; if the effect were more complicated, the timeline could quickly become messy and difficult to work with.

Creating simple motion using the timeline in this manner can also be accomplished within Flash MX 2004 and later versions via Timeline Effects (more on this in Chapter 4).

ActionScripted Animation Example

Let's take another look at this animation, but this time, let's build it in Action-Script.

1. Draw a simple shape (like a circle) on the stage and convert it to a movie clip symbol named `Scripted_Animation`. Position the symbol instance on the stage at (0, 0), and name the instance `scripted_animation`.

2. With the Actions Panel open and the first frame of the main timeline selected, add the following code:

```
var endX = scripted_animation._x + 100;
var endY = scripted_animation._y + 100;
var stepX = (endX - scripted_animation._x) / 10;
var stepY = (endY - scripted_animation._y) / 10;

scripted_animation.onEnterFrame = function ()
{
  if (this._x < endX) this._x += stepX;
  if (this._y < endY) this._y += stepY;
};
```

First, we set variables for the x and y endpoints (`endX` and `endY`) to equal the starting coordinates plus 100 pixels along each axis. We then use these values to calculate how much the object will have to move per frame along each axis (`stepX` and `stepY`) to reach its destination in ten frames. We then introduce an event handler that moves the object along the two axes by the calculated distances until it reaches its destination.

This code takes the previous example a step further, though, because you can place this movie clip anywhere on the stage. Regardless of its starting location, the clip will move 100 pixels along each axis from its starting position.

You may be looking for more code to complete the effect, but that's it! Simple, isn't it? Of course, ActionScript becomes more complicated as you add more interesting effects, but this method certainly saves a lot of clutter on the timeline.

Animations built using the timeline and motion tweening are useful for testing and for implementation as part of a larger animation (for example, creating simple rotation for a loading animation). The real benefits of developing animations with ActionScript are scalability and the opportunity for dynamic movement in response to user input or other variables.

Once you start animating with ActionScript, it's difficult to stop—this method really does act as a springboard for your creativity. And, don't forget to save your experimental FLA files even if you don't use them straight away. You never know when you might need them!

Creating Function Libraries

Once the ActionScript bug has bitten you, you'll be infected permanently, and there's no known antidote! You'll create many FLAs over time, and will no doubt build up your own core set of scripts and methods. But, rather than reinventing the wheel every time you need to carry out a particular function, why not save your scripts in `.as` (ActionScript) files? These files can then be included dynamically in your creations as you need them.

I maintain a core of scripts that I've created over the past few years, and which I back up regularly. I'm always careful to sort my ActionScript files into a logical folder structure. That way, when I start a new project, I can go and grab my existing script files without any hassle.

Any scripts that are still in development, or that I haven't had time to finish, I place in a file called `unfinished.as`. This way, I don't lose the code or accidentally delete it, and I can come back to it later to finish or develop it further.

Hotmail for backups

If I lost all of my code snippets, I'd be very unhappy! And, even though I perform regular backups, I can never be sure of their integrity. For this reason, I set up a free mail account with Hotmail, and created an archive folder. Now, every month, I mail myself a ZIP archive of my .as files. This may seem a little extreme, but if you've ever lost your work in a hard drive or backup failure, you'll understand why I go to such lengths to protect my code.

Creating a Simple Function Library

A simple animation library can help you clean up your timeline and make things more manageable. To create your own library, follow these steps, or simply locate Simple_Motion.fla and Simple_Motion.as in the code archive:

1. Look at the code from the ActionScript animation example you completed above; specifically, look at the onEnterFrame event handler. We can write a function that does the same job for a specified clip, given stepX, stepY, endX, and endY values:

    File: **Simple_Motion.as**
    ```
    function SimpleMovement (stepX, stepY, endX, endY, clip)
    {
      if (clip._x < endX) clip._x += stepX;
      if (clip._y < endY) clip._y += stepY;
    }
    ```

    The structure of the SimpleMovement function is similar to the event handler, except that it accepts parameters to tell it exactly what to do (and what clip to do it to), instead of relying on predefined variables.

    Type the code for this function into a text editor (e.g., Notepad on PC, or BBEdit on Mac) and save it as Simple_Motion.as.

2. To use this file, add the following line of ActionScript to the root of any movie, in the first frame

    File: **Simple_Motion.fla**   Actions : 1 (excerpt)
    ```
    #include "Simple_Motion.as"
    ```

This compiles the code from the `Simple_Motion.as` file into the SWF file when it is created, providing access to the `SimpleMovement` function we created above.

3. Alter the `onEnterFrame` event handler to use the imported function as follows:

File: **Simple_Motion.fla**   Actions : 1 (excerpt)

```
scripted_animation.onEnterFrame = function ()
{
  SimpleMovement(stepX, stepY, endX, EndY, this);
};
```

Here, we've created a simple function call, passing the four variables defined on the root of the timeline, as well as the movie clip we wish to animate.

4. Preview you movie in Flash, and you'll see it works exactly as before.

Including the function in another project is as simple as saving the `.as` file to the directory containing the FLA you're working on, and adding the `#include` directive to the project. You can then use the function as often as you like.

Creating Master Libraries

When you're working on a series of projects that share a similar theme, you may find they also share bitmaps and vector and sound objects. If you've forgotten which FLA these shared objects reside in, you're left to choose between a time-consuming search or laborious replication.

To avoid this situation, I create what I call **master libraries** for my buttons, movie clips, and animations, which I name according to their content. For example, I might create an FLA file that contains all plastic- or glossy-looking buttons, and call it `Buttons - Plastic_Gloss.fla`. I would then save this in a master directory. When I need them, I simply select File > Import > Import to Library..., locate my FLA file and, presto! The buttons appear in the Library Panel for use in the current project.

Even after several months, you may come back to a project to enhance it or add extra functionality. If you can't remember where the source FLA files are, you're going to waste a lot of time. Using this procedure allows you to be smart with your time and resources, and maintain a consistent look and feel across projects.

I think that, by now, we've covered most of the best practices and methods for increasing productivity when you work with Flash. The practices I've outlined here are only guidelines to make your life a little easier; they're not hard and fast rules. So, feel free to embrace as many or as few of them as you wish.

Now it's time again to "holster up" and get ready for a showdown with some very cool ActionScripted effects!

Random Motion

Have you ever wanted to create random movement for an object or a number of objects? There's a simple technique that will take a single movie clip, create many copies of the object, and randomly place these on the canvas. It then creates the illusion of constant random movement. Best of all, this technique is easily extensible, allowing you, for example, to dynamically alter many of the properties of the object, including opacity and scale.

If you'd like to see the finished product before you proceed, have a look at `Random_Motion.fla` in the code archive.

Setting the Scene

First, you'll need to create a new Flash movie to showcase your effect.

1. Select File > New to create a new Flash movie.

2. Select Modify > Document and set both the width and height of the movie to 300 pixels.

In order to randomly place and move copies of your object, you'll first need an object to use. In this example, we'll create a movie clip container named `MCWorld`, which will contain another movie clip, called `World`.

3. Select Insert > New Symbol, select Movie clip, and name the clip `MCWorld`. Click on the Advanced button to view the clip's linkage parameters, select Export for ActionScript, and name the identifier `MCWorld`, as shown in Figure 3.1.

Figure 3.1. Set linkage properties for the parent movie clip.

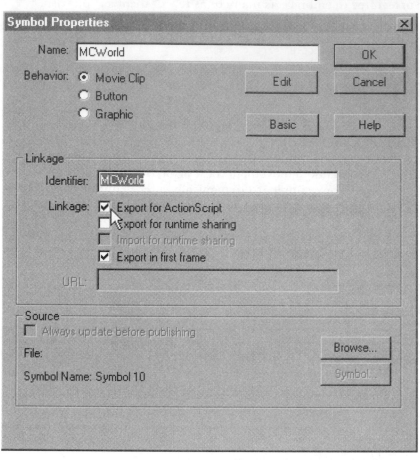

 We select the Export for ActionScript button because, in a moment, we'll use ActionScript dynamically to create instances of this clip. To do that, we need to make it available to ActionScript by choosing this option and assigning the clip a unique identifier.

4. Create a graphic symbol that contains the object or image to which you want to assign random movement. Select Insert > New Symbol… and choose Graphic. Name this symbol World, then create the object either with the drawing tools, or by importing an image or other object from an external source.

The Library Panel should now contain a graphic symbol named World, as in Figure 3.2.

Figure 3.2. Add the child movie clip.

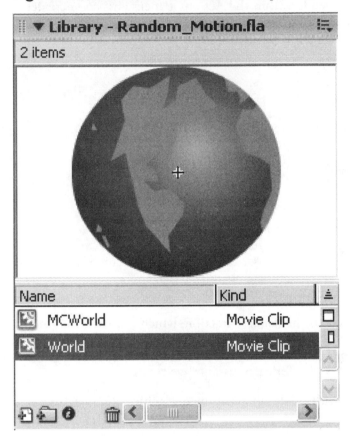

5. Double click the MCWorld movie clip to open it. Drag an instance of the World symbol into it and name the instance World.

Adding the ActionScript

Great! We've created a clip called MCWorld that contains a graphic called World. Now, we can begin to add the ActionScript that will control what takes place on the stage:

6. Select Layer 1 within the main timeline, and give it the name ActionScript. Expand the Actions Panel (select Window > Development Panels > Actions or press **F9**).

7. Add the following code within the Actions Panel. This code creates thirty instances of the MCWorld clip and places them on the canvas at random. It also randomly alters the clips' opacity.

File: **Random_Motion.fla**   ActionScript : 1

```
var numObjects = 30;
for (i = 0; i < numObjects; i++)
{
  var randomObject = attachMovie ('MCWorld', 'MCWorld' + i, i);
  randomObject._x = random (300);
  randomObject._y = random (300);
  randomObject._alpha = random (100);
}
```

The key here is the attachMovie method, which lets you add a new movie clip to the current movie. The parameters we pass to this method are: the identifier we gave the clip in the library (MCWorld), a unique name for each clip instance (in this case, MCWorld with a number appended to it), and a number that indicates where to place the clip in the stacking order.

Also of note in this code is the random function, which returns a random integer between zero (inclusive) and the specified number (exclusive). So random (300) returns a number from 0 to 299. We use this function to generate the position on the stage and the opacity for each instance we create.

With our stage filled with randomly-positioned graphics, it's now time to move them around.

8. Double-click the MCWorld movie clip in the Library Panel to open it. Select Layer 1 and rename it ActionScript.

9. Add the following code within the Actions Panel. It uses setInterval (a standard JavaScript function) to move the graphic symbol instance (World) to a new random position within two pixels of its current position every tenth of a second.

File: **Random_Motion.fla**   MCWorld : ActionScript : 1

```
setInterval (Randomizer, 100);
function ()
```

```
{
  var xShift = random (5) - 2;
  var yShift = random (5) - 2;
  World._x += xShift;
  World._y += yShift;
}
```

We could instead have used an `onEnterFrame` event handler to do this, but `setInterval` allows us to define the speed of the motion independent of the movie's frame rate, which can be useful in many circumstances.

Testing the Movie

You've created your movie clips; now, let's take the movie for a test-drive.

10. Select Control > Test Movie to preview your movie.

Figure 3.3. Preview the movie within Flash.

If everything has gone according to plan, you should see an animated random movie similar to the one shown in Figure 3.3, where the x and y coordinates of the graphics change every tenth of a second.

Random movement is simple to achieve using the basic building blocks outlined here. With experimentation, you'll realize that the possible applications of this technique are limitless.

Modifications

It's easy to modify the `Randomizer` function to alter the presentation of the movie. Changing various properties of the object at different points within the code can have quite dramatic effects—as we're about to see.

Flickering Opacity

Returning to the `Randomizer` function, let's add an extra line that alters the opacity of the graphic.

11. Locate the `Randomizer` function in the first frame of the `MCWorld` movie clip, and adjust it as follows:

File: **Random_Motion_Alpha.fla**   MCWorld : ActionScript : 1 (excerpt)

```
function ()
{
  var xShift = random (5) - 2;
  var yShift = random (5) - 2;
  World._x += xShift;
  World._y += yShift;
  World._alpha = random(100);
}
```

12. Save and preview the movie.

Every tenth of a second, at the same time each graphic is given a little nudge, the opacity is now reset to a random value between zero and 99%, producing a flickering effect. How easy was that?

You can even insert additional object properties to, for example, alter the horizontal and vertical scale of the object. Adding the following lines to the above code will randomly scale the graphic objects:

```
World._xscale = random(100);
World._yscale = random(100);
```

Increasing the Redraw Rate

As I mentioned earlier, using `setInterval` to trigger the changes to our graphics disconnected this animation from the frame rate of the movie. To increase the rate of the animation, simply change the delay specified when calling `setInterval`:

File: **Random_Motion.fla**   MCWorld : ActionScript : 1 (excerpt)

```
setInterval(Randomizer, 100);
```

Reducing this value will increase the redraw rate (how often the `Randomizer` function is called). Bear in mind that these values are counted in milliseconds. To change the redraw rate to one second, you'd set the value to 1000. Keep in mind that decreasing the amount of time between redraws will increase the load on the CPU. If your movie uses a large number of objects, or objects that are complex, the user's computer might have a tough time keeping up with the changes.

Increasing the Number of Objects

To increase the number of objects initially drawn on the screen, simply change the `numObjects` variable in the main timeline code:

File: **Random_Motion.fla**   ActionScript : 1 (excerpt)

```
var numObjects = 30;
for (i = 0; i < numObjects; i++)
{
```

The `for` loop uses this variable to control the number of objects created, so changing the number of objects couldn't be easier!

If those objects are complex, the CPU load will also increase proportionally. Be careful!

Altering the Random Shift Value

After the objects are originally placed on the canvas at random, the `Randomizer` function shifts the x and y coordinates of the graphics every tenth of a second to give an appearance of jittery nervousness. To increase or decrease this quality, simply locate and edit the following lines within the `Randomizer` function:

File: **Random_Motion.fla**   MCWorld : ActionScript : 1 (excerpt)

```
var xShift = random(5) - 2;
var yShift = random(5) - 2;
```

To keep your graphics from wandering off the stage, make sure that the first number on each line is twice the second number plus one. This relationship ensures that the calculated shift values tend to average out to zero. Of course, the easiest way to maintain this relationship is to make it explicit in the code:

```
var nervousness = 2;
var xShift = random(nervousness * 2 + 1) - nervousness;
var yShift = random(nervousness * 2 + 1) - nervousness;
```

As you can see, once you become comfortable with editing the properties of objects, and randomizing their values, you can create some very interesting effects. The key to finding out what you can do is to experiment with values, explore the ActionScript reference, and have fun!

Simple Scripted Masking

In this example, we'll animate a mask from one point to another, based on input parameters we provide. I created this example to illustrate the traffic received by two Web servers hosting a number of Websites. The movie accepts two input parameters, then animates the mask accordingly. For this simple example, we'll populate the variables statically by declaring them in the root of the timeline. A more realistic scenario would see the movie embedded in a database-driven Web page and the variables passed to the movie dynamically. We'll cover importing external data in Chapter 8.

Figure 3.4. This simple scripted masking effect animates a mask between two points.

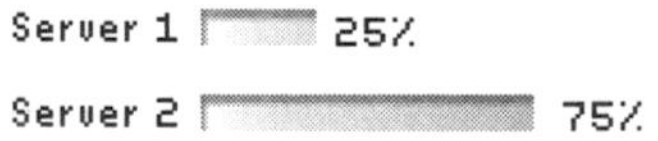

Server 1 ▢▢▢ 25%
Server 2 ▢▢▢▢▢▢ 75%

The finished product is shown in Figure 3.4. Let's look at how this effect is accomplished. To skip straight to modifying the effect , locate the file called `Simple_Animation_Masking.fla` in the code archive.

1. Create a new movie that's 200 pixels wide and 40 pixels high. Alter the frame rate to 24 fps for a nice, smooth animation.

2. Create the folders and layers shown in Figure 3.5 below.

Figure 3.5. Organize the layers and folders for the scripted masking effect.

We now need to create the background bar that we'll mask. In this example, I created a bar that's white on the left and gradually became red toward the right, indicating the increase in server load as traffic levels grow.

3. Add two static text fields within the `textlabels` layer and enter text that reads, `Server 1` and `Server 2`, to let users know what each bar represents. We don't need to convert these to movie clips, as we won't reference them in our ActionScript. Move them to (1, 0) and (1, 25) respectively.

4. Within the Server1Background layer, create a new rectangle that's 100 pixels wide and 9 pixels high. Select a gradient fill that changes from white on the left, through yellow and orange, to red on the right of the rectangle. Select the rectangle, then select Insert > Convert to Symbol.... Choose to create a Graphic named `Background`.

5. Name the existing instance of `Background` `backg1` and move it to (50, 3). Drag a second instance of the graphic from the Library Panel into the Server2Background layer naming it `backg2`, and move it to (50, 29). Lock these two layers; we don't need to modify them any further.

Now that we've created the backgrounds, we can build the masks we'll control via ActionScript:

6. Create a new rectangle, with no stroke and a solid white fill, that's 5 pixels wide and 9 pixels high (this exactly matches the height of the movie clip we will mask). Convert the rectangle to a graphic symbol named `ServerAnimation`, and place instances of the graphic in the Server1Mask and Server2Mask layers.

    Name the instances `server1Mask` and `server2Mask` respectively. (This is important as we will reference these clips in ActionScript later.) Move them to (50, 3) and (50, 29), so they're flush with the left edge of the `backg1` and `backg2` movie clips.

7. To achieve the desired effect, we need to set up the `server1Mask` and `server2Mask` graphics so that they work as **masks** for the background graphics beneath them. Locate the Server1Mask and Server2Mask layers, right-click on each, and select Mask (see Figure 3.6).

Figure 3.6. Convert the dynamic movie clips into masks.

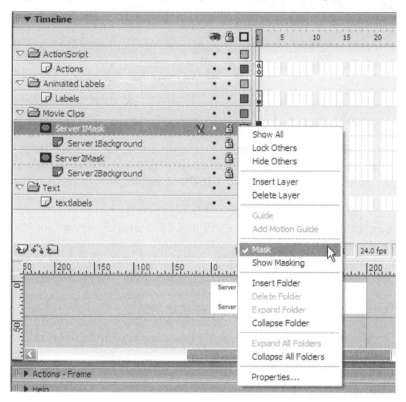

When the movie runs, only those portions of the Background graphics in Server1Background and Server2Background that are covered by the ServerAnimation graphics in Server1Mask and Server2Mask will be visible.

8. We now need to animate the two mask graphics so that they reveal the appropriate portions of the Background graphics. Select the Actions layer, and, with the Actions Panel open, add the following code to the first frame:

File: **Simple_Animation_Masking.fla**   Actions : 1 (Excerpt)

```
var server1load = 25;
var server2load = 75;

function animate (server, serverload)
{
  server.onEnterFrame = function ()
  {
```

```
    if (this._width <= serverload)
      this._width += 2;
  };
}
animate (server1Mask, server1load);
animate (server2Mask, server2load);
```

That's all the code we need to alter the rectangles to make the two bar graphs grow to their assigned lengths. Let's look at how it's done.

First, we create two variables with values that represent (as a percentage) how much of the Background graphic we want to display for each server. The math is kept simple because the backg1 and backg2 graphics are exactly 100 pixels wide.

The animate function takes a reference to one of our mask graphics and sets up an onEnterFrame event handler to increase its width by two pixels per frame up to a specified value. The code finishes by calling animate for each of the two mask graphics, passing each of the two server load values.

Save your movie and preview it. Notice how the two masks grow to sizes dictated by the server1load and server2load variables. It's a pretty cool effect that you can easily include in your projects, creating bar graphs or other visual displays of increases occurring over time.

Adding Text Labels

So far, we've managed to animate masks over time to create a slick, animated bar graph. This is great, but we don't know what values the bars represent. Let's add a text label to each graph to complete the effect:

9. Create a new graphic symbol named serverinfo containing a dynamic text field that's 34 pixels wide and 15 pixels high. In the Property Inspector for the text field, set the Var name to serverload (which we'll use to set the value to be displayed for each server). Also in the Property Inspector, click Character... and make sure that Embed font outlines for is set to Basic Latin (or All Characters in Flash MX).

10. Drag two instances of this new symbol into the first frame of the Labels layer of the Animated Labels folder. Name the instances server1info and server2info. Position them at (54, 1) and (54, 27) respectively.

11. Navigate back to the first frame of the Actions layer in the root of the movie. Insert the following code below the first two variables:

File: **Simple_Animation_Masking.fla**   Actions : 1 (excerpt)

```
server1info.serverload = server1load + "%";
server2info.serverload = server2load + "%";
```

This code sets the `serverload` variable inside each of the two `serverinfo` symbols, controlling the text they display.

12. Save and preview your work.

You'll notice that the values for each of the bars now simply sit where we placed them. They look a little out of place, given the movement that is occurring. We'd better animate them so that they fit in.

13. Still in the first frame of the Actions layer, add the following function declaration:

File: **Simple_Animation_Masking.fla**   Actions : 1 (excerpt)

```
function moveText (serverinfo, serverload)
{
  var startPos = serverinfo._x;
  serverinfo.onEnterFrame = function ()
  {
    if (this._x <= startPos + serverload)
      this._x += 2;
  };
}
```

This function works just like the `animate` function, but it moves the graphic we pass to it horizontally instead of setting its width.

Tip

Try some speedy text

For a slightly different effect that adds to the movie's visual appeal, you could have the text move more quickly than the bars by increasing the step size of the movement from two to four.

All that's left is to call this function for each of our text labels to kick off their animation.

14. Add the following code:

File: **Simple_Animation_Masking.fla**   Actions : 1 (excerpt)

```
moveText (server1info, server1load);
moveText (server2info, server2load);
```

---

15. Save your movie and preview it.

That's it! This scripted animation of the text fields completes the effect and looks very cool!

Modifications

You can easily modify this effect to include more items. Simply create more bars, and reference them when the movie loads, to produce interesting graphs. This effect could also generate moving bars that slide into place as the movie is loaded. The direction in which you choose to take this effect really is up to you.

Raindrops Keep Falling on My Head

One of the quickest ways to create an animated effect is to take an animation and duplicate it multiple times on the stage. The success of this technique depends on the original animation being cool enough to warrant this kind of replication. In this example, we'll create a quick rainfall effect by duplicating a movie clip several times on the canvas. Sound simple? Let's look at how it's done.

To skip the details and jump straight into the effect, locate the `Duplication.fla` file in the code archive.

Figure 3.7. This simple raindrop effect is created using duplication.

Setting the Scene

First, we need to create the movie clip we'll reference in our control code.

1. Create a new movie that's 350 pixels wide and 400 pixels high. Increase the frame rate to 18 fps. Create three layers and name them Actions, Raindrops and Background.

2. Create a graphic symbol named Raindrop and use the drawing tools to draw a falling drop of water.

3. Create a new movie clip symbol, also named Raindrop. Make sure it's open for editing, then drag an instance of the Raindrop graphic from the Library

Panel onto the stage. Name the instance `Raindrop`. Position it at (0, 0) within the clip.

4. Create a new keyframe within the movie clip at frame 40. Select frame 1, right-click, and select Motion Tween. Shift back to frame 40 and move the raindrop graphic to the bottom of the stage—about (0, 390).

5. In the Library Panel, duplicate the `Raindrop` movie clip you created, and name this duplicate `RaindropSlow`. Edit the `RaindropSlow` movie clip, grab the end keyframe in the timeline, and drag it out to frame 80. This will produce a slower animation.

We will use these two Raindrop clips to create a subtle effect a little later. Now let's assemble the main scene:

6. Drag one instance each of the `Raindrop` and `RaindropSlow` movie clips into the Raindrops layer. Name them `raindrop` and `raindropSlow`, respectively.

7. Move the two clips so they sit near the top of the stage, but outside its left edge. I placed them at (-45, 10) and (-30, 10). If you can't see past the edge of the stage, you may have to choose View > Work Area first. The goal here is to have the drops as part of the scene, but not visible on stage.

8. Select the Background layer and add some rolling hills and a storm cloud to it using the drawing tools. To finish, lock this layer.

Adding the Control Code

All the graphics are created and in place on the stage; we just need to duplicate them a few times. If you were to preview the movie now, you'd see two single raindrops, one falling faster than the other, off the side of the stage. I think we'd better spice things up with a little ActionScript.

9. Navigate to the first frame of the Actions layer within the timeline and add the following code:

File: **Duplication.fla**   Actions : 1

```
for (i = 0; i < 50; i++)
{
  var newDrop = raindrop.duplicateMovieClip ("raindrop" + i,
      i);
  newDrop._x = random (350);
```

```
newDrop._y = random (20);
}
```

Here, we use the `duplicateMovieClip` method to create 50 copies of the `raindrop` clip that resides on the root of the timeline. If you want more raindrops, you can change the number 50 in the `for` loop to whatever you like. However, beware of the increased CPU load that comes with large numbers of movie clips.

As with the `attachMovie` method we saw earlier in this chapter, `duplicateMovieClip` requires parameters that set the instance name for the new movie clip (in this case, `raindrop` with a number appended to it) and its position in the stacking order.

After we duplicate the movie clip, we assign each duplicate a random horizontal location between zero and the right-hand side of the stage (x=350). We also shift each instance of the clip vertically using a random value between zero and twenty, to make it look as if the raindrops are falling out of different parts of the cloud.

10. Save your movie and preview it within Flash. You'll notice that, even though the raindrops appear to be randomly spaced along the x and y axes, they fall in a straight line. It certainly doesn't rain like this in my neighborhood! We can quickly remedy the situation by introducing more random elements to the code.

11. Replace the code in the Actions Panel with the following:

File: **Duplication.fla**   Actions : 1 (excerpt)

```
for (i = 0; i < 50; i++)
{
  var newDrop = raindrop.duplicateMovieClip ("raindrop" + i,
     i);
  newDrop._x = random (350);
  newDrop._y = random (20);
  newDrop.gotoAndPlay(random(40) + 1);
}
```

Notice the extra line of code within this block, shown in bold. This little snippet may look insignificant, but it brings the animation to life. Using the `gotoAndPlay` method of each new clip, the animation is advanced to a random frame between 1 and 40 (remember, `random(40)` generates values from 0 to 39) and then played from that point.

12. Save and preview your movie. You'll notice that the raindrops now fall much more naturally than they did before.

Although this animation is simple to accomplish, it's effective in its execution. There are numerous ways to extend this example and make it more interesting. Let's take a little time to examine them now.

Add Some Randomness

To make this effect more engaging, we can modify the horizontal scale and alpha values of each drop of rain as it's created:

13. Modify the code in the Actions layer as follows:

File: **Duplication.fla**   Actions : 1 (excerpt)

```
for (i = 0; i < 50; i++)
{
  var newDrop = raindrop.duplicateMovieClip ("raindrop" + i,
      i);
  newDrop._x = random (350);
  newDrop._y = random (20);
  newDrop._xscale = random (100);
  newDrop._alpha = random (50);
  newDrop.gotoAndPlay (random (40) + 1);
}
```

Save and preview the movie. You'll see raindrops with differing widths—from little, skinny drops to big, fat ones. Each drop's opacity value is also picked at random between zero and 50%.

And the Heavens Opened...

Remember the movie clip we created earlier that was slower than the original raindrop? We have a use for it now! Not all raindrops fall at the same speed, and we can use that clip to make our animation more realistic. Let's add some code that will include the second raindrop movie clip in our animation.

To edit this effect for your own needs, locate `Duplication_Modification.fla` in the code archive.

14. Add the following code below the existing code in the first frame of the Actions layer:

```
File: Duplication_Modification.fla                          Actions : 1 (excerpt)
for (j = i; j < i + 100; j++)
{
  var newDrop = raindropSlow.duplicateMovieClip (
      "raindropSlow" + j, j);
  newDrop._x = random (350);
  newDrop._y = random (20);
  newDrop._xscale = random (100);
  newDrop._alpha = random (25);
  newDrop.gotoAndPlay (random (80) + 1);
}
```

This works just like the previous block of code: the `for` loop creates a number of duplicates of the movie clip, then uses the `random` function to set values for various properties of the duplicates. Here are the differences in this second block of code:

❏ Our `for` loop counts to 100, instead of 50, so we'll create twice as many duplicates.

❏ We create duplicates of the `raindropSlow` clip this time.

❏ We use a new counter variable for this loop (`j`), and add it to the count at the end of our previous loop (`i`) when setting the stacking order of the new duplicates. This ensures that all the drops get their own place in the stacking order. (Otherwise, the slow raindrops would replace the fast raindrops on the stage!)

❏ We set alpha values between zero and 25% for our slow raindrops, to make them appear further away.

❏ Because `RaindropSlow` is 80 frames in length instead of forty, we have adjusted the value we pass to `random` on the last line.

That's it for the raindrops! Now let's see if we can further enhance the scene with some more complicated effects.

Creating a Parallax Cloud Structure

Like raindrops, the movement of clouds is extremely random—each cloud moves at a different speed. With some clever math and a few simple cloud movie clips, you can create an interesting effect that adds depth to the scene (see Figure 3.8).

Figure 3.8. By choosing the right random values, you can create this smooth cloud movement.

We'll start where we left the example in the previous section. To jump straight to the finished product, locate in the code archive.

15. Create two new movie clip symbols, named `LargeCloud` and `SmallCloud`, and place an image that resembles a cloud in each. Make the cloud in the `SmallCloud` clip about half the size of its counterpart in `LargeCloud`.

16. Create above the RainDrops layer a new layer called Clouds, and drag instances of the two new movie clips into this layer. Name them according to their master movie clips (`largeCloud` and `smallCloud`, respectively). Again, place them off the side of the stage.

We'll use these two clouds in a manner similar to our work with the two raindrops, duplicating them with ActionScript code to create a random scene. To add a feeling of depth to our cloud structure, we'll create a **parallax** effect. This involves making faraway objects (our small clouds) move more slowly than nearby objects (our large clouds), which creates a sense of perspective and depth.

17 Add the following code to frame 1 of the Actions layer, beneath the existing code:

File: **Duplication_Modification_Clouds.fla**   Actions : 1 (excerpt)

```
for (i = j; i < j + 60; i++)
{
  var newCloud = smallCloud.duplicateMovieClip (
      "smallCloud" + i, i);
  newCloud._alpha = random (100);
  newCloud._x = random (450) - 100;
  newCloud._y = random (60) + 10;
  newCloud.step = random(4);
  newCloud.onEnterFrame = cloudStep;
}
for (j = i; j < i + 30; j++)
{
  var newCloud = largeCloud.duplicateMovieClip (
      "largeCloud" + j, j);
  newCloud._alpha = random (100);
  newCloud._x = random (450) - 100;
  newCloud._y = random (40) - 20;
  newCloud.step = random(4) + 2;
  newCloud.onEnterFrame = cloudStep;
}
function cloudStep()
{
  if (this._x >= 350) this._x = -100;
  this._x += this.step;
}
```

As you can probably figure out by examining the code, we're creating 60 duplicates of the small cloud and thirty duplicates of the large cloud. Our loops continue to use the i and j variables so that the clouds are added to the top of the stacking order and the raindrops appear to come from behind or within them.

For each cloud we assign a random opacity between 0% and 99%, and a random horizontal position between -100 and 350. Remember that this is the position of the left edge of the cloud, so we need those negative values to allow for clouds partially obscured by the left edge of the stage.

To develop the sense of depth even further, and to ensure our small clouds aren't obscured by the large clouds, we make our small clouds sit lower on the stage (with random vertical positions from 10 to 69) than our large clouds (from -20 to 19). With the small clouds closer to the horizon, they will seem further away.

Now for the crux of our parallax effect: the motion of the clouds. All of our clouds will move across the stage from left to right. Each cloud will have its own randomly assigned step size, which indicates the number of pixels per frame it should move. For the small clouds, we generate step sizes from zero to three pixels, while the large clouds will get step sizes from two to five pixels. We store each cloud's step size into a variable called `step` within the cloud's movie clip (`newCloud.step`).

Finally, we add an `onEnterFrame` event handler for each of the clouds, all of which will use a common function called `cloudStep`. This uses the clip's step size to move it to the right until it reaches a horizontal position of 350 pixels, at which point it's sent back to -100.

18. Save the movie and preview it. To see how the effect looks without the objects running off the stage, export the movie to a SWF file and double-click it to view the movie in Flash Player.

That's a pretty cool effect! All the clouds move at different speeds, so the effect doesn't look "manufactured." But there is still more we can add to this scene...

Creating a Lightning Flash

That storm we just created looks pretty good, but it could do with some sheet lightning to add that finishing touch.

We'll pick up where we left off in the previous section. To jump straight to the end of this example, locate `Duplication_Modification_Clouds_And_Flash.fla` from the code archive.

19. Create a new movie clip named `LightningFlash` and add a rectangle that fills the stage (350x400 pixels). Give it a white gradient fill, fading from 100% opacity at the center of the rectangle to 0% opacity at the bottom edge of the rectangle.

20. Back in the main timeline, create a new layer named Flash above the Clouds layer and drag an instance of the new movie clip into it. Name the instance `flash`. You can lock and hide the layer—we won't need to edit it again.

Now that we've created the movie clip, we can add the control code:

21. Once again, add the following code to the end of frame 1 of the Actions layer:

File: **Duplication_Modification_Clouds_And_Flash.fla**   Actions : 1 (excerpt)

```
flash._alpha = 0;
flash.onEnterFrame = function ()
{
  var flashControl = random (10);
  if (flashControl >= 9 ||
      flash._alpha > 0 && flashControl >= 5)
  {
    flash._alpha += random (65);
    if (flash._alpha > 65)
    {
      flash._alpha = 0;
    }
  }
};
```

We start by setting the `flash` movie clip's opacity to zero, so that the lightning doesn't appear until we want it to.

Next, we tackle the `onEnterFrame` event handler, which will control the opacity of the lightning for each frame of the movie.

Even in the worst storms, lightning is an intermittent thing. After some fiddling, I've decided I want a 10% chance that a flash of lightning will occur in any given frame. So I use `random` to generate a number (`flashControl`) between zero and nine and write my code so that it initiates a lightning flash whenever that number is nine.

Within the body of the `if` statement, the code goes on to add a random value between 0 and 64 to the opacity of the `flash` movie clip. Once this takes place, we want the lightning to continue to grow in brightness until it hits the maximum brightness for a flash of lightning (which, after some experimentation, I've decided is 65% opacity. At that point, we set the opacity back to zero and wait for the next flash of lightning.

When a lightning flash occurs, we don't want to wait for that one-in-ten chance of lightning to make the existing flash brighter. And, at the same time, we can add some variety to our lightning flashes by not having them grow brighter with every frame. That's why the condition in the `if` statement is so complex—if a lightning flash is in progress (which we detect by checking if `flash._alpha` is greater than zero), then we allow the flash to grow brighter 50% of the time (whenever `flashControl` is five or greater).

22. Save the movie and preview it in Flash.

The conditions we've employed here, including the use of random values, cause the `_alpha` value of the `flash` movie clip to flash in and out, producing quite a stormy scene. Feel free to experiment with the probabilities I've put in place to make the storm more or less severe.

Creating User-driven Motion

In this example, we'll create motion based on user input. When the user clicks one button, objects slide into place; when another button is clicked, the objects slide back to their starting points (see Figure 3.9). This example builds upon previous animation examples and is fully scripted—there's not a motion tween in sight!

Figure 3.9. This effect is driven by user input.

If you don't feel like creating this effect from scratch, locate `User_Drive_Motion.fla` in the code archive.

Setting the Scene

1. Start by creating a new movie that's 400 pixels wide and 185 pixels high, and has the folder and layer structure shown in Figure 3.10.

   ### Figure 3.10. Create the folder structure for the user-driven motion effect.

2. Create a new movie clip named `Animation_Base`. In it, place a 190x10 pixel rectangle. Feel free to replace this rectangle with whatever you wish, as we'll be using it only to illustrate the effect of this animation.

3. Drag four instances of the `Animation_Base` movie clip into the Movie Clips layer, naming them `line1`, `line2`, `line3`, and `line4`, and positioning them at (10, 10), (10, 20), (10, 30), and (10, 40) respectively.

4. Set the Color for each `Animation_Base` instance to an Alpha value of 0%, so that the clips start off invisible.

5. Create two new button symbols called `Trigger_Show` and `Trigger_Hide`, and create instances of them in the Buttons layer called `trigger_show` and `trigger_hide`, respectively. Don't be too concerned about the way they look—you can redesign them later when you modify the effect for your own use.

Adding the ActionScript

Now, we'll create a function that will take care of all the movement in this effect, including the speed at which the objects move into and out of position:

6. Select the first frame of the Actions layer, and add the following code within the Actions Panel:

File: **User_Drive_Motion.fla**   Actions : 1 (excerpt)

```
function MoveTo (clip, fadeType, xTo, yTo, speed)
{
  clip.onEnterFrame = function ()
  {
    this._x += (xTo - this._x) * speed;
    this._y += (yTo - this._y) * speed;
    if (fadeType == "in" && this._alpha < 100)
    {
      this._alpha += 5;
    }
    else if (fadeType == "out" && this._alpha > 0)
    {
      this._alpha -= 5;
    }
  };
}
```

The `MoveTo` function accepts the following parameters:

clip   The clip we're animating

fadeType   The type of fade effect to display (`"in"` or `"out"`)

xTo   The final horizontal position for the animation

yTo   The final vertical position for the animation

speed   The speed of the clip's movement (between 0 and 1 for smooth animation)

Looking over the code, it should be pretty obvious what `MoveTo` does. It sets up an `onEnterFrame` event handler for the specified movie that will ease the clip to the specified coordinates while fading its opacity in or out.

The effect will be triggered by the `trigger_show` button, and reversed by the `trigger_hide` button. So all we really need to do is call `MoveTo` with the proper parameter values whenever one of these buttons is clicked.

Adding the Button Trigger Code

Now, we'll add the button trigger code that will make the function work.

7. Add the following code beneath the function declaration we created in the previous section:

```
trigger_show.onPress = function ()
{
  MoveTo (line1, "in", 50, 10, 0.3);
  MoveTo (line2, "in", 100, 20, 0.3);
  MoveTo (line3, "in", 150, 30, 0.3);
  MoveTo (line4, "in", 200, 40, 0.3);
};
```

When the `trigger_show` button is pressed, the `MoveTo` function will be called, moving the clips to their new positions. In this example, we move the movie clips horizontally, as the vertical coordinate matches their starting positions on the stage.

Let's now add the code that will be called when the `trigger_hide` button is pressed, returning the clips to their resting states:

8. Add the following code:

```
trigger_hide.onPress = function()
{
  MoveFromTo(line1, "out", 10, 10, 0.3);
  MoveFromTo(line2, "out", 10, 20, 0.3);
  MoveFromTo(line3, "out", 10, 30, 0.3);
  MoveFromTo(line4, "out", 10, 40, 0.3);
};
```

9. Save and preview your work.

The effect you see is smooth and crisp. Clicking the first button moves the objects into place, while clicking the second option tucks them away.

Tip

Looks like a menu to me!

You could easily build this effect into a navigation element by nesting buttons within the movie clips and altering the passed parameters to suit your needs.

Subtle Flame Animation

With the right balance of subtle animation, you can create effects that are both interesting and visually appealing. In this example, we'll create a realistic flame animation for our hot-rod server (Figure 3.11).

Figure 3.11. Use random movement to create subtle animation effects.

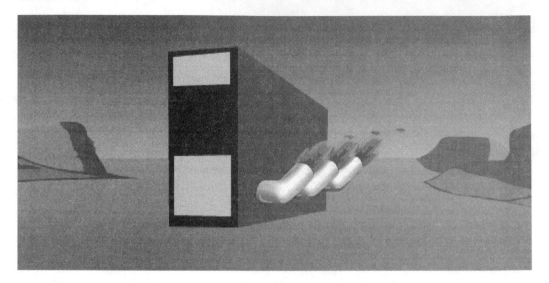

You can grab the finished version of this example and edit it for your own needs by locating `Flaming_Server.fla` in the code archive.

1. Create a new movie that's 600 pixels wide and 300 pixels high; set the frame rate to 24 fps.

2. Create the layer and folder structure shown in Figure 3.12.

Figure 3.12. Use this folder and layer structure.

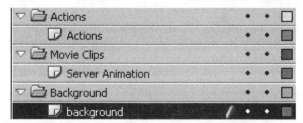

3. Create a background graphic that will serve as the backdrop for the effect within the background layer. In Figure 3.11, I've used a Grand Canyon background.

4. Create a new movie clip named `Flame`, and create three keyframes. Using the pen tool, create three different flames, one on each keyframe, as shown in Figure 3.13. We'll use these to create the random flame effect.

Figure 3.13. Create three different flames for a subtle animation effect.

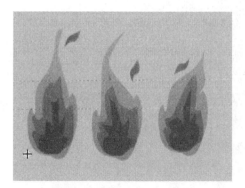

5. Drag three instances into the first frame of the Server Animation layer, naming them `flame1`, `flame2`, and `flame3`.

6. Add the following code to the first frame of the Actions layer on the root of the timeline:

```
function randomBetween (a, b)
{
```

```
    return Math.min (a, b) + random (Math.abs (a - b) + 1);
};
```

What we have here is a useful function that will provide a random integer between the two given numbers (inclusive). Work through the math if you like—`Math.min` returns the smaller of two numbers, while `Math.abs` returns the absolute (positive) value of a number. We'll be using this function throughout this example to create additional subtlety and randomness.

7. Add the following code:

```
Flame1.gotoAndPlay (randomBetween (1, 3));
Flame2.gotoAndPlay (randomBetween (1, 3));
Flame3.gotoAndPlay (randomBetween (1, 3));
```

This randomly starts the animation of each flame between frames one and three.

Now, we have a subtly alternating effect. The next section of code adds a little more randomness—in the real world, flames aren't always the same length. Let's make the size of each flame change at random.

8. Add the following code:

```
Flame1.onEnterFrame = function ()
{
  this._yscale = randomBetween (100, 140);
  this._alpha = randomBetween (60, 100);
};
Flame2.onEnterFrame = function ()
{
  this._yscale = randomBetween (100, 180);
  this._alpha = randomBetween (60, 100);
};
Flame3.onEnterFrame = function ()
{
  this._yscale = randomBetween (100, 200);
  this._alpha = randomBetween (60, 100);
};
```

This assigns an `onEnterFrame` event handler to each of the flames. These handlers randomly modify the opacity and vertical scale of the clips for each frame of the animation. Feeding different values to `randomBetween` gives a different quality to each of the flames.

9. You're done! Preview the movie in Flash.

In the completed example that I've created for you, I've put the flame movie clips behind three exhaust pipe graphics and rotated them to make them look realistic when bolted onto the side of a server box, which is a simple graphic symbol.

Conclusion

This chapter has been an adventure in ActionScript animation techniques, and we've covered a lot of ground—from simple animation, to scripted masking and complex duplication techniques. I hope you'll grab the source files from the code archive and rip them apart! Use the techniques that you've learned here to improve your own projects and create new effects.

In Chapter 4, we'll apply these same techniques to create some truly intriguing text effects—effects that really harness the new powers of Flash MX 2004!

4

Text Effects

One of the most common applications of Flash is in the production of animated text effects. In movies across the Web, text is slid into view, animated, and manipulated to convey dynamic movement. There are hundreds upon hundreds of variations of interesting and engaging text effects, many of which you may see every day as you surf the Web, visit the cinema, or kick back watching television. And, sure, they all look good. But it's important to remember that the basic purpose of text effects is to enhance the delivery of a message or theme from the screen to the user.

Planning is critical to the success of text effects, so always take the time to plan them. Complex effects can easily get off track if they haven't been thought through, so it's worth the effort to sketch them out in storyboard fashion first. This will help you identify and fill any gaps, and will highlight points at which the effect may fail.

As a rule of thumb, you can use text effects and animation however you wish, but be judicious. If the effect is basically pointless, or fails to engage or communicate clearly with the user, then leave it out. There's no point in adding a sub-standard effect—you may as well just paste static text on the page. And, as we noted in the previous chapter, over-animation can be counterproductive. So always ask yourself whether a text effect is needed before you invest time to develop it.

Get inspired: hit the couch!

When your well of creative inspiration runs dry at the end of a long day, put your feet up and take a break in front of the television. But, don't just zone out! Some of the introductory sequences to programs, movies, and even ads can contain inspirational concepts: take note! Those ideas can act as a great source of stimulation for current and future Flash projects.

Advertisements can be particularly useful. Most ads have to make an impact on the viewer within just 15 or 30 seconds. Look out for tricks and techniques that advertisers use to get attention, and think about how you can transfer those concepts to your Flash projects. Keep a pad and pen next to the couch for making note of the most interesting effects and transitions.

When to Use Text Effects

Text effects can add real value to your Flash movies by helping you achieve two important goals:

Focus users' attention

When an object moves around the screen, or is revealed in an interesting way, users will focus their attention on it until they understand what's going on. This can be a great technique for telling stories, or setting user expectations before they move further into your application. Once you have their attention, they represent a sort of captive audience, which can make it easy to convey the message you want to get across.

Convey a message

Once you have users' attention, you can present your message in a manner that befits the application. Be careful, though—if your message isn't strong, or relevant to the theme that you've set aesthetically, the user will soon loose interest and move on. Having established momentum, you must carry that impetus through the rest of the presentation in order to communicate your message successfully.

Types of Text Effects

There are two basic types of text effects.

Interactive Text Effects

Interactive effects call upon the user—you guessed it—to interact. They can be as simple as a basic click-response feedback mechanism, or as complex as fractal-like word structures that unfold after each click, drawing the user through a message. It's up to you to design the text effect that best suits your project and message, but be careful that you don't complicate things unnecessarily. There's a fine line between giving users an engaging display to explore and confusing them with an interface that takes an unreasonable amount of time and energy to decipher. Let your effects create an experience that users can understand— there is, after all, no point designing the coolest delivery on the planet if only 1% of your audience can comprehend it.

Static Text Effects

If you can keep users interested with static text effects, you've done a good job. They run without any user interaction whatsoever. If the user clicks on the text (assuming it doesn't link to another location), nothing happens—the effect serves purely informational purposes. Static effects are typically linear and either run once or in an infinite loop.

When Not to Use Text Effects

It can be very simple to create text effects that look great, and are easy to incorporate into your interface. The problems arise when you view each text effect as a separate entity rather than as part of the whole. Interfaces can quickly become cluttered with multiple effects. And, because each of the animations uses a share of processor time, the more effects, the more intensive the load becomes on the client machine.

Don't fall into the trap of adding text effects to your projects just for the sake of it; you risk overloading users, who will quickly leave in search of a less burdensome online experience at a competitor's site. In general, when creating text effects, ask yourself these questions:

❑ Do I need this effect to complete my movie?

❑ Will the addition of this effect enhance the overall impact of my movie?

❑ Does the effect help make my movie more coherent?

If you answered in the negative to any of those questions, think twice about including the effect. It's always better to err on the side of fewer effects, rather than risk disturbing users and losing the opportunity to convey your message.

Lighting Effects

This section discusses the creation of effects you can find anywhere in the typical urban environment, from neon signs to reflecting chrome imagery. Because they exist in the environment in which many of us live, they're easily recognizable and can be storyboarded without difficulty. They're also very extensible—small tweaks to the code and source imagery can produce a unique experience.

Dazzling Chrome Effect

To ease you into this chapter, I thought I'd begin by introducing you to a technique that's straightforward and can easily be included in your projects. It uses simple ActionScript animation to create a subtle highlight effect (Figure 4.1). The highlight is animated across the text to give the impression that a light is being shone across the front of it. If you wish to dissect the finished product, locate `chromesweep.fla` in the code archive and dive straight in!

Figure 4.1. Create a subtle chrome highlight effect.

Setting the Scene

1. Create a new 500x400 pixel scene with a white background.

2. Create the layer structure shown in Figure 4.2.

Figure 4.2. Use this layer structure for the chrome effect.

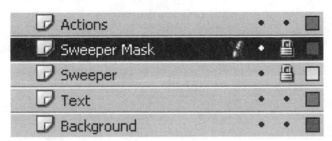

3. Import `background.png` from the code archive into the Background layer. This will serve as a backdrop for the effect.

4. Create the text you wish to highlight in a graphics editor, and import it into the Text layer. Alternatively, create the text within Flash and apply a gradient fill from white through gray, finishing with a light blue, to simulate the appearance of chrome.

    This text forms the basis for the effect, but keep in mind that it doesn't necessarily have to represent chrome—you can run the highlight across any text design.

5. In either Flash or Fireworks MX 2004, create three skewed rectangles with a white linear gradient fill that fades at the edges (Figure 4.3 illustrates how these are created in Fireworks MX 2004). Place the rectangles in the Sweeper layer, and convert them to a movie clip named `Sweeper` with the instance named `sweeper`.

Figure 4.3. Create the highlight gradient.

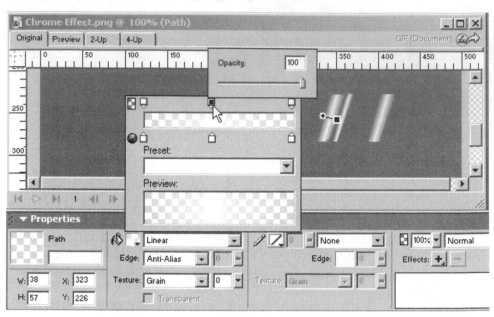

6. Position the sweeper to the left of the text, as shown in Figure 4.4, so that it's ready to move across it horizontally.

Figure 4.4. Position the sweeper and understand the script.

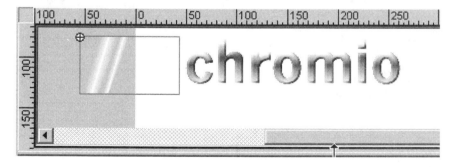

7. To make sure the effect works on any type of background, copy the text from the Text layer and paste it in place (Edit > Paste in Place) into the Sweeper Mask layer. Right-click the Sweeper Mask layer in the timeline and choose

Mask to turn the layer into a mask for the Sweeper layer. This ensures that the effect highlights the text only, avoiding any other elements that may be in the background of your composition.

Animating the Sweeper

We've created the graphic we'll highlight and the highlighting element that will be animated across it. Let's now add some simple code to bring the effect to life.

8. Select the first frame of the Actions layer and add the following code within the Actions Panel:

File: **chromesweep.fla**   Actions : 1

```
sweeper.onEnterFrame = function ()
{
  var step = 7;
  if (this._x > 270)
  {
    this._x = -55;
  }
  this._x += step;
};
```

9. Preview your work and marvel at how such a pleasing effect can be created in such a short time!

The code is fairly simple: as long as the _x coordinate of the sweeper movie clip doesn't exceed 270, we continue to increment the position of the sweeper across the screen. When the _x coordinate exceeds 270, the sweeper has finished its movement across the text, so we reset its position to the beginning.

Modifications

A simple modification to this effect involves creating a duplicate of the sweeper within the Sweeper layer, and having it move in the opposite direction. You'll find chromesweep-duplicate.fla in the code archive.

10. Create another instance of the Sweeper movie clip, name it sweeper2, and move it to the right so that it doesn't overlap the text. Add the following code to the first frame of the Actions layer:

```
File: chromesweep-duplicate.fla                           Actions : 1 (excerpt)
sweeper2.onEnterFrame = function ()
{
  var step = 7;
  if (this._x < -55)
  {
    this._x = 270;
  }
  this._x -= step;
}
```

Here, we simply reverse the direction of the sweeper using the code we created earlier.

11. Preview the effect and save it. This effect was quick and easy!

Neon Text Effect

I couldn't talk about text effects without including a funky neon-type effect. In this section, we'll produce a broken neon sign (Figure 4.5) that flickers constantly, complete with an electric crackle that occurs when certain conditions are met. What's nice about this effect is the inclusion of a dynamic sound object, which is called when the opacity of the neon highlight hits a certain level, by adding an air of realism to the final product.

Figure 4.5. The effect of crackling electricity gives this neon text a realistic appearance.

To jump straight in and modify this effect for your own needs, locate `neon.fla` in the code archive. you'll find the source graphics for the effect, which were created with Fireworks MX 2004, in the `neon.png` file in the code archive.

Setting the Scene

We need to start by creating the elements that we'll manipulate within Flash. We'll create two elements—the neon tube, and the highlight effect—within an image editor of your choice (the examples shown in Figure 4.6 were created in Fireworks MX 2004 and then imported into Flash). They'll need to be separate entities, as we'll manipulate the neon highlight via ActionScript a little later on.

Figure 4.6. The neon tube and neon highlight layers were created within Fireworks 2004.

Flash MX 2004 can't create glow effects like this, which is why we create them as bitmaps rather than vector images within Flash. This procedure is a necessary evil—it will increase the file size of the exported SWF file—but it's one we can live with on this occasion.

1. Create two separate images, one for the neon tube and one for the neon highlight. Alternatively, copy each object from `neon.png` in the code archive, as shown in Figure 4.6. Paste the bitmaps into two layers (Neon Tube and Neon Highlight) within a new Flash document. Add another layer called Actions above them.

2. Make sure that Neon Highlight (containing the image with the yellow glow) is beneath the Neon Tube layer in the stacking order, by reordering the layers if necessary.

3. Give the highlight image an instance name of `neonHighlight`. We'll reference this later in our ActionScript, so it's important to name it now.

4. Import `fizzle.mp3` from the code archive into your library. Right-click on the object within the Library Panel and edit the linkage properties as shown in Figure 4.7.

Figure 4.7. Set up the linkage properties for the sound byte.

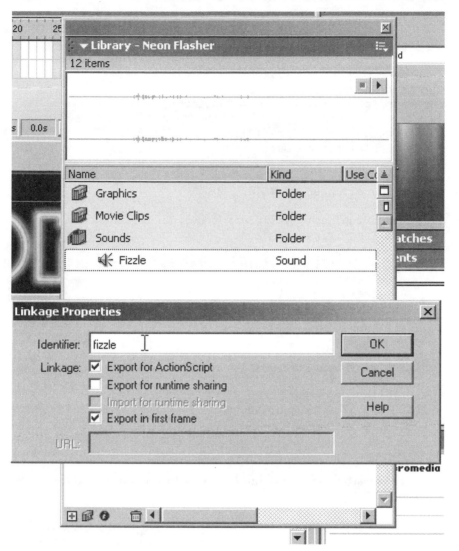

Now that we've added the elements to the stage, we can move on to look at the ActionScript that will make our neon sign blink into life, along with some crackly sound effects.

Adding the ActionScript

5. Select the first frame of the Actions layer and add the following code to the Actions Panel:

File: **neon.fla**   Actions : 1

```
var neonTrigger = 75;
neonHighlight.onEnterFrame = function ()
{
  neonTrigger += random (10);
  if (neonTrigger >= 50)
  {
    neonHighlight._visible = !neonHighlight._visible;
    if (neonTrigger >= 75)
    {
      neonHighlight._visible = true;
      if (neonTrigger >= 200)
      {
        neonHighlight._visible = false;
        playSound("fizzle");
        neonTrigger = 0;
      }
    }
  }
};
function playSound (sound)
{
  var initSound = new Sound ();
  initSound.attachSound (sound);
  initSound.start ();
}
```

The code is quite straightforward, but let's walk through it now and see how the effect is achieved.

The goal, of course, is to make our blinking highlight mimic the behavior of a faulty neon sign. To this end, we want the light to start out lit, but then at some point we want it to blink off with a fizzle. After a moment or two, we'd like it to begin to flicker on and off with each frame of the animation, before finally coming back on.

The code above uses a single variable called `neonTrigger`, whose value is incremented with each frame of the animation by a random number between zero and nine:

```
neonTrigger += random (10);
```

When `neonTrigger` reaches a value of 50, the first `if` statement becomes true and the light begins blinking on and off with each frame:

```
if (neonTrigger >= 50)
{
  neonHighlight._visible = !neonHighlight._visible;
```

When `neonTrigger` reaches a value of 75, the second `if` statement kicks in and the light remains on:

```
if (neonTrigger >= 75)
{
  neonHighlight._visible = true;
```

And when `neonTrigger` reaches a value of 200, the final `if` statement switches off the light, plays the fizzle sound, and sets `neonTrigger` back to zero:

```
if (neonTrigger >= 200)
{
  neonHighlight._visible = false;
  playSound("fizzle");
  neonTrigger = 0;
}
```

The `playSound` function takes as a parameter the name of the sound clip, uses it to attach the sound in the library to a new ActionScript `Sound` object, and then starts it playing:

```
function playSound (sound)
{
  var initSound = new Sound ();
  initSound.attachSound (sound);
  initSound.start ();
}
```

Save your movie and preview it. Wow! The ActionScript really makes the effect work—as the lettering sputters out, we can hear the electric sparking of the neon tube.

By changing the conditions under which the neonHighlight movie clip is switched on or off, you can easily tweak the effect to your liking.

For example, decreasing the value in the final if statement, as shown below, produces a *very* broken neon sign!

```
if (neonTrigger >= 100)
{
  neonHighlight._visible = false;
  playSound("fizzle");
  neonTrigger = 0;
}
```

Try playing with the conditions and values until you find an effect you're happy with.

This effect can form the foundation for many more "urban environment" effects based around electricity, flickering light bulbs, car headlights—the list goes on! Experiment further to see how you can use this effect in your projects.

Glow in the Dark Effect

Well, we've built a neon sign. Now, let's develop another illuminating project—a text effect (Figure 4.8) that looks like a glowing bulb! This effect is simple to achieve, but, like the previous example, can really look great.

Figure 4.8. Build this great dynamic bulb effect.

You can apply this effect to any item you might want to fade in and out. The object doesn't have to be a bulb; it could be a car headlight, part of an inter-face—anything you please!

Setting the Scene

To skip the discussion and play with the finished effect, locate `bulb.fla` in the code archive. You'll find the source files, created with Fireworks 2004, in `bulb.png`.

1. Create two separate bitmaps in an image editor, one for the actual bulb, and one for the "glow." Alternatively, you could copy and paste each object from the sample source file (`bulb.png`), as shown in Figure 4.9. Paste the images into two layers called Bulb and Bulb Glow within a new Flash document, then line them up.

    Figure 4.9. Separate layers are used for the glowing bulb effect.

2. Making sure that the Bulb Glow layer appears beneath the Bulb layer in the stacking order

3. Give the glow object an instance name of `bulbGlow`.

4. Create another layer at the top of the stacking order and call it Actions.

Adding the ActionScript to Create the Glow

Now that the images have been imported, it's time to add the ActionScript that will make the effect work. But this time, we'll use a prototype function in our code, as we first saw in Chapter 2.

To refresh your memory, adding a method to the `MovieClip.prototype` object effectively adds that method to all `MovieClip` objects, that is, all movie clips in the movie. That's exactly what we're about to do.

5. Select the first frame of the Actions layer and add the following code within the Actions Panel:

File: **bulb.fla**   Actions : 1

```
MovieClip.prototype.Glow = function (max, min, step)
{
  this.glowMax = max;
  this.glowMin = min;
  this.glowStep = step;
  this.glowDir = true;
  this._alpha = glowMin;
  this.onEnterFrame = function ()
  {
    if (this.glowDir)
    {
      this._alpha += this.glowStep;
    }
    else
    {
      this._alpha -= this.glowStep;
    }
    if (this._alpha >= this.glowMax ||
        this._alpha <= this.glowMin)
    {
      this.glowDir = !this.glowDir;
    }
  };
};
bulbGlow.Glow (100, 50, 5);
```

This is quite a chunk of code to take in all at once! What we're doing here is extending the functionality of the `MovieClip` class to include a new custom method, called `Glow`, to be used.

This function stores the parameters you provide (maximum opacity, minimum opacity, and step size) into the movie clip and sets its opacity to the minimum value. It then sets up an `onEnterFrame` event handler that will smoothly fade from that minimum opacity up to the maximum, and then back down to the minimum, and so on.

The last line of the code simply calls the newly-added method on the `bulbGlow` movie clip, specifying a maximum opacity of 100%, a minimum opacity of 50%, and a step size of 5%.

It's very easy to produce effects in this way. They make clear, logical sense, and you can see at a glance what will happen to the clips on the stage.

Modifications

You can produce a more subtle effect by decreasing the range over which the effect will last, but be careful—the more subtle the effect, the more difficult it may be to spot within your interface.

A more subtle effect might be appropriate for some interface buttons, providing visual clues that help users make a selection. You could also increase the speed of the effect by increasing the `step` parameter value, or modify it for a mouseover effect using the `onRollOver` and `onRollOut` event handlers—the choice is yours.

This example gives you the basics from which you can create many different effects to draw attention to areas of your interface as required.

Motion Effects

Let's further explore text animation. There are many motion effects you can develop, but, as we don't have the time or space to include them all, let's focus on some of the more common, funky effects.

Jiggling Text Effect

Applying quick movement—a little jiggle!—can be a fantastic way to draw attention to a headline or banner ad. This quickfire effect, shown in Figure 4.10, can be included in any of your projects with relative ease, and can quickly be modified to accomplish new tasks.

Figure 4.10. This jiggling text is a great effect.

Setting the Scene

To jump straight in and modify this effect for your own needs, access `jiggle.fla` from the code archive.

1. Create two layers, named Actions and Letters, within a new Flash document.

2. Create a word in whatever text size and font you desire. Select Modify > Break Apart to separate it into individual letters.

Import bitmaps if you like

You don't have to create the letters from a font within Flash—you can import bitmap images created in another program. Remember, though, that bitmaps will increase the file size more than vector images will. Whichever method you choose, make sure you separate each individual letter to give this effect its maximum impact.

3. Convert each letter into a movie clip and name each instance accordingly. In this example, the word "jiggle" has been separated into movie clip instances with the following names: j, i, g1, g2, l, and e.

Adding the Jiggle Script

Now it's time to get those letters jiggling! Let's add the ActionScript to control motion.

4. Select the first frame of the Actions layer and enter the following code into the Actions Panel:

File: **jiggle.fla**   Actions : 1 (excerpt)

```
function randomBetween (a, b)
{
  return Math.min (a, b) + random (Math.abs (a - b) + 1);
}
```

This is the same `randomBetween` function we used in Chapter 3; it returns an integer between the two numbers you specify (inclusive).

5. Add this code to what you already have:

File: **jiggle.fla**   Actions : 1 (excerpt)

```
MovieClip.prototype.Jiggle = function ()
{
  var mc = this.createEmptyMovieClip ("Jiggle", 0);
  mc.onEnterFrame = function ()
  {
    var jiggle = randomBetween (-20, 20);
    this._parent._rotation = jiggle;
  };
};
```

As with the previous example, we're using a prototype function to extend the `MovieClip` class, in this case, with a new method called `Jiggle`. `Jiggle` is a parameterless method that randomly rotates the movie clip within a range of 40 degrees.

The important difference here is how we have applied this effect. Rather than attach an `onEnterFrame` event handler to the clip itself, we dynamically create a new, empty movie clip using the `createEmptyMovieClip` method of the existing clip. We then assign the `onEnterFrame` event handler to the new clip. This event handler picks a random value between -20 and 20 and assigns this as the rotation of its *parent* movie clip (the clip for which we called the `Jiggle` method).

Why bury the event handler in an empty movie clip, you ask? This approach allows us to apply more than one effect to a single movie clip. A movie clip can have only one `onEnterFrame` event handler, so using it to apply one effect prevents us from using it for another. As an exercise, go back to the glowing bulb example in the previous section and modify it to use an empty clip for its `onEnterFrame` event handler. Then, if you're feeling *really* adventurous, try applying the glow effect to the jittering letters in this example! The two effects should coexist happily, since each is managed by a separate clip.

Back to the example at hand, all that remains is to call the `Jiggle` method for each of the movie clip instances that appear on the stage. As we'll see, it's very easy to include additional letters and scale the effect for your needs.

6. Beneath the existing code, insert the following:

File: **jiggle.fla**   Actions : 1 (excerpt)

```
j.Jiggle();
i.Jiggle();
g1.Jiggle();
g2.Jiggle();
l.Jiggle();
e.Jiggle();
```

7. Save your document and preview it in Flash.

See how the letters jiggle between the ranges we've set for them? I really like this animation—it's so effective, yet so easy to accomplish.

Modifications

With just a few modifications, this can become a really compelling effect that we can use anywhere, anytime. By applying the following modification, we'll quickly be able to assign individual ranges to each of the movie clips, achieving tighter control over each letter. To skip the talk and start modifying the effect for your own needs, locate `jiggle-control.fla` in the code archive.

8. Modify the `Jiggle` prototype code to resemble the following:

File: **jiggle-control.fla**   Actions : 1 (excerpt)

```
MovieClip.prototype.Jiggle = function (min, max)
{
  var mc = this.createEmptyMovieClip ("Jiggle", 0);
```

```
   mc.min = min;
   mc.max = max;
   mc.onEnterFrame = function ()
   {
      var jiggle = randomBetween (this.min, this.max);
      this._parent._rotation = jiggle;
   };
};
```

Notice that the function now accepts two parameters, min and max. These are passed to the randomBetween function, providing us precise control over what happens within the effect.

Having extended the function, we can now change the code to make individual letters move more or less than their neighbors. The overall effect is to make the letters look as if they're squashed together, jostling for position like sardines in a tin. Let's make the changes.

9.   Alter the individual method calls for the movie clips as follows:

File: **jiggle-control.fla**   Actions : 1 (excerpt)
```
j.Jiggle (-20, 20);
i.Jiggle (-12, 12);
g1.Jiggle (-5, 5);
g2.Jiggle (-5, 5);
l.Jiggle (-12, 12);
e.Jiggle (-20, 20);
```

10.   Save and preview your work.

As you can see, the closer any letter is to the center of the arrangement, the narrower is its range of movement—just like in real life! If you thought the original looked good, I think you'll agree that this effect looks even better! It really looks as if the letters are fighting for room—albeit unsuccessfully.

Let's alter this effect even more. Instead of adjusting the rotation of the text, let's alter the horizontal scale of the movie clips instead. To access the code for this effect and modify it to suit your needs, locate jiggle-scale.fla from the code archive.

11.   Modify the Jiggle prototype function code as follows:

File: **jiggle-scale.fla**   Actions : 1 (excerpt)

```
MovieClip.prototype.Jiggle = function (min, max)
{
  var mc = this.createEmptyMovieClip ("Jiggle", 0);
  mc.min = min;
  mc.max = max;
  mc.onEnterFrame = function ()
  {
    var jiggle = randomBetween (this.min, this.max);
    this._parent._xscale = jiggle;
  };
};
```

12. Alter the controlling code for each of the movie clips as follows:

File: **jiggle-scale.fla**   Actions : 1 (excerpt)

```
j.Jiggle (100, 150);
i.Jiggle (100, 150);
g1.Jiggle (100, 150);
g2.Jiggle (100, 150);
l.Jiggle (100, 150);
e.Jiggle (100, 150);
```

13. Save your work and preview it.

The effect we've created here also can be used in an environment other than the rotational example we produced earlier. It is possible to modify the effect in order to couple both scaling and rotation. This can easily be achieved by altering the function and incoming parameters. We'll do so now, by passing in a few more parameters and adding both rotational and horizontal scaling code to this function.

To jump straight to the completed code for this effect, locate `jiggle-scale-rotate.fla` in the code archive.

14. Modify the `Jiggle` prototype function code as follows:

File: **jiggle-scale-rotate.fla**   Actions : 1 (excerpt)

```
MovieClip.prototype.Jiggle = function (minRot, maxRot,
    minScale, maxScale)
{
  var mc = this.createEmptyMovieClip ("Jiggle", 0);
  mc.minRot = minRot;
  mc.maxRot = maxRot;
```

```
mc.minScale = minScale;
mc.maxScale = maxScale;
mc.onEnterFrame = function ()
{
  var jiggleScale = randomBetween (this.minScale,
     this.maxScale);
  this._parent._xscale = jiggleScale;
  var jiggleRot = randomBetween (this.minRot, this.maxRot);
  this._parent._rotation = jiggleRot;
};
};
```

15. Modify the movie clip function calls as follows:

File: **jiggle-scale-rotate.fla**   Actions : 1 (excerpt)

```
j.Jiggle (-20, 20, 100, 120);
i.Jiggle (-20, 20, 100, 120);
g1.Jiggle (-20, 20, 100, 120);
g2.Jiggle (-20, 20, 100, 120);
l.Jiggle (-20, 20, 100, 120);
e.Jiggle (-20, 20, 100, 120);
```

16. Save your movie and preview it within Flash.

Effects like this may seem complicated, but as we've built the effect, and added the extra functionality ourselves, we can see what it does. It looks cool and could easily find a home in many of your future projects.

Zooming In Effect

There are many different variations of the zooming effect, but let's start out with a simple one. We'll zoom text items into place on the canvas from a large value to a predefined standard value (Figure 4.11). The opacity of each zooming object will also increase as the minimum scaling value is approached.

Figure 4.11. Zooming text effects can capture user attention.

Setting the Scene

To edit the finished effect for your own needs, locate `zoom.fla` within the code archive.

1. Create a new Flash document and alter the frame rate to 24 fps (Modify > Document...).

2. Create two new layers: Actions and Words.

3. Create three new static text objects in the first frame of the Words layer, containing the text to which you wish to apply the effect. In this example we have used the words "scale," "me," and "down." Convert these three text objects to movie clips (press **F8**, or Modify > Convert to Symbol...) and name their instances according to their content: `scale`, `me`, and `down`.

Zooming the Objects with ActionScript

4. Select the first frame of the Actions layer and insert the following code:

File: **zoom.fla**   Actions : 1 (excerpt)

```
MovieClip.prototype.ScaleDown = function (maxScale, minScale,
    minAlpha, alphaStep, scaleStep)
```

```
{
  var mc = this.createEmptyMovieClip ("ScaleDown", 0);
  this._xscale = maxScale;
  this._yscale = maxScale;
  this._alpha = minAlpha;
  mc.minScale = minScale;
  mc.scaleStep = scaleStep;
  mc.alphaStep = alphaStep;
  mc.onEnterFrame = function ()
  {
    if (this._parent._xscale > this.minScale)
    {
      this._parent._xscale -= this.scaleStep;
      this._parent._yscale -= this.scaleStep;
    }
    if (this._parent._alpha < 100)
    {
      this._parent._alpha += this.alphaStep;
    }
  };
};
scale.ScaleDown (500, 100, 0, 2, 6);
me.ScaleDown (500, 100, 0, 2, 6);
down.ScaleDown (500, 100, 0, 2, 6);
```

In the code above, we're passing a whole caravan of parameters to the function. They control the minimum and maximum scale values, the minimum alpha value for the objects as they zoom into view, and the step increments for both the scale and alpha values.

Having created an empty movie clip to manage the effect, we then set the initial values for the opacity, horizontal scale, and vertical scale of the current movie clip.

Next, we store the remaining parameters as variables in the empty clip for use by the onEnterFrame event handler, the code of which should seem relatively straightforward by now.

5.   Save your and preview the effect.

Great! The text zooms into place, fading from invisibility to an opacity of 100%. The best thing about this effect is that it's so easy to insert extra words or sentences.

We can easily extend this basic effect by altering the parameters that we pass to the function. Let's look at this now.

Modifications

As with all ActionScript-based effects, we can alter the display simply by changing the parameters we pass. In the following example, we'll change the starting scales of our words so they settle into their final positions one at a time. To edit the effect and modify it for your own needs, locate `zoom-step.fla` in the code archive.

6. Locate the control code that calls the functions, and alter it as follows:

File: **zoom-step.fla**   Actions : 1 (excerpt)
```
scale.ScaleDown (300, 100, 0, 2, 6);
me.ScaleDown (400, 100, 0, 2, 6);
down.ScaleDown (500, 100, 0, 2, 6);
```

7. Save and preview the effect.

You'll notice that the first words appear to move in more quickly than the others. This is because we've reduced the initial scale for the movie clips `scale` and `me`. Quite a simple change, yet it has a dramatic impact (Figure 4.12).

Figure 4.12. Altering the ActionScript produces varied effects.

Now, if we alter a few more of the parameters that are passed, we can make this effect look even funkier! The adjusted version of the code can be found in as `zoom-step2.fla`.

8. Change the control code as follows:

File: **zoom-step2.fla** Actions : I (excerpt)
```
scale.ScaleDown (300, 100, 0, 6, 6);
me.ScaleDown (400, 100, 0, 4, 4);
down.ScaleDown (500, 100, 0, 2, 2);
```

9. Save your document again, and preview your work.

That's how easy it is to control the way the zoom effect works. With a little thought, we can also control the timing of the appearance of the words. This can be very useful—you could, for example, produce an entire animated poem in this manner. To skip forward and access the finished code for this effect , locate `zoom-timed.fla` in the code archive.

10. To begin, delete the three `ScaleDown` calls from the previous example. To achieve the desired effect, we want these calls made on cue, rather than immediately.

11. Add the following code in their place:

File: **zoom-timed.fla** Actions : 1 (excerpt)
```
scale._visible = false;
me._visible = false;
down._visible = false;
```

This code initially switches off the visibility of the text movie clips, placing the timing of the calls under our control.

12. Finally, add the following code:

File: **zoom-timed.fla** Actions : 1 (excerpt)
```
var marker = 20;
ScheduleTrigger = function ()
{
  marker--;
  if (marker == 15)
  {
    scale.ScaleDown (300, 100, 0, 6, 6);
```

```
    scale._visible = true;
  }
  if (marker == 10)
  {
    me.ScaleDown (400, 100, 0, 6, 6);
    me._visible = true;
  }
  if (marker == 5)
  {
    down.ScaleDown (500, 100, 0, 6, 6);
    down._visible = true;
  }
};
setInterval (ScheduleTrigger, 200);
```

You can see here that our calls to ScaleDown have been moved into another function, called ScheduleTrigger. We start by setting a variable named marker with an initial value of 20. This variable is decremented each time the function is called. When it reaches 15, we call ScaleDown on the scale movie clip, and make it visible. We do the same for me and down when it reaches 10 and five, respectively.

The final line of this code uses the built-in setInterval function to call ScheduleTrigger every 200 milliseconds (i.e. five times per second).

13. Save your document and preview your work.

Now the effect occurs when you want it to; approximately once each second, one of the words appears and zooms into place. Using this method to control the timing of the effect allows us to say what happens and when—a very useful ability!

Zooming Out Effect

The zooming out effect we are about to create (Figure 4.13) shares 80% of its code with the zooming in effect we saw before, but is sufficiently different that it warrants its own discussion. In this effect, the text will zoom towards us, but, at a given point that we'll control, it will leap forward as if given a sudden boost of speed.

To edit the completed effect for your own needs, locate zoom-out.fla within the code archive.

Figure 4.13. The Zooming In effect can be modified to zoom out.

Setting the Scene

1. Start by creating a new Flash document with a frame rate of 24 fps (Modify> Document...). Create two new layers called Actions and Words.

2. Create three new text objects containing relevant content. In this example, I used the text "scale," "me," and "up." Convert the text objects to movie clip symbols and name the instances according to their content (`scale`, `me`, and `up`).

Adding the ActionScript

3. Select the first frame of the Actions layer and add the following code within the Actions Panel:

File: **zoom-out.fla** Actions : 1 (excerpt)

```
MovieClip.prototype.ScaleUp = function (maxScale, minScale,
    minAlpha, alphaStep, scaleStep)
{
  var mc = this.createEmptyMovieClip ("ScaleUp", 0);
  this._xscale = minScale;
  this._yscale = minScale;
  mc.minScale = minScale;
  mc.maxScale = maxScale;
  mc.scaleStep = scaleStep;
  mc.alphaStep = alphaStep;
  mc.onEnterFrame = function ()
  {
    if (this._parent._xscale < this.maxScale)
    {
      var multiplier = 1;
      if (this._parent._xscale >= this.minScale * 1.6)
      {
        multiplier = 10;
      }
      this._parent._xscale += this.scaleStep * multiplier;
      this._parent._yscale += this.scaleStep * multiplier;
    }
    if (this._parent._alpha > 0)
    {
      this._parent._alpha -= this.alphaStep;
    }
  };
};
```

I won't go into the construction of the method again, as we covered it in detail in the previous example. Suffice to say that the effect is now inverted—it zooms out instead of in—with a twist. Here, we've included an extra condition: when the **_xscale** property reaches a certain value, the text is given that extra boost of speed I mentioned a moment ago.

```
if (this._parent._xscale >= this.minScale * 1.6)
{
  multiplier = 10;
}
```

As soon as the condition is met—whoosh! The text rapidly flies off into the ether at a rate of knots.

4. Insert the following code beneath the method you just added:

File: **zoom-out.fla**   Actions : 1 (excerpt)

```
scale.ScaleUp (500, 100, 0, 2, 2);
me.ScaleUp (500, 100, 0, 2, 2);
up.ScaleUp (500, 100, 0, 2, 2);
```

5. Save the document and preview your work.

This revision is largely the same as that which was used in the previous example, yet the effect achieves a fairly different result. As we wrote everything in Action-Script, the natural beauty of the beast comes into play—to our advantage! This makes it easy for us to tweak the settings and add extra functionality without the headache of juggling keyframes on the timeline.

Modifications

Figure 4.14. Add a `triggerPoint` parameter to produce a speedy "chase" effect.

Presently, all the movie clips we're controlling are speeding away at the same rate. We can modify the effect so that the clips zoom off one after another, almost like they're involved in a high-speed car chase!

To skip the details and jump straight to editing the effect, locate `zoom-out-race.fla` in the code archive.

6. Modify the `ScaleUp` method definition as follows:

File: **zoom-out-race.fla**   Actions : 1 (excerpt)

```
MovieClip.prototype.ScaleUp = function (maxScale, minScale,
    minAlpha, alphaStep, scaleStep, triggerPoint)
{
  var mc = this.createEmptyMovieClip ("ScaleUp", 0);
  this._xscale = minScale;
  this._yscale = minScale;
  mc.minScale = minScale;
  mc.maxScale = maxScale;
  mc.scaleStep = scaleStep;
  mc.triggerPoint = triggerPoint;
  mc.alphaStep = alphaStep;
  mc.onEnterFrame = function ()
  {
    if (this._parent._xscale < this.maxScale)
    {
      var multiplier = 1;
      if (this._parent._xscale >= this.triggerPoint)
      {
        multiplier = 10;
      }
      this._parent._xscale += this.scaleStep * multiplier;
      this._parent._yscale += this.scaleStep * multiplier;
    }
    if (this._parent._alpha > 0)
    {
      this._parent._alpha -= this.alphaStep;
    }
  };
};
```

We've altered the function to accept another parameter, triggerPoint, which will be sent in via the control code. This allows us to set the point at which each clip races off into the distance.

All that remains is to alter the control code for each clip, in order to send the staggered values through:

7. Alter the remaining code as follows:

File: **zoom-out-race.fla**   Actions : 1 (excerpt)

```
scale.ScaleUp (2000, 100, 0, 1, 2, 150);
me.ScaleUp (2000, 100, 0, 1, 2, 180);
up.ScaleUp (2000, 100, 0, 1, 2, 210);
```

8.   Save the movie and preview it.

Now we see a staggered race to the finish! We've set a `triggerPoint` parameter for each movie clip—the lower the value, the sooner the clip reaches the threshold before it whizzes off into the distance!

Circulating Text Effect

There comes a time in every Flash designer's life when the desire to create non-linear, "off the wall" effects develops. We will now satisfy that need! Although this next project works well on its own, it could also be used subtly in the background of another effect.

The project involves rotating a number of letters, each around its own axis. Figure 4.15 doesn't really do it justice.

Figure 4.15. Circulating text could form a subtle background for another effect.

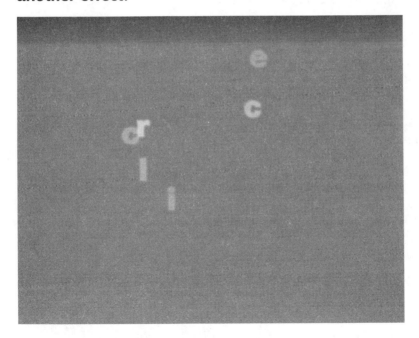

The effect centers upon the rotation of a movie clip around a central point with given values for radius and speed. And, as we'll see, it lends itself to several modifications.

To jump right in and edit the effect to suit your needs, locate `rotate.fla` in the code archive.

Setting the Scene

1. Start by creating some text as single letters or phrases in Flash. To apply special effects to the text, such as shadows or glows, create the text in an image editor.

    Feel free to use the same graphics I created; you'll find them in <`rotate.png`> in the code archive.

    In this example, I used Fireworks MX 2004 to create the word "circle." I converted the text to paths, applied a subtle glow to each letter, flattened them into individual bitmaps, and saved each as a `.png` file. Finally, I imported these files into Flash.

2. Create a new Flash document and alter the frame rate to 24 fps (Modify > Document...). Create three new layers, named, from the top layer down, Actions, Animated Text and Background. Place a background of your choice within the Background layer and lock it.

    Use the 500x400 pixel background file, called `background.png`, from the code archive if you're struggling for ideas.

3. Import your letters into Flash (File > Import > Import to Stage...). Locate the letters or phrases you wish to animate, and convert each into an individual movie clip instance in the Animated Text layer of the stage. Name these movie clip instances according to their content. In this example, I named them `letterC` through `letterE` (the second letter C is called `letterC2`).

4. Scatter the clips randomly about the stage, as shown in Figure 4.16. You can place them wherever you like—just make sure they're not too far from the center.

Figure 4.16. Randomly place the movie clips on the stage.

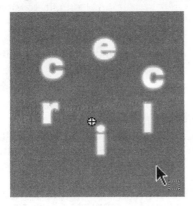

Now that we've got the clips in order, it's time to add the code that will control the effect.

Adding the ActionScript

Once again, we'll use a prototype function to implement this effect as a method of the `MovieClip` class. Creating the effect this way makes it easy to understand and simple to update and tweak.

5.   Add the following code to the first frame of the Actions layer:

File: **rotate.fla**   Actions : 1 (excerpt)

```
Math.randomBetween = function (a, b)
{
  return Math.min (a, b) + random (Math.abs (a - b) + 1);
}
```

This is our faithful random number generator. This time we've made it a method of the ActionScript `Math` object to keep things neat.

6.   Add the following code beneath the `randomBetween` function:

File: **rotate.fla**   Actions : 1 (excerpt)

```
Movieclip.prototype.Spin = function (radius, speed)
{
  this.centerX = this._x;
  this.centerY = this._y;
```

```
  this.radius = radius;
  this.speed = speed;
  this.degrees = Math.randomBetween(0, 359);
  this.onEnterFrame = function ()
  {
    this.degrees += this.speed;
    var radians = this.degrees * Math.PI / 180;
    this._x = this.centerX + this.radius * Math.cos (radians);
    this._y = this.centerY + this.radius * Math.sin (radians);
    this._alpha = Math.randomBetween (0, 80);
  };
};
```

The function accepts two parameters: radius, which specifies how far from its original location the clip should rotate, and speed, the number of degrees the clip should rotate per frame (the higher this value, the faster the clip will spin).

As with most effects, we start by storing a number of values in our movie clip, and then assign an onEnterFrame event handler to work the magic. We store the clip's starting position (to use as the center of rotation), the values given for the radius and speed parameters, and an initial angle of rotation between 0 and 359.

The onEnterFrame event handler is quite straightforward, except for some basic trigonometry. For each frame of the animation, we add our stored speed value to the angle of rotation. Since ActionScript's trigonometric features work in radians, not degrees, we need to convert our angle of rotation into radians with this formula:

radians = degrees × /180

Finally, we multiply the specified radius by the cosine of the angle of rotation to get the horizontal position of the clip for this frame. Similarly, we multiply the radius by the sine of the angle of rotation to get the vertical position. Used in this way, the sine and cosine functions (Math.cos and Math.sin) produce a perfectly circular, clockwise path for the clip to follow.

Add some backspin!

Tip

If you'd like the animation to produce a counterclockwise spin, simply swap Math.cos and Math.sin in the code.

For good measure, the event handler gives the movie clip a random opacity value between zero and 80%.

If you preview your work now, the clips will sit still, as we haven't yet added the control code that applies the spin effect. Let's do that now.

7.   Add the following code beneath the `Spin` method in the Actions Panel:

File: **rotate.fla**   Actions : 1 (excerpt)

```
letterC.Spin (50, 3);
letterI.Spin (47, 3);
letterR.Spin (70, 4);
letterC2.Spin (36, 7);
letterL.Spin (130, 3);
letterE.Spin (100, 5);
```

Here, we specify arbitrary widths (the first parameter) and speeds (the second parameter) for each of our clips. This makes the position and shape of the axis on which the letters will spin appear random.

8.   Save your document and preview the effect.

That's a pretty strange effect. The letters circle away, blinking as if they're running out of energy.

Modifications

To make the effect a little more random, we can harness the power of the `Math.randomBetween` method for both the spin radius the speed of each of the movie clips. To go ahead and edit the effect to your linking, locate `rotate-random.fla` in the code archive.

9.   Alter the control code for each clip as follows:

File: **rotate-random.fla**   Actions : 1 (excerpt)

```
LetterC.Spinner(randomBetween(5, 150), randomBetween(1, 10));
LetterI.Spinner(randomBetween(5, 150), randomBetween(1, 10));
LetterR.Spinner(randomBetween(5, 150), randomBetween(1, 10));
LetterC2.Spinner(randomBetween(5, 150), randomBetween(1, 10));
LetterL.Spinner(randomBetween(5, 150), randomBetween(1, 10));
LetterE.Spinner(randomBetween(5, 150), randomBetween(1, 10));
```

10. Save and preview your work.

Every time you view the movie, you'll see a different effect—not a bad modification! Try altering the ranges of values to create an effect you really like.

Bouncing Text Effect

The world is full of subtle effects, from falling snowflakes to rocks tumbling down a mountainside. In this example, we'll produce a bouncing text effect (Figure 4.17) that brings text onto the stage with more energy than the slides we've seen so far.

Figure 4.17. The bouncing text effect is realistic and familiar.

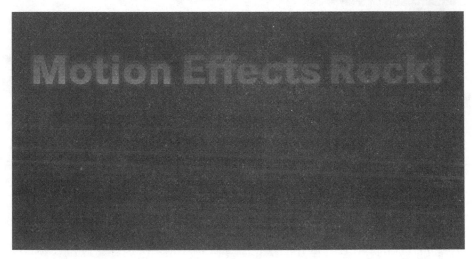

I like this effect, as it has its feet firmly in the real world and is instantly recognizable. We'll drop three text movie clips from the top of the screen to a point that we define. When they "land," they'll bounce, but, as if in response to gravity, the bounces will become smaller until the clips come to rest.

To edit this effect to suit your needs, locate `bounce.fla` in the code archive.

Setting the Scene

1. Create a new Flash movie and alter the frame rate to 24fps (Modify > Document...). This will allow for a smooth animation.

2. Start by creating your text in Flash or an image editor (Fireworks MX 2004 was used in this example). Create the word or phrase you want to animate. If necessary, import the images onto the stage.

   To view the source file for the text we'll use here, locate `bounce.png` within the code archive.

3. Create two new layers, named `Actions` and `Animated Text`. Alter the background color of your movie to suit your needs, or import a background of your choice.

4. Create movie clip symbols out of your text (whether imported or drawn from scratch), naming them and their instances appropriately. I named the symbols `Motion`, `Effects`, and `Rock`, and their instances `motion`, `effects`, and `rock`.

5. Move the clips into the Animated Text layer and arrange them to your liking, positioned about 100 pixels above where you'd like them to end up after they fall.

Adding the ActionScript

6. Add the following code the first frame of the Actions layer:

File: **bounce.fla**   Actions : 1 (excerpt)

```
MovieClip.prototype.DropIn = function (yTarget, accel, spring,
    alphaEnd, alphaStep)
{
  this._alpha = 0;
  this.speed = 0;
  this.accel = accel;
  this.spring = spring;
  this.yTarget = yTarget;
  this.alphaEnd = alphaEnd;
  this.alphaStep = alphaStep;
  this.onEnterFrame = function ()
  {
    this._y += this.speed;
    if (this._y + this._height >= this.yTarget)
    {
      this._y = yTarget - this._height;
      this.speed *= -this.spring;
    }
    this.speed += this.accel;
    if (this._alpha < this.alphaEnd)
```

```
   {
      this._alpha += this.alphaStep;
   }
 };
};
```

Since the words will fall vertically, this code is concerned only with manipulating the _y value of the clip. However, the function could easily be modified to work on the _x value.

It accepts a number of parameters, all of which are used to create the effect.

yTarget	The vertical position on the stage to which the bottom of the clip will move—the "ground level"
accel	The acceleration that the clip will be subject to, in pixels per frame squared; controls how fast the clip will fall.
spring	The fraction of the clip's downward speed that's converted to upward speed when it bounces—the coefficient of restitution; controls how bouncy the clip will be
alphaEnd	The percentage opacity at which the clip finishes fading in
alphaStep	The speed (in percentage of opacity per frame) at which the clip will fade in

This effect works much like our previous efforts, setting up a bunch of variables in the movie clip and then assigning an onEnterFrame event handler to use them.

First, we set the initial _alpha property of the clip to 0 so that we can fade it into view.

```
this._alpha = 0;
```

We also initialize a variable for the speed of the falling clip to zero. The rest of the variables come directly from the function parameters.

As we step into the onEnterFrame event handler, the code starts by increasing the _y value of the clip in accordance with its current speed. If this motion takes it past the "ground level", we set the _y value to exactly ground level and multiply its speed by the negative of the spring variable (the coefficient of restitution) to produce the bounce.

```
this._y += this.speed;
if (this._y + this._height >= this.yTarget)
{
  this._y = yTarget - this._height;
  this.speed *= -this.spring;
}
```

Next, to simulate the effect of gravity on the falling clip, we increase its speed by the acceleration value specified:

```
this.speed += this.accel;
```

Again, we use only a small piece of code to fade the clip into view:

```
if (this._alpha < this.alphaEnd)
{
  this._alpha += this.alphaStep;
}
```

7.   Add the following code beneath the `DropIn` method:

File: **bounce.fla**   Actions : 1 (excerpt)
```
motion.DropIn (170, 2, 0.6, 100, 4);
effects.DropIn (170, 2, 0.6, 100, 4);
rock.DropIn (170, 2, 0.6, 100, 4);
```

We've specified the same parameters for each of our words, so they will all drop and fade in the same way.

8.   Save the document and preview your work!

It's a great little effect—the movie clips drop into view, bounce, and come to rest. It's a joy to watch! And it lends itself to a few interesting modifications, as outlined in the following section.

Modifications

Physics aside, it might make sense for the purposes of our effect to have the smallest (lightest) of the clips bounce more than the largest (heaviest). We can accomplish this in our example by modifying the parameters that are passed to the function.

To modify this effect for your own needs, locate `bounce2.fla` within the code archive.

9. Modify the code for each of the movie clips as follows:

File: **bounce2.fla**   Actions : 1 (excerpt)

```
motion.DropIn (170, 2, 0.6, 100, 4);
effects.DropIn (170, 2, 0.5, 100, 3);
rock.DropIn (170, 2, 0.75, 100, 2);
```

Notice that we allocate the "heaviest" movie clip the lowest value for the `spring` parameter. To add a little more visual interest, I've also given the clips different `alphaStep` values, so they fade in at slightly different rates.

10. Save the document and preview the effect.

That's more like it! Now, the effect looks much more realistic—all it needed was a little planning. Try playing with the other parameters and see how obvious or subtle you can make the effect.

Look around you; there's inspiration at every turn! Keep your eyes open, and you'll gain countless ideas for effects that will look great in your Flash projects.

Opacity Effects

One of the best ways to grab user attention is to reveal elements of your movie in an interesting way. One of the first things you may have learned as you played with animation in Flash was how to smoothly fade an object into view. In this section, we'll use that basic approach of fiddling with an object's opacity to create a number of captivating effects.

Random Fading Text Effect

One of the questions I hear most is, "How can I fade in a string of text, letter by letter?" It's an interesting question, and as you can see from Figure 4.18, we'll answer it in this example.

Figure 4.18. Fade in a string of text using the random fading text effect.

RANDOM FADE E F CT

Because the effect is not just the modification of a movie clip and its properties, it's a little more complex than those we've looked at so far. In this effect, we need to split up the letters and place them in duplicate clips on the stage. We can then modify the properties of the clips as we please to create the effects we want.

Setting the Scene

This really is powerful—the effects we can accomplish using this method of splitting words into their individual letters are virtually limitless.

To modify the finished product to your own requirements, locate `randomfade.fla` in the code archive.

1. Create a new Flash document with a width of 60 pixels and alter the frame rate to 24 frames per second (Modify > Document...).

2. Create a new dynamic text field with 40-point text. Set its Var value to `WhatLetter` (as shown in Figure 4.19). Make sure the character set is Basic Latin (or All characters in Flash MX).

Figure 4.19. Set the `Var` value for the dynamic text field.

3. Convert the dynamic text field to a movie clip symbol. Name that symbol `TextToDuplicate`, and give the instance the name `textToDuplicate`.

In a moment, we'll duplicate this dynamic text field several times and populate it with the letters of the text.

Adding the ActionScript

Now, let's add the control code that splits our string into individual letters and creates the duplicate movie clips that we can then control.

4. Select the first frame of the Actions layer within the Actions Panel. Put in our trusty `randomBetween` function:

File: **randomfade.fla**   Actions : 1 (excerpt)

```
function randomBetween (a, b)
{
    return Math.min (a, b) + random (Math.abs (a - b) + 1);
}
```

5. Next, add the code that controls the effect:

File: **randomfade.fla**   Actions : 1 (excerpt)

```
var textMessage = "RANDOM FADE EFFECT";
var positioning = 60;
var letterSpacing = 30;
for (i = 0; i < textMessage.length; i++)
{
    var mc = textToDuplicate.duplicateMovieClip (
        "letterDuplicate" + i, i);
    mc._x = positioning;
    mc.WhatLetter = textMessage.charAt (i);
    mc.FadeIn ();
    positioning += letterSpacing;
}
```

First, we specify the string we wish to display:

```
var textMessage = "RANDOM FADE EFFECT";
```

We use another couple of variables to control the horizontal position of the first letter and the number of pixels to allow for each letter:

```
var positioning = 60;
var letterSpacing = 30;
```

We then enter a for loop, which executes once for each letter of the text to be displayed. Each time through the loop, we create a new duplicate of the textToDuplicate clip, position it horizontally, assign it a letter taken from the message, and instruct it to fade in with the clip's FadeIn method, which we'll write in a moment. Finally, we increment the positioning variable by the letter width specified by letterSpacing in preparation for the next letter.

To assign a letter for each duplicate clip to display, we populate the WhatLetter variable within the clip. The dynamic text field we created earlier is set to display the value of that variable. To populate WhatLetter, we use the charAt method of the ActionScript String object, which picks out the character at each position in the string.

Regardless of how long the string is, the code we've written here can cope with it.

Controlling the Dynamically Created Movie Clips

All that's left is to write the FadeIn method, which makes the letters appear in random order:

6. Insert the following code *above* that which was added in the previous steps:

File: **radomfade.fla**   Actions : 1 (excerpt)

```
MovieClip.prototype.FadeIn = function ()
{
  this._alpha = randomBetween (-200, 0);
  this.onEnterFrame = function ()
  {
    if (this._alpha < 100)
    {
      this._alpha += 10;
    }
  };
};
```

Our FadeIn method, which will be called for each letter of the text, sets the _alpha property of the movie clip to a random value between -200 and 0. You may read that and think, "Negative 200 opacity? What's going on here?" In fact, Flash will display any _alpha value that is less than or equal to zero as completely transparent. By assigning random negative values to each of the letters and then incrementing those values at an even rate, we get the random fade-in effect we're after!

7. Save your document and preview your work.

The effect is really enjoyable and works well. If you decide to change the text, provided the string is in upper case, it will all fit together using the code we've seen here. If you change the size of the font, you'll need to decrease the value of the `letterSpacing` variable to accommodate the new text size.

Also, be aware that, as our code provides a fixed number of pixels for the width of all letters, short kerning letters, such as 'i' and 'l,' will produce odd spacing.

Of course, there is a way to modify the code to account for letters that are especially narrow, as we'll see in the following example. To edit the completed effect for your own needs, locate `randomfade-kern.fla` in the code archive.

8. Leave the declarations for the `FadeIn` method and the `randomBetween` function alone, but replace the remaining code with the following modified version:

File: **`ramdomfade-kern.fla`**   Actions : 1 (excerpt)

```
var textMessage = "Splendid Effect In Flash";
var positioning = 60;
var letterSpacing = 30;
for (i = 0; i < textMessage.length; i++)
{
  var mc = textToDuplicate.duplicateMovieClip (
      "letterDuplicate" + i, i);
  mc._x = positioning;
  mc.WhatLetter = textMessage.charAt (i);
  mc.FadeIn ();
  positioning += letterSpacing +
      adjustFor (textMessage.charAt (i));
}
function adjustFor(char)
{
  if (char == 'i' || char == 'l' || char == 'I' ||
      char == '1' || char == 'f' || char == 'j' ||
      char == ' ')
  {
    return -10;
  }
```

```
    return 0;
}
```

As you can see, we've modified the last line of the `for` loop that creates and positions the movie clip for each letter to be displayed. Specifically, we've changed the line that sets the `positioning` variable for the next letter to be displayed. In addition to the fixed `letterSpacing` value of 30 pixels, the line calls the new `adjustFor` function, passing it the current letter. This function returns zero for most characters, but for especially skinny ones ('i', 'l', 'f', and so on) it returns `-10`, significantly reducing the space between the current letter and the next.

9. Save and preview the effect.

Adjusting this code is by no means foolproof. A little tinkering is required to get the effect working once you've increased or decreased the size of the text, but it does bring us one step closer to solving the problem! Unfortunately, ActionScript currently provides no practical way to calculate the width of an arbitrary character in an arbitrary font, which means that accurate kerning on the fly simply isn't possible. The `adjustFor` function is a nice compromise, though.

Simple Opacity Transition

Flash provides an effective means of building transitions between different parts of a message. Available methods range from employing a simple opacity fade between sentences, to the application of complex masking techniques. In this and following sections, we'll explore several different methods of producing effective text transitions.

In this example, we'll cycle through a message in parts or steps, as shown in Figure 4.20. We'll fade each part of the message in and out by increasing and decreasing its opacity. As the opacity of the object reaches zero, this cues the next part of the message. When that fades out, we return to the first message and the process begins again. Sound simple enough? Let's see how it's done.

Figure 4.20. Develop this great opacity transition effect.

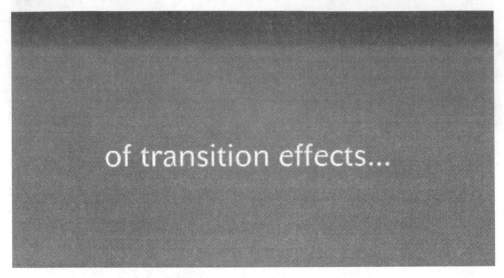

To modify this effect for your own needs, locate `Transition_Opacity.fla` in the code archive.

Setting the Scene

1. Create a new Flash document that's 500 pixels wide and 400 pixels high, setting the frame rate to 24 fps (Modify > Document...).

2. Create three layers, named Actions, Text and Background.

3. Place a background of your choice into the Background layer and lock it.

    Use the 500x400 pixel background file (`background.png`) in the code archive if you're struggling for ideas.

4. Within the Text layer, create a new dynamic text field named `messagetext`. Set its Var value to `message` in the Property Inspector so that it will display the variable by that name. Also click on Character... and set it to include Basic Latin (All Characters in Flash MX). Make sure the text box is wide enough to hold at least 25 characters.

5. Create a new movie clip symbol out of the text area. Name the symbol `Message` and name the instance `message`.

Adding the ActionScript

Although we could modify all the movie clip's properties, we're interested only in the opacity of each of the messages in this example.

6. Select the first frame of the Actions layer and add the following code to the Actions Panel:

File: **opacity.fla**   Actions : 1 (excerpt)

```
MovieClip.prototype.OpacityTransition = function (max, min,
    step)
{
  this.messages = new Array (
    "this is",
    "the simplest",
    "of transition effects...",
    "...simple but effective"
  );
  this.max = max;
  this.min = min;
  this.step = step;
  this.counter = 1;
  this.fadeIn = true;
  this._alpha = min;
  this.message = this.messages[0];
  this.onEnterFrame = function ()
  {
    if (this.fadeIn)
    {
      this._alpha += this.step;
    }
    else
    {
      this._alpha -= this.step;
    }
    if (this._alpha <= this.min || this._alpha >= this.max)
    {
      this.fadeIn = !this.fadeIn;
      if (this.fadeIn)
      {
        this.message = this.messages[this.counter++];
        if (this.counter >= this.messages.length)
        {
          this.counter = 0;
        }
```

```
          }
      }
   };
};
```

As before, we extend the functionality of the MovieClip class by adding a new method to it: OpacityTransition. This writes an array containing the messages we want to display to a variable in the movie clip (messages). We also store the min, max, and step values passed to the method, a counter variable to track which message is currently displayed, and a fadeIn variable to track whether it's fading in or out. Finally, we initialize the _alpha value to the specified minimum and display the first message in the messages array. To do so, we assign it as the value of the message variable, which our dynamic text field is set to display.

With all this in mind, the onEnterFrame event handler should make sense. It increases the _alpha value until it reaches the specified maximum value, then decreases it until it reaches the minimum, at which point the next message in the array is displayed. When the counter variable gets to the end of the array, it is reset to zero to start over at the beginning.

All that remains is to add the trigger code that brings the effect to life.

7. Add the following beneath the previous code:

File: **opacity.fla**   Actions : 1 (excerpt)
```
message.OpacityTransition(100, 0, 2);
```

Remember, message is the instance name of the movie clip on the stage. Here, we pass the maximum opacity, minimum opacity, and opacity step size to the new OpacityTransition method.

8. Save the document and preview the movie.

It's a neat effect that, although programmatically simple, works well and can easily be modified to suit your needs. By changing the alpha values that are passed to the method, you also change the trigger points for the text values, producing other interesting effects.

Modifications

Extending the functionality of this effect is easy. We can, for example, simply add to the mix another movie clip with a different message.

To make this effect scalable, we need to move away from using hard-coded messages. Instead, we'll accept the array of messages as another parameter.

The completed effect is `opacity-multiple.fla` in the code archive.

9. Drag another instance of the **Message** movie clip onto the stage and align it beneath the previous clip. Name this instance **message2**.

10. Make the indicated changes to the start of the **OpacityTransition** method:

File: **opacity-multiple.fla**   Actions : 1 (excerpt)

```
MovieClip.prototype.OpacityTransition = function (max, min,
    step, messages)
{
  this.messages = messages;
  this.max = max;
  this.min = min;
  this.step = step;
  this.counter = 1;
  this.fadeIn = true;
  this._alpha = min;
  this.message = this.messages[0];
  this.onEnterFrame = function ()
  {
    ...
```

The method now receives its array of messages as a parameter, but is otherwise identical to its previous incarnation.

We also need to update the code that calls this method, both to supply a value for this new parameter and to apply the effect to the second clip.

11. Replace the existing call to **OpacityTransition** with the following code:

File: **opacity-multiple.fla**   Actions : 1 (excerpt)

```
message.OpacityTransition (100, 0, 5, new Array("Mary", "had",
    "a", "little", "lamb"));
message2.OpacityTransition (100, 0, 4, new Array("its",
    "fleece", "was", "white", "as", "snow"));
```

12. Save and preview your Flash document.

Notice how the first clip fades in and out slightly faster than the one at the bottom? This occurs because that clip's `step` value is higher, causing it to reach the upper and lower values more quickly than does the second clip.

Slides

Sliding a series of words or letters into view is a technique that's commonly employed in advertising and cinematic productions. Let's look at how these effects can easily be added to your projects for maximum impact.

The vertical sliding effect shown in Figure 4.21 is a handy method for introducing messages quickly and efficiently without being too intrusive.

Figure 4.21. Create this cool vertical sliding transition effect.

To edit this effect for your own needs, locate `mask.fla` in the code archive.

Setting the Scene

This example uses some of the code and structure we saw in the previous transition example, altered to suit our needs.

1. Create a new Flash document that's 500 pixels high and 400 pixels wide. Set the frame rate to 24 fps (Modify > Document...).

2. Create the following layers from the top down: Actions, Simple Mask, Text, and Background.

3. Add a background of your choice to the Background layer, and lock the layer. If you're lacking inspiration, a 500x400 pixel background file, called `background.png`, has been provided in the code archive.

4. Within the Text layer, create a new dynamic text field. Name it `messagetext`, set its Var setting to `message`, and click Character... to select Basic Latin (All Characters in Flash MX).

5. Convert this dynamic text field to a movie clip symbol named `Message` and name the instance `message`.

6. With the Rectangle Tool selected, click the fill selector within the Property Inspector. Select the white to black gradient chip at the bottom left of the pop-up.

7. Select the Simple Mask layer and create a small rectangle (the exact dimensions don't matter). Fill it with a solid color of your choice, but don't give it an outline (or remove the outline if it has one).

Flash masks ignore color and opacity

This rectangle will be used as a mask in the effect, so its color (and even its opacity) is inconsequential.

8. Select the rectangle you've just created, and convert it to a movie clip symbol named `Simple Mask`. Name the instance `simplemask`.

We can safely move the rectangle offstage, as we'll place and animate it dynamically through the ActionScript later on.

9. Move the `simplemask` movie clip off the stage (e.g. to the coordinates (-100, 0)).

Adding the ActionScript

Now that we've added the relevant movie clips to the scene, we can insert the code that will create the effect.

10. Select the first frame of the Actions layer. Add the following code to the Actions Panel. Since this code so closely resembles that of the previous example, I've indicated the differences in bold.

File: **mask.fla**   Actions : 1

```
MovieClip.prototype.SlideTransition = function (max, min,
    step, messages, mask)
{
```

```
this.mask = mask;
this.messages = messages;
this.max = max;
this.min = min;
this.step = step;
this.counter = 1;
this.fadeIn = true;
this._alpha = min;
this.message = this.messages[0];
mask._x = this._x;
mask._y = this._y;
mask._width = this._width;
mask._height = 0;
this.setMask(mask);
this.onEnterFrame = function ()
{
  if (this.fadeIn)
  {
    this._alpha += this.step;
    this.mask._height += this.step * this._height / 100;
  }
  else
  {
    this._alpha -= this.step;
  }
  if (this._alpha <= this.min || this._alpha >= this.max)
  {
    this.fadeIn = !this.fadeIn;
    if (this.fadeIn)
    {
      this.message = this.messages[this.counter++];
      this.mask._height = 0;
      if (this.counter >= this.messages.length)
      {
        this.counter = 0;
      }
    }
  }
};
};
message.SlideTransition (100, 0, 5, new Array("one", "two",
    "three", "four", "five", "six", "seven", "eight", "nine",
    "ten"), simplemask);
```

We've used the code from the previous transition example as the starting point for this effect. However, we've made some pretty important alterations here, so let's look under the hood and see how it all works.

The method (which is now called `SlideTransition`) takes an additional parameter, `mask`, which provides a reference to the movie clip that will be used to mask the message and thus produce the slide effect. The method stores that reference to a variable in the clip to be masked.

```
MovieClip.prototype.SlideTransition = function (max, min, step,
    messages, mask)
{
  this.mask = mask;
```

Creating the mask on the fly

If you intend to use this effect on more than one element in the movie, it would make sense to create the clip on the fly from the symbol in the library using the `attachMovie` method, rather than using an existing clip sitting offstage. We saw how to do this in the section called "Random Motion" in Chapter 3.

Later, in the initialization phase, the method sets the dimensions (`_x`, `_y`, `_width`, and `_height`) of the mask clip to match the clip to be masked, with the exception of height, which it sets to zero. As a result, no part of the message is initially visible. Finally, it uses the `setMask` method of the movie clip to specify that the mask clip should be used as a mask.

```
  mask._x = this._x;
  mask._y = this._y;
  mask._width = this._width;
  mask._height = 0;
  this.setMask(mask);
```

Next we make two simple adjustments to the `onEnterFrame` event handler. The first increases the height of the mask along with the opacity of the message, producing our vertical slide reveal. The formula ensures that the mask will match the height of the clip at the same time it reaches an opacity of 100%.

```
    this._alpha += this.step;
    this.mask._height += this.step * this._width / 100;
```

The second adjustment sets the height of the mask back to zero when the effect moves to a new message:

```
        this.message = this.messages[this.counter++];
        this.mask._height = 0;
```

The final change is the actual call to the effect. We must use the new method name and pass it a reference to the mask movie clip to be used for the effect:

```
message.SlideTransition (100, 0, 5, new Array("one", "two",
    "three", "four", "five", "six", "seven", "eight", "nine",
    "ten"), simplemask);
```

11. Save and preview your Flash document.

This effect works really well. As each subsequent message is displayed, it appears gradually, almost as though it's being wiped in. Of course, as this effect is based in ActionScript, modifications are easy to make.

Modifications

Let's see how easy it is to modify this effect to work horizontally instead of vertically, as shown in Figure 4.22.

Figure 4.22. Modify the opacity transition effect to make it work horizontally.

To pull apart the finished product, locate the mask-horizontal.fla file within the code archive.

12. Select the first frame of the Actions layer and modify the lines indicated here in bold:

File: **mask-horitzonal.fla**   Actions : 1
```
MovieClip.prototype.SlideTransition = function (max, min,
    step, messages, mask)
{
  this.mask = mask;
  this.messages = messages;
```

```
    this.max = max;
    this.min = min;
    this.step = step;
    this.counter = 1;
    this.fadeIn = true;
    this._alpha = min;
    this.message = this.messages[0];
    mask._x = this._x;
    mask._y = this._y;
    mask._width = 0;
    mask._height = this._height;
    this.setMask(mask);
    this.onEnterFrame = function ()
    {
      if (this.fadeIn)
      {
        this._alpha += this.step;
        this.mask._width += this.step * this._width / 100;
      }
      else
      {
        this._alpha -= this.step;
      }
      if (this._alpha <= this.min || this._alpha >= this.max)
      {
        this.fadeIn = !this.fadeIn;
        if (this.fadeIn)
        {
          this.message = this.messages[this.counter++];
          this.mask._width = 0;
          if (this.counter >= this.messages.length)
          {
            this.counter = 0;
          }
        }
      }
    };
};
message.SlideTransition (100, 0, 5, new Array("one", "two",
    "three", "four", "five", "six", "seven", "eight", "nine",
    "ten"), simplemask);
```

The modifications are self-explanatory; we simply change the width of the
mask instead of its height.

13. Save and preview your work.

How easy was that? Very easy! Once you have an understanding of how to manipulate the properties of movie clips, the possibilities are endless! You can create a literally infinite variety of transitions and text effects to suit the requirements of your projects.

Advanced Text Effects

These effects don't really fit into any other category—they're text-based effects, and they're advanced in nature. Let's dive in!

Falling Text

This example is straight out of a winter scene and reminds me of the arrival of the first snowflakes each year. We'll create all the necessary objects on the canvas, then duplicate them several times. We'll animate them in a natural manner, bringing them to rest at the bottom of the screen and fading them away before the process starts over.

Figure 4.23. This effect makes text appear to fall like snowflakes.

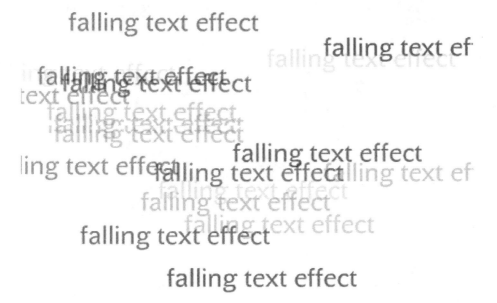

To edit the effect and modify it for your own needs, locate `fall.fla` in the code archive.

Setting the Scene

1. Create a new Flash document that's 400 pixels high and 500 pixels wide. Set the frame rate to 24 fps (Modify > Document...).

2. Create a new layer called Actions and, with this layer selected, create a new dynamic text field, naming it `textholder`. Make sure the Character... options are set to Basic Latin (or Include All for Flash MX). Add some text to the text area and convert it to a movie clip symbol named `textholder`. Delete the instance from the stage.

3. From within the Library Panel, select the `textholder` movie clip symbol, right-click, and select Linkage.... Select the Export for ActionScript option, accept the default name it suggests, and click OK.

We must select the Export for ActionScript option so that we can use the `attachMovie` method to create instances of the clip in a moment.

That's all that we need to do here! With nothing but an empty stage before us, let's add the ActionScript to create the effect!

Adding the ActionScript

4. Select the first frame of the Actions layer and add the following code to the Actions Panel:

File: **fall.fla**   Actions : 1

```
function randomBetween (a, b)
{
  return Math.min (a, b) + random (Math.abs (a - b) + 1);
}
MovieClip.prototype.Waterfall = function (speed, yGround)
{
  this.speed = speed;
  this.yGround = yGround;
  this._alpha = randomBetween (0, 90);
  this._y = randomBetween (-100, -mc._height);
  this.onEnterFrame = function ()
  {
    this._y += this.speed;
```

```
      if (this._y > this.yGround - this._height)
      {
        this._y = this.yGround - this._height;
        this._alpha -= 2;
        if (this._alpha <= 0)
        {
          this._y = randomBetween (-100, -mc._height);
          this._alpha = randomBetween (0, 90);
        }
      }
    };
};
for (var i = 1; i < 20; i++)
{
  var mc = attachMovie ("textholder", "textholder" + i, i);
  mc._x = randomBetween (-mc._width, 500);
  mc.Waterfall (randomBetween (1, 5), 300);
}
```

Let's take a look at what's going on here, starting with the first code that's executed upon running the Flash movie (the `for` loop at the bottom). As we made the `textholder` movie clip available for ActionScript export, we can create a new movie clip instance from the symbol with this line:

```
var mc = attachMovie ("textholder", "textholder" + i, i);
```

As the `for` loop increments the counter (in this case, `i`), we assign the number dynamically to the instance name and depth of the new movie clip.

Once we've created the clip, we set its horizontal position to a random value that will make it at least partially visible on stage:

```
mc._x = randomBetween (-mc._width, 500);
```

The clip's vertical position and other visual characteristics will be handled by the effect. This is applied with the `Waterfall` method, to which we pass a random speed and a ground level, as we'll discuss momentarily.

```
mc.Waterfall (randomBetween (1, 5), 300);
```

The code for the `Waterfall` method adopts the familiar pattern of storing variables in the movie clip, setting its initial properties (random `_alpha` and `_y` position offstage), then applying an `onEnterFrame` event handler.

The handler increases the _y property of the clip by adding the speed variable to the _y position until the text reaches the specified ground level, at which point the code sets the _y property so that it remains at ground level, while reducing the _alpha property to fade the clip out. Once the clip's _alpha value reaches zero, we randomly reset it to a value between zero and 90, and move the clip to a random vertical position above the top of the stage.

5.   Save the document and preview your work.

All in all, the code is quite tight and efficient, and produces a pleasing effect. We haven't finished there, though! You can apply many different modifications to make this really effective.

Modifications

One modification that immediately springs to mind is to make the text dynamic. You can display any message you like, based on an easily managed array of strings that you define (or even an XML file, as we'll see in Chapter 5). The message in Figure 4.24 is a series of keywords taken from a corporate Internet security Website, but you can easily change the message to suit your own needs.

Figure 4.24. Modify the floating text effect.

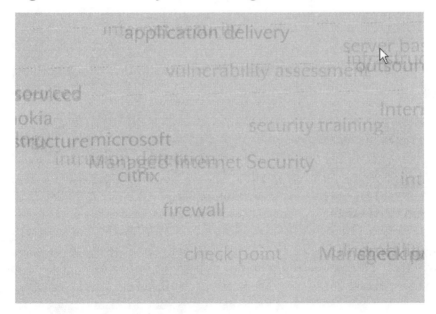

To edit this effect, locate `fall-array.fla` in the code archive.

6. Select the first frame of the Actions layer and make the changes shown in bold below:

File: **fall-array.fla**   Actions : 1

```
function randomBetween (a, b)
{
  return Math.min (a, b) + random (Math.abs (a - b) + 1);
}
MovieClip.prototype.Waterfall = function (message, speed,
    yGround)
{
  this.textholder.text = message;
  this.speed = speed;
  this.yGround = yGround;
  this._alpha = randomBetween (0, 90);
  this._y = randomBetween (-100, -mc._height);
  this.onEnterFrame = function ()
  {
    this._y += this.speed;
    if (this._y > this.yGround - this._height)
    {
      this._y = this.yGround - this._height;
      this._alpha -= 2;
      if (this._alpha <= 0)
      {
        this._y = randomBetween (-100, -mc._height);
        this._alpha = randomBetween (0, 90);
      }
    }
  };
};
var messages = new Array(
  "Internet Security", "application delivery",
  "server based computing", "infrastructure",
  "managed services", "firewall", "intrusion detection",
  "vulnerability assessment", "outsourced",
  "security training", "portal technology", "citrix",
  "microsoft", "check point", "nokia", "nfuse elite"
);
for (var i = 1; i < messages.length; i++)
{
  var mc = attachMovie ("textholder", "textholder" + i, i);
  mc._x = randomBetween (-mc._width, 500);
```

```
    mc.Waterfall (messages[i], randomBetween (1, 5), 300);
}
```

These changes require little explanation, especially since we've already used an array to store a list of messages in the slide example earlier in this chapter. In brief, we have declared an array of short messages and modified our `for` loop to execute once for each of them. We pass each message as a parameter to the Waterfall method, which now sets the text to be displayed by the `textholder` field in the clip.

7.   Save and preview the movie.

Wow! The effect now accepts dynamic messages that you can easily modify for your own needs.

So far, we've been concerned with populating the dynamic text fields and animating the vertical movement of the movie clips. Let's now concentrate on altering the horizontal movement as well. To edit the effect, locate `fall-sway.fla` in the code archive.

8.   Select the first frame of the Actions layer and make the changes shown in bold below:

File: **fall-sway.fla**   Actions : 1

```
function randomBetween (a, b)
{
   return Math.min (a, b) + random (Math.abs (a - b) + 1);
}
MovieClip.prototype.Waterfall = function (message, speed,
     yGround)
{
   this.textholder.text = message;
   this.speed = speed;
   this.yGround = yGround;
   this.xStart = this._x;
   this._xscale = speed * randomBetween(0, 80);
   this._yscale = this._xscale;
   this._alpha = randomBetween (0, 90);
   this._y = randomBetween (-100, -mc._height);
   this.onEnterFrame = function ()
   {
      this._y += this.speed;
      if (this._y > this.yGround)
      {
```

```
      this._y = this.yGround;
      this._alpha -= 2;
      if (this._alpha <= 0)
      {
        this._y = randomBetween (-100, -mc._height);
        this._alpha = randomBetween (0, 90);
      }
    }
    this._x = this.xStart + 20 * Math.cos(this._y / 50 *
      Math.PI);
  };
};
var messages = new Array(
  "Internet Security", "application delivery",
  "server based computing", "infrastructure",
  "managed services", "firewall", "intrusion detection",
  "vulnerability assessment", "outsourced",
  "security training", "portal technology", "citrix",
  "microsoft", "check point", "nokia", "nfuse elite"
);
for (var i = 1; i < messages.length; i++)
{
  var mc = attachMovie ("textholder", "textholder" + i, i);
  mc._x = randomBetween (-mc._width, 500);
  mc.Waterfall (messages[i], randomBetween (1, 5), 300);
}
```

These changes introduce a number of improvements. First, we make the clips sway from side to side as they fall. As with most examples of oscillating motion in Flash, this involves a bit of trigonometry. First, we set aside the starting horizontal position of the clip:

```
this.xStart = this._x;
```

Then, after the onEnterFrame event handler has adjusted the vertical position of the clip for each frame, we use that vertical position to generate a horizontal offset based on the cosine function:

```
this._x = this.xStart + 20 * Math.cos(this._y / 50 * Math.PI);
```

If you aren't strong on math, this might be a bit of a puzzler. Math.cos (the cosine function) returns values oscillating between 1 and -1 as you feed it steadily increasing values. It oscillates once for every 2 (2 * Math.PI) increase in the value it is fed. So by feeding it this._y / 50 * Math.PI, we ensure that the value will oscillate once for every 100 pixels the clip travels vertically. We multiply the outcome by twenty to get values between 20 and -20, and then add that to the starting horizontal position of the clip. The result is a clip that sways from side to side as it moves down the screen.

We've also added code that chooses a random scale for the clip:

```
this._xscale = speed * randomBetween(0, 80);
this._yscale = this._xscale;
```

As you can see, the scale is a random value whose magnitude is controlled by the speed assigned to the clip. This generally makes slow-falling clips smaller than those that fall more rapidly, creating an illusion of depth.

Finally, we've tweaked the code that determines where the clips touch down. Previously, we factored the height of the clips into these calculations, but doing this now would diminish the illusion of depth by making the smaller (more distant) clips stop further down the screen. Removing the clip height from the equation has the opposite effect, further enhancing the illusion of depth.

```
if (this._y > this.yGround)
{
   this._y = this.yGround;
```

9.   Save and preview your work in Flash.

This horizontal movement improves the animation, but the modifications don't stop there! Other mathematical functions can also be applied. For instance, changing the cosine function we've used for horizontal movement can produce some really crazy effects. Try a variation based on the exponential function and see what happens!

```
this._x = this.xStart + 20 * Math.exp(this._y / 50 * Math.PI);
```

Spend some time exploring the impact that other functions available from the Actions Panel can have on this effect.

Let's take this example one step further with the addition of user interaction. In the following example, we'll detect the proximity of the cursor to the duplicated movie clip. As the cursor approaches the clip, we'll stop the message in question and scale it up as shown in Figure 4.25. When the cursor moves away, the clip will scale back to its original size.

Figure 4.25. Modify the floating text effect to respond to user interaction.

To edit this effect, locate `fall-stop.fla` in the code archive.

10. Open the `textholder` movie clip symbol from the library, select the dynamic text field, and align it to the center of the stage (Modify > Align > …). Then return to the main stage.

To make the effect appear uniform when we scale up one of the clips, we must ensure that the **registration point** of the symbol (the little + visible on the stage) is at the center of the symbol's contents. If the registration point were at the top-left corner, the clip it would expand downward and to the right when scaled up.

11. Select the first frame of the Actions layer and make the changes shown in bold:

File: **`fall-stop.fla`**   Actions : 1
```
function randomBetween (a, b)
{
  return Math.min (a, b) + random (Math.abs (a - b) + 1);
```

```
}
MovieClip.prototype.Waterfall = function (message, speed,
    yGround)
{
  this.textholder.text = message;
  this.speed = speed;
  this.yGround = yGround;
  this.minScale = speed * randomBetween (0, 80);
  this.minAlpha = randomBetween (0, 90);
  this.xStart = this._x;
  this._xscale = this.minScale;
  this._yscale = this._xscale;
  this._alpha = this.minAlpha;
  this._y = randomBetween (-100, -mc._height);
  this.onEnterFrame = function ()
  {
    if (this.hitTest(_root._xmouse, _root._ymouse, true)) {
      this._y += 0.5;
      if (this._xscale < 100) {
        this._yscale = this._xscale += 10;
      }
      if (this._alpha < 100) {
        this._alpha += 10;
      }
    } else {
      this._y += this.speed;
      if (this._xscale > this.minScale) {
        this._yscale = this._xscale -= 10;
      }
      if (this._alpha > this.minAlpha) {
        this._alpha -= 10;
      }
    }
    if (this._y > this.yGround)
    {
      this._y = this.yGround;
      this._alpha -= 2;
      if (this._alpha <= 0)
      {
        this._y = randomBetween (-100, -mc._height);
        this._alpha = randomBetween (0, 90);
      }
    }
    this._x = this.xStart + 20 * Math.cos(this._y / 50 *
        Math.PI);
  };
```

```
};
var messages = new Array(
  "Internet Security", "application delivery",
  "server based computing", "infrastructure",
  "managed services", "firewall", "intrusion detection",
  "vulnerability assessment", "outsourced",
  "security training", "portal technology", "citrix",
  "microsoft", "check point", "nokia", "nfuse elite"
);
for (var i = 1; i < messages.length; i++)
{
  var mc = attachMovie ("textholder", "textholder" + i, i);
  mc._x = randomBetween (-mc._width / 2, 500 + mc._width / 2);
  mc.Waterfall (messages[i], randomBetween (1, 5), 300);
}
```

Once again, the changes are relatively straightforward. Let's take them one at a time.

First, we adjust the range of horizontal positions for the movie clips in the for loop to recognize that the registration point of each clip (i.e., the point represented by the coordinates assigned to each clip) is now at its center rather than the top-left corner.

```
mc._x = randomBetween (-mc._width / 2, 500 + mc._width / 2);
```

We then modify the initialization code so that it stores the starting opacity and scale of the clip in a pair of variables.

```
this.minScale = speed * randomBetween (0, 80);
this.minAlpha = randomBetween (0, 90);
...
this._xscale = this.minScale;
...
this._alpha = this.minAlpha;
```

Finally, we replace our simple one-liner that made the clip fall steadily in each frame of the animation with a new block of code.

```
if (this.hitTest(_root._xmouse, _root._ymouse, true)) {
  this._y += 0.5;
  if (this._xscale < 100) {
    this._yscale = this._xscale += 10;
  }
  if (this._alpha < 100) {
```

```
      this._alpha += 10;
    }
  } else {
    this._y += this.speed;
    if (this._xscale > this.minScale) {
      this._yscale = this._xscale -= 10;
    }
    if (this._alpha > this.minAlpha) {
      this._alpha -= 10;
    }
  }
}
```

This uses the hitTest method we saw in Chapter 2 to detect when the cursor is over the movie clip. When it is, the downward motion of the clip is slowed to 0.5 pixels per frame, and both the scale and opacity of the clip are increased by 10% per frame until they reach a value of 100%. (Clips that have an initial scale larger than this will not grow larger.) Otherwise, the else branch moves the clip at its normal speed, gradually returning the scale and opacity to their original values.

12. Save and preview your work.

Now, when your cursor "catches" a message, the words may scale up (the big ones won't), and they will certainly slow down. This allowance for user interaction has added even more finesse to an already cool effect!

3D Barrel Roll

Thiseffect is rather different. The movie clips roll around a pivotal axis, fading and reducing in scale as they move away, and increasing in opacity and scale as they move closer. This creates the illusion of movement in a three-dimensional space. You can get a sense of this from Figure 4.26.

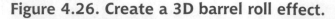

Figure 4.26. Create a 3D barrel roll effect.

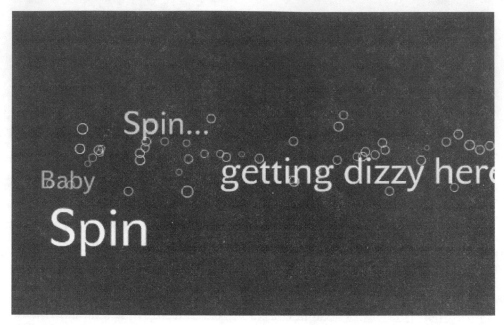

Setting the Scene

To edit this effect, access the file named `barrel.fla` in the code archive.

1. Create a new Flash document that's 550 pixels wide and 450 pixels high. Alter the frame rate to 24 fps and click OK.

2. Rename the default layer Actions, and create beneath it a new layer called Animated Text.

3. Create four movie clip symbols containing static text. In this example, the text in the static boxes is "spin," "baby," "spin…," and "getting dizzy here!" If the clips are not already on the stage, drag an instance of each into the Animated Text layer, naming the instances `spin`, `baby`, `spin2`, and `dizzy`.

   Feel free to change the text within the clips, but don't forget to give the clip instances names that relate to their contents—this will make it easier to reference them later.

Now, we can add the ActionScript necessary to produce the three-dimensional movement.

Adding the ActionScript

4. Select the first frame of the Actions layer and add the following code within the Actions Panel:

File: **barrel.fla**   Actions : 1

```
function randomBetween (a, b)
{
  return Math.min (a, b) + random (Math.abs (a - b) + 1);
}
MovieClip.prototype.threeDee = function (angle, radius)
{
  this.angle = angle;
  this.radius = radius;
  this.yAxis = 200;
  this._x = randomBetween(0, Stage.width - this._width);
  this.onEnterFrame = function ()
  {
    var y = this.radius * Math.cos(this.angle * Math.PI /
        180);
    var z = this.radius * Math.sin(this.angle * Math.PI /
        180);
    var scaling = 100 / (z + 100);
    this._yscale = this._xscale = scaling * 100;
    this._y = this.yAxis + y * scaling;
    this._alpha = scaling * 80;
    this.speed = (Stage.height / 2 - _root._ymouse) / 50;
    this.angle -= this.speed;
  };
};
spin.threeDee (0, 50);
baby.threeDee (90, 50);
spin2.threeDee (180, 50);
dizzy.threeDee (270, 50);
```

Let's review the code to see how it all fits together.

The code at the bottom calls the `threeDee` method for each of the clips, passing two parameters: `angle` and `radius`.

```
spin.threeDee(0, 50);
```

The first parameter, `angle`, sets the position of the clip on the imaginary rotating cylinder, with zero being the top. If we wanted ten different movie clips evenly spaced around the cylinder, we would give the first an angle of zero degrees, then increase the angle for each subsequent clip by 36 degrees.

The second parameter, `radius`, controls the distance of the clip from the axis of rotation.

In the `threeDee` method itself, we store the `angle` and `radius` parameters as variables in the clip, then set the vertical position of the axis of rotation. Finally, we assign the clip a random horizontal position that will keep it visible on the stage.

In the `onEnterFrame` event handler, we populate two variables: y and z. These represent the vertical position of the clip and its depth in 3D space. To make these clips trace a circular path around the axis of rotation, we use the cosine and sine functions to calculate these respective coordinates:

```
var y = this.radius * Math.cos(this.angle * Math.PI /
    180);
var z = this.radius * Math.sin(this.angle * Math.PI /
    180);
```

Convert degrees to radians

As the sine and cosine functions require values in radians, we multiply the `this.angle` value by `Math.PI / 180` to convert the angle from degrees to radians.

Having the 3D position of our clips is one thing, but using these coordinates to display them on a 2D stage is quite another. We must use these coordinates to calculate the 2D position, scaling, and opacity that will make the clips look as if they're moving in a 3D space.

Our code starts by calculating a variable called `scaling`, which we'll use to control the size of the clip on the stage. The closer the clip is supposed to appear to the viewer (i.e. the lower the value of z), the larger this value should be.

```
var scaling = 100 / (z + 100);
```

If you have an aptitude for math, you can probably draw out a graph of this equation with a bit of thought. In summary, though, `scaling` will be 1 when z is 0. As z grows bigger, the `scaling` gets smaller, tending towards zero. As z grows smaller, the `scaling` gets bigger, spiking to infinity when z reaches -100. This means the user's virtual "point of view" in 3D space is 100 pixels away from the axis of rotation.

Play with the virtual camera!

If you feel like tweaking, you can increase the strength of the 3D effect by replacing the two literal values in the equation (the two **100**s) with smaller positive values. You can also increase the camera's distance from the point of view by increasing only the second literal value in the equation. In movie-making terms, the first number controls the zoom of the virtual camera, while the second controls the dolly.

Having calculated a value for `scaling`, we use it to set the `_xscale` and `_yscale` properties of the clip. The variable also factors into our calculation for the vertical position of the clip, as a given vertical position in 3D space will appear closer to the axis of rotation the further it is from the viewer:

```
this._y = this.yAxis + y * scaling;
```

For added measure, we also tie the `_alpha` property of the movie clip to the `scaling` variable, which makes the effect even more realistic. The clip appears less opaque at a distance, as if shrouded in a haze.

```
this._alpha = scaling * 80;
```

All that's left is to rotate the clip about the axis. To do this, we simply increment or decrement the `angle` variable. To add a bit of interactivity to the effect, we'll calculate a rotational speed based on the position of the user's cursor:

```
this.speed = (Stage.height / 2 - _root._ymouse) / 50;
this.angle -= this.speed;
```

`Stage.height` gives us the total height of the movie as it is currently displayed.

5.   Save and preview the effect.

To see exactly how the cursor interaction works, you'll want to publish the movie to an SWF file and view it in Flash Player, as the preview in Flash itself presents the movie on a stage larger than the movie clip.

When you move your cursor over the top half of the animation, the objects appear to be rolling away from you around a central axis. Move your cursor to the lower half of the movie and the animation occurs in reverse—the objects roll toward you.

Because the speed of rotation is related to the vertical position of the cursor, the effect provides feedback to the user. The scaling and fading of the clips, coupled with the rotation, successfully fool the eye—we believe we're seeing movement in three dimensions.

Modifications

Several modifications can be made to this effect. Most notably, we can toy with the parameters that are passed to the `threeDee` prototype.

Another subtle modification is to add some randomly placed "background noise" that exhibits behavior similar to the existing movie clips. We can introduce this extra noise easily, by creating a new clip within the Library Panel, then instantiating it several times and controlling the clips using our existing effect.

To edit the finished effect, locate `barrel-noise.fla` in the code archive.

6. Create a new movie clip symbol within the Library Panel. Name the clip `noise`. It can contain anything you like (this example uses a very small circle).

7. Select the `noise` movie clip within the Library Panel, right-click, and select Linkage.... Select Export for ActionScript and enter the identifier value as `noise`.

We can now reference the movie clip from the Library Panel without adding it to the stage. We can begin to create instances of it with the aid of ActionScript.

8. Select the first frame of the Actions layer, navigate to the bottom of the Actions Panel, and add the following code:

File: **barrel-noise.fla**   Actions : 1

```
for (i = 0; i < 50; i++)
{
  var mc = attachMovie ("noise", "noise" + i, i);
  mc.threeDee (randomBetween (0, 359), randomBetween (0, 50));
}
```

By now, this code should be quite familiar to you. We're creating 50 instances of the `noise` movie clip dynamically, then applying the 3D rotation effect to each, using random values for angle and radius.

9. Save your work and preview the results.

The "noise" certainly adds to the effect and makes it more interesting. Because we're using random values for the placement of the duplicated `noise` movie clips, we see some interesting effects, including movie clips that look like they're coming out of the screen at us!

Experiment with different content for your `noise` movie clips, and ranges for your random values, to see the cool modifications you can create!

Timeline Effects

A brand new feature within Flash MX 2004 is Timeline Effects. These allow for the rapid creation of commonly used effects, such as drop shadows, opacity changes, and blurs. You can then alter these effects via a Property Inspector *after* you've applied them—change the effect's settings and the alterations will be applied to your selection!

Timeline Effects can be applied to any selected object. Simply click Insert > Timeline Effects and choose the effect you wish to apply.

Several effects are available and, while they do save a lot of time, they probably will not deliver many benefits to your everyday projects.

There are, however, a few exceptions, most notably the Transform and Transition effects found under Insert > Timeline Effects > Transform/Transition. These effects can be used to create basic movement, or to build simple transitions, respectively. They can also be used as building blocks for ActionScripted effects that can, in turn, be enhanced by small amounts of tweened movement or transitions.

Try experimenting with the effects discussed in this chapter. Apply different Timeline Effects to some of the base movie clips we've used to see what can be accomplished.

Don't go overboard!

The application of Timeline Effects to clips that you're manipulating via ActionScript can slow things down substantially, due to the amount of processing they require. For example, if you were to create a simple movie clip containing a rectangle, apply a thirty-frame blur timeline effect, then duplicate the movie clip several times and preview your movie in Flash, you'd notice the (negative) impact of the Timeline Effects on processing speed!

Using the new Flash JavaScript API, it is possible to create complicated and intricate Timeline Effects of your own. Alternatively, you can download free, non-commercial Timeline Effects from the Flash Exchange[1].

There are several other, third-party companies that produce Timeline Effects, some of which show how truly extensible the Flash architecture can be, given a little clever forethought.

Conclusion

Well, that wraps up this chapter—and *what* a chapter! I hope you've been inspired to experiment with the examples offered here, or have found new inspiration to complete some of your own unfinished projects with one or two of these effects.

We've covered a lot of ground, but there's one thing all these examples have in common. They were all designed for use in the real world. Adapt them to your needs and see what you can accomplish.

With text out of the way, it's time to move into the realm of sound. In the next chapter, we'll see how you can spruce up your projects with a little sound byte here or there, or even base a whole project around the creation and playback of sound.

---

[1] http://www.macromedia.com/exchange/flash/

5

Sound Effects

Sadly, sound within Flash projects is often included as an afterthought—if it's included at all. Hurried, last-minute sound additions typically amount to no more than a clichéd loop that serves little purpose. If you ever find yourself in the position of importing a sound clip into a project without a clear idea of why you're doing it, stop and repeat the Flash designers' mantra: *bad use of sound can destroy the entire user experience.*

In this age of digital media, sound can and should be a part of the online environment. A little sound can go a long way toward enhancing and solidifying the user experience. Even a simple "click" sound can provide valuable auditory feedback, provided it's used in the right manner. But beware overloading your projects with sound "just for the sake of it." The use of sound, then, is a question of balance.

When Should You Use Sound in Your Projects?

This is one of those golden questions, and the answer depends on the type of project you're developing . Some productions don't require any sound when viewed in isolation; yet, when incorporated into a larger project, they call for some degree of aural enhancement. If a project is heavily related to sound, then it should definitely involve an appropriate variety of audio clips.

Always consider your work from the perspective of users: will the addition of sound increase their enjoyment of the project? Including short or long musical loops, sound bytes, or a narrative can greatly increase the appeal of an interface, but may also detract from other content and become extremely annoying after just a short while. Consider the following examples of possible Flash projects and think about sound might benefit them. Your choice could include sound effects, musical loops, narratives, or, of course, nothing at all.

❏ Looping animation

❏ Single level menu system

❏ Multilevel menu system

❏ Multi-paged Flash site

❏ Flash form

❏ Streaming video content

Quickly run through these examples in your head. It's not difficult to see what will and won't work for different projects. Over time, you'll become increasingly adept at making decisions about when and how to add sound to your projects.

Selecting Sound Clips

One of the major benefits of digital sound is its flexibility. Audio processing software such as Steinberg Wavelab[1] makes it easy to edit, modify, loop, and add effects to sounds. You can take a ten-second section from one audio loop, paste it into another, or paste it across multiple tracks, with no more difficulty than editing a Word document. The advanced sound processing tools that are now available, combined with a microphone and your own imagination, allow you to create a huge array of audio clips. If you're pushed for time or need extra inspiration, there are many online resources from which you can download free clips or purchase collections of clips for use in your projects.

---

[1] http://www.steinberg.net/en/products/audio_editing/wavelab/

The application of sound to your projects should not be taken lightly. You need to pay attention to a number of factors if the effects are to be successful—most notably, timing, volume, and composition. Remember, you're seeking to enhance your visual messages rather than work against them, so your choice of sound is important. A manic techno loop attached to the submit button of a Flash form may well provoke visitors to close the browser. On the other hand, if you give users subtle feedback that the form has been submitted, they'll likely gain confidence in the interface and continue to interact.

As you can see, it's all about context. The appropriate integration of sound into a project can support the efficient communication of the message.

Importing and Exporting Sound Clips

Flash MX 2004 offers a built-in sound editor, which is fine for simple editing tasks. However, this tool is too basic for most needs: it doesn't allow you to add effects to your sound selections, for example. I definitely advocate the use of a more powerful sound processor, especially when it comes to trimming, duplicating, and looping clips.

You can import a sound clip from the File menu just as you would any other media type. Imported sounds can be applied directly to buttons and button states (Up, Down, Over, etc.), incorporated via streaming external files, included through ActionScripted control in the Action Panel, or added via other means.

The addition of a "click" sound to a button's Down state to simulate a real world mouse click is an example of a basic sound effect. It doesn't *require* ActionScript knowledge, but it certainly can be created via script. In the following example, the necessary code is applied to a button called `myButton`, which references a sound clip that has a linkage identifier of `mySound` in the Library Panel:

```
myButton.onPress = function ()
{
  newSound = new Sound ();
  newSound.attachSound ("mySound");
  newSound.start ();
}
```

For more advanced effects, including streaming and abstract playback mechanisms, we need to look under the hood of the ActionScript `Sound` class to see how we can control sound from within the interface and code conditions. It's an exciting arena in which you can create interesting and dramatic effects quickly, with just a little imagination.

As this book is concentrated on the creation of effects via ActionScript, we won't cover the integration of sound effects into buttons and frames on the timeline. For examples of this, refer to the Flash MX 2004 documentation.

Let's start with an interesting volume control that's linked to an animation.

Dynamic Volume Control

In the following demonstration, we scale the vertical height of a movie clip dynamically, tying the volume of a sound associated with the clip to its height. It's an important example, as it forms the basis for many of the effects you'll create in future.

To edit a completed version of the effect, locate `volcontrol.fla` in the code archive.

Setting the Scene

1. Create a new Flash document that's 500 pixels wide and 400 pixels high. Set the frame rate to 24 fps (Modify > Document...).

2. Rename the default layer Actions, and create two new folders in the Library Panel: Movie Clips and Sound.

3. Create a new movie clip symbol in the Movie Clips folder with some arbitrary content. The example in the code archive includes a static text area in which the text "sound effect" appears.

4. Drag an instance of the movie clip to the stage and name it `clipper`.

5. Select File > Import to Library... and either select `reverb.mp3` from the code archive, or import another sound file of your choice. Place it in the Sound folder.

    The file used here is a short, three-second clip of medium quality chosen primarily because it's a small file.

6. Select the sound clip from the Library Panel, right-click and select Linkage.... Check the Export for ActionScript checkbox and enter `reverb` as the identifier.

Having added the element we're going to animate and linked the sound clip for ActionScript export, we can now add the control code.

Adding the ActionScript

7. Select the first frame of the Actions layer and add the following code to the Actions Panel:

File: **volcontrol.fla**   Actions : 1 (excerpt)

```
MovieClip.prototype.WaveFade = function (minValue, maxValue,
    period)
{
  this.period = period;
  this.minValue = minValue;
  this.maxValue = maxValue;
  this.count = O;
  this.onEnterFrame = function ()
  {
    var value = (1 + Math.cos (this.count++ * 2 * Math.PI /
        this.period)) / 2;
    this._yscale = this.minValue + value *
        Math.abs (this.maxValue - this.minValue);
  };
};
clipper.WaveFade (20, 100, 48);
```

Here, we extend the movie clip class with a new method called WaveFade, which scales the clip up and down vertically in a smooth, regular pattern. The method is relatively straightforward, with the exception that careful use of the cosine function is required to produce the values that control the scaling.

The method takes three parameters: minValue, the minimum scale for the clip (as a percentage); maxValue, the maximum scale for the clip; and period, the number of frames in one oscillation (from the maximum scale to the minimum and back again).

The value variable is assigned a value using the cosine function. We add one and then divide the result by two to get values oscillating between zero and one. (Cosine oscillates between one and minus one.) We then multiply that by the difference between the maximum and minimum scaling values to determine the vertical scaling of the clip for each frame.

8. Save and preview your work.

Notice that the `_yscale` of the movie clip oscillates smoothly from its full height down to 20% and then back up again. Now that we have the animation in place, we can add the sound clip:

9. Add the lines shown in bold to the existing code in the Actions Panel:

File: **volcontrol.fla**   Actions : 1

```
MovieClip.prototype.WaveFade = function (minValue, maxValue,
    period)
{
  this.period = period;
  this.minValue = minValue;
  this.maxValue = maxValue;
  this.count = 0;
  this.reverb = new Sound ();
  this.reverb.attachSound ("reverb");
  this.reverb.start (0, 999);
  this.onEnterFrame = function ()
  {
    var value = (1 + Math.cos (this.count++ * 2 * Math.PI /
        this.period)) / 2;
    this._yscale = this.minValue + value *
        Math.abs (this.maxValue - this.minValue);
    this.reverb.setVolume (this.minValue + value *
        Math.abs (this.maxValue - this.minValue));
  };
};
clipper.WaveFade (20, 100, 48);
```

We start by creating a new Sound object and attaching the sound from the Library Panel. We start the clip at the beginning (0), and set it to loop **999** times.

Meanwhile, within the onEnterFrame event handler, we set the percentage volume of the sound clip using the same calculation we employed for its `_yscale`:

```
    this.reverb.setVolume (this.minValue + value *
        Math.abs (this.maxValue - this.minValue));
```

This is the same code we used to control the clip's `_yscale`; in theory, we could replace it with the following:

```
    this.reverb.setVolume(this._yscale);
```

However, we avoid using this code as it's less readable. When you revisit your code at a later date, you might easily become confused if you saw sound properties linked to movie clip properties.

10. Save and preview your work.

Notice that, as the scale of the clip decreases, so does the volume of the sound. As the scale increases, so does the volume. The addition of scripted sound has enhanced this simple effect, which strengthens the message and creates a more powerful experience.

Dynamic Panning Control

In this example, we animate an object across the screen and alter the panning of sound in accordance with the object's location. Panning involves the movement of a sound in stereo, which can add dynamism to even a single continuous tone. This builds on the previous example to increase your skills with the `Sound` class using a new method: `setPan`.

By default, the panning of a sound is set to `0`, but we can use `setPan` to alter that between the limits of `-100` (all sound to the left channel) and `+100` (all sound to the right channel).

Let's mirror the movement of a simple animation from left to right with an effect that moves the sound from the left channel to the right.

To skip ahead and modify this effect, locate `pancontrol.fla` in the code archive.

Setting the Scene

1. Create a new Flash document that's 500 pixels wide and 400 pixels high. Set the frame rate to 24 fps (Modify > Document...).

2. Rename the default layer Actions, and create two new folders within the Library Panel: Movie Clips and Sound.

3. Create a new movie clip symbol in the Movie Clips folder with arbitrary content. The example in the code archive uses a static text area in which the text "Sound Effect" appears.

4. Drag an instance of the movie clip to the stage and name it `clipper`.

5. Select File > Import to Library... and choose `reverb.mp3` from the code archive, or import a sound file of your choice.

6. Select the sound clip from the Library Panel, then right-click and select Linkage.... Check the Export for ActionScript checkbox, and enter `reverb` as the identifier.

Adding the ActionScript

We're done setting the scene. It's time to add the code to bring it all together.

7. Select the first frame of the Actions layer and add the following code within the Actions Panel. As this is so similar to the previous example, I've high-lighted the differences in bold:

File: **pancontrol.fla**   Actions : 1

```
MovieClip.prototype.WavePan = function (minValue, maxValue,
    period)
{
  this.period = period;
  this.minValue = minValue;
  this.maxValue = maxValue;
  this.count = 0;
  this.reverb = new Sound ();
  this.reverb.attachSound ("reverb");
  this.reverb.start (0, 999);
  this.onEnterFrame = function ()
  {
    var value = (1 + Math.cos (this.count++ * 2 * Math.PI /
        this.period)) / 2;
    this._x = this.minValue + value *
        Math.abs (this.maxValue - this.minValue);
    this.reverb.setPan (-100 + value * 200);
  };
};
clipper.WavePan (50, Stage.width - 100, 48);
```

We give the method a new name (`WavePan`), we've, set the horizontal position (instead of the vertical scale) of the movie clip to oscillate between the maximum and minimum values, and have the sound pan between the left and right speakers.

In our call to `WavePan`, we pass minimum and maximum values to ensure that the movie clip covers most of the stage:

```
clipper.WavePan (50, Stage.width - 100, 48);
```

All that remains is to test-drive the effect!

8. Save your Flash document and preview your work.

Move your speakers apart or put your headphones on, so you can enjoy this effect to the full.

This simple effect can serve multiple purposes within your projects. It can really bring your creations to life, adding pizzazz to animations, navigation systems, and more!

Mini Sound Player

It's time to stretch our legs! We've covered the fundamentals of sound control. Now, let's move into the development of a fully functional sound playback device. In this example, we'll create a random sound player that provides visual feedback about various properties of the random sound clips it plays, as shown in Figure 5.1.

Figure 5.1. Create a mini sound player.

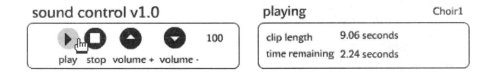

To jump forward and edit this effect, locate `miniplayer.fla` in the code archive.

Setting the Scene

1. Create a new Flash document that's 450 pixels wide and 100 pixels high. Set the frame rate to 24 fps (Modify > Document...).

2. Create three new layers, naming the top layer Actions, the middle Elements, and the bottom Background.

3. Select the Background layer and create a background element that will sur-round the controls, as shown in Figure 5.1. Lock the Background layer.

4. Create four buttons (as symbols in the Library) that visually reflect the fol-lowing functions: Play, Stop, Increase Volume, and Decrease Volume. Refer to `miniplayer.fla` in the code archive or Figure 5.1 for examples.

5. Drag instances of the buttons into the first frame of the Elements layer, naming them `PlayClip`, `StopClip`, `VolumeUp`, and `VolumeDown`. Arrange the buttons so they sit within the bounds of the background you created in step 3.

6. Add a static text box beneath each of the buttons to identify the tasks they perform. In the example file, I labeled them `play`, `stop`, `volume +` and `volume -`, respectively.

7. Locate the following files in the code archive and import them into your library (File > Import to Library...): `choir1.mp3`, `choir2.mp3`, `choir3.mp3`, `choir4.mp3`, and `choir5.mp3`.

8. Select each sound clip within the Library Panel, then right-click and select Linkage.... Check the Export for ActionScript checkbox and accept the default identifier value (which should be `choir1`, `choir2`, etc.).

    As I've explained before, this allows us to access the sound clips dynamically without having to drag them onto the stage.

We've successfully created the objects and imported the sounds we need to achieve basic functionality. All that remains is to add the ActionScript that con-trols the application.

Adding the ActionScript

First, we'll add the code that controls the playback of the sounds we imported.

9. Select the first frame of the Actions layer and add the following code within the Actions Panel:

File: **miniplayer.fla**   Actions : 1 (excerpt)

```
function randomBetween (a, b)
{
  return Math.min (a, b) + random (Math.abs (a - b) + 1);
}
```

```
PlayClip.onPress = function ()
{
  stopAllSounds ();
  _root.orchestra = new Sound ();
  _root.orchestra.attachSound ("choir" + randomBetween (1, 5));
  _root.orchestra.start ();
};
```

As the music player plays clips at random, our familiar `randomBetween` function comes in handy.

As the heart of this example, the `onPress` event handler of the `PlayClip` button definitely merits further study. The first thing it does is stop any sound that may already be playing, so that multiple sound clips aren't played at the same time if the `PlayClip` button is clicked repeatedly. The built-in `stopAllSounds` function handles this:

```
stopAllSounds ();
```

Next, we create a new `Sound` object and store it in a variable in the main movie (_root) called `orchestra`. We then use `attachSound` to load one of the five sounds from the library start it playing:

```
_root.orchestra = new Sound ();
_root.orchestra.attachSound ("choir" + randomBetween (1, 5));
_root.orchestra.start ();
```

10. Save and preview your work.

Press the Play button and a randomly selected clip will begin to play; press it again and another random clip will play. It's all functioning as expected.

Now, we'll add the Stop button's control code. This is much the same as the code we used with the Play button to remove the movie clips and stop all sound on the stage:

11. Add the following code beneath what you already have:

File: **miniplayer.fla**   Actions : 1 (excerpt)
```
StopClip.onPress = function ()
{
  stopAllSounds ();
  _root.orchestra = null;
};
```

We use `stopAllSounds` to stop any playing sounds, and throw away the `Sound` object we'd stored in the `orchestra` variable. This frees up the memory the object was using.

12. Save and preview your work.

When you press the Play button, the sound plays; when you hit the Stop button, it stops. Let's add the volume control buttons and finish this example.

13. Insert the following code beneath what you already have:

File: **miniplayer.fla**   Actions : 1 (excerpt)

```
VolumeUp.onPress = function ()
{
  if (_root.orchestra.getVolume () < 100)
  {
    _root.orchestra.setVolume (_root.orchestra.getVolume () +
      10);
  }
};
VolumeDown.onPress = function ()
{
  if (_root.orchestra.getVolume () > 0)
  {
    _root.orchestra.setVolume (_root.orchestra.getVolume () -
      10);
  }
};
```

When the volume of a sound clip is less than 100, we increase it in increments of ten each time the `VolumeUp` button is pressed. Conversely, when its volume is greater than zero, it's decreased in steps of ten each time the `VolumeDown` button is pressed.

14. Save and preview your work.

You can select a random clip by pressing the Play button, stop the dynamically loaded clip with the Stop button, and increase or decrease the volume of the clip using the volume controls. You may want to experiment with sound clips of your own, as those distributed in the code archive are quite short.

Modifications

We've successfully created an interface for the playback of random sound clips! We can extend it easily to provide visual feedback about the duration of the loaded track, the play time remaining, the name of the playing clip, and the volume level.

To edit these additions, locate `miniplayer-feedback.fla` in the code archive.

15. Working from the previous example, add a new layer below the Actions layer, and name it Labels. This will hold our text labels, which provide feedback about what's going on.

16. Select the first frame of the Labels layer and create a new dynamic text field to the right of the volume buttons, as depicted in Figure 5.1. Name the instance `volume`.

17. With the text box selected, click Character... in the Property Inspector and select Basic Latin (All Characters in Flash MX). Click OK.

18. Referencing Figure 5.1 for placement, create the titles `clip length` and `time remaining` using static text areas.

19. Insert three dynamic text fields beside the relevant titles, naming the fields `clipname`, `cliplength` and `timeleft`. Repeat step 3 for each of the text boxes. Make sure each box is large enough to hold the required information.

20. Select the first frame of the Actions layer and replace the existing code with the following. The changes are extensive, but once again I've highlighted them in bold:

File: **miniplayer-feedback.fla**   Actions : 1

```
function roundNumber (toRound, numDecimals)
{
  return Math.round (toRound * Math.pow (10, numDecimals)) /
     Math.pow (10, numDecimals);
}
function randomBetween (a, b)
{
  return Math.min (a, b) + random (Math.abs (a - b) + 1);
}
_root.createEmptyMovieClip ("tracker", 1);
PlayClip.onPress = function ()
```

```
{
  stopAllSounds ();
  _root.orchestra = new Sound ();
  var clipnumber = randomBetween (1, 5);
  _root.orchestra.attachSound ("choir" + clipnumber);
  _root.orchestra.start ();

  _root.tracker.onEnterFrame = function ()
  {
    _root.timeleft.text = roundNumber (
        (_root.orchestra.duration - _root.orchestra.position)
        / 1000, 2) + " seconds";
  };
  _root.cliplength.text = roundNumber (
      _root.orchestra.duration / 1000, 2) + " seconds";
  _root.clipname.text = "Choir" + clipnumber;
  _root.volume.text = _root.orchestra.getVolume ();
};
StopClip.onPress = function ()
{
  stopAllSounds ();
  _root.orchestra = null;
  _root.cliplength.text = "";
  _root.clipname.text = "";
  _root.timeleft.text = "";
};
VolumeUp.onPress = function ()
{
  if (_root.orchestra.getVolume () < 100)
  {
    _root.orchestra.setVolume (_root.orchestra.getVolume () +
        10);
    _root.volume.text = _root.orchestra.getVolume ();
  }
};
VolumeDown.onPress = function ()
{
  if (_root.orchestra.getVolume () > 0)
  {
    _root.orchestra.setVolume (_root.orchestra.getVolume () -
        10);
    _root.volume.text = _root.orchestra.getVolume ();
  }
};
```

Let's dissect the changes we've made, so we understand how it all works!

First, we introduce a new math function, roundNumber, which rounds figures to a specified number of decimal places. This will be used to show both the play time remaining for each clip and the clip's total duration.

```
function roundNumber (toRound, numDecimals)
{
  return Math.round (toRound * Math.pow (10, numDecimals)) /
    Math.pow (10, numDecimals);
}
```

We'll be updating the track time remaining with each frame of the movie, so we'll need an onEnterFrame event handler. Unfortunately, we don't have any obvious movie clip to hook that handler to. We could attach it to one of the buttons in our interface, but it's tidier to create an empty movie clip called tracker to host it:

```
_root.createEmptyMovieClip ("tracker", 1);
```

We then add the following code to the PlayClip button's onPress handler that sets up the event handler itself:

```
_root.tracker.onEnterFrame = function ()
{
  _root.timeleft.text = roundNumber ((_root.orchestra.duration -
    _root.orchestra.position) / 1000, 2) + " seconds";
};
```

This continuously updates the timeleft dynamic text field we created earlier. We constantly monitor the position of the sound clip using the duration and position properties of the Sound object, calculating the remaining time in milliseconds. We then convert this to a value in seconds, rounding to two decimal places with the help of our roundNumber function.

We also update the other dynamic text fields that hold the length of the clip being played, its name, and its volume.

```
_root.cliplength.text = roundNumber (_root.orchestra.duration /
    1000, 2) + " seconds";
_root.clipname.text = "Choir" + clipnumber;
_root.volume.text = _root.orchestra.getVolume ();
```

Within the `StopClip` button's `onPress` event handler, we include the following code, which clears the dynamic text fields of the information associated with the clip played previously:

```
_root.cliplength.text = "";
_root.clipname.text = "";
_root.timeleft.text = "";
```

Finally, the `VolumeUp` and `VolumeDown` `onPress` event handlers are updated. This ensures that any changes to the clip's volume are reflected in the `volume` dynamic text field.

```
_root.volume.text = _root.orchestra.getVolume ();
```

That's it for the code changes.

21. Save your Flash document and preview it.

There! We have a fully-fledged random clip player that provides information on the duration of the current clip, its name, and the play time remaining.

This example can easily be extended through the addition of more clips to the library. Export them for ActionScript reference, and alter the code that selects the clip to play within the `PlayClip` button's `onPress` event handler.

 Tip

Use an array!

A useful variation would be to store the linkage names of available clips in an array, so that the number of clips available would not have to be hard-coded.

Random Track Sequencer Effect

This effect is different from others in the book in that it has no interface! There's nothing to see, but plenty to hear. We're aiming to overlay random tracks to create a unique sound—something that's a little different from what a user might normally hear. The composition contains four ten-second loops comprising a random selection from the following categories:

❑ Background: a selection of five background bed tracks

❑ Drums: a selection of five drum tracks

❑ Guitar: a selection of five guitar loops

❑ Overlay: a selection of different overlays

As the movie loads, a random selection is made from each category. The tracks are then combined to create one of 625 possible soundtracks.

That's enough of the introduction—let's get cracking! To edit this effect, locate random.fla in the code archive.

Setting the Scene

1. Create a new Flash document that's 200 pixels wide and 200 pixels high. Modify the frame rate to 24 fps (Modify > Document...).

2. Rename Layer1 as Actions.

3. Select File > Import > Import to Library... and select the following MP3 files from the code archive: Background1.mp3, Background2.mp3, Background3.mp3, Background4.mp3, Background5.mp3, Drum1.mp3, Drum2.mp3, Drum3.mp3, Drum4.mp3, Drum5.mp3, Guitar1.mp3, Guitar2.mp3, Guitar3.mp3, Guitar4.mp3, Guitar5.mp3, Overlay1.mp3, Overlay2.mp3, Overlay3.mp3, Overlay4.mp3, and Overlay5.mp3.

4. Select these sound clips within the Library Panel, then right-click and select Linkage.... Check the Export for ActionScript checkbox, accept the provided identifier (remove the .mp3 extension if you're using Flash MX 2004), and click OK.

That's all the setting up we need to do for this example. As we're not adding an interface or allowing any user interaction, no other elements need to be included, apart from the ActionScript to produce the sound composition.

Adding the ActionScript

5. Select the first frame of the Actions layer and add the following code to the Actions Panel:

File: **random.fla**   Actions : 1
```
function randomBetween (a, b)
{
  return Math.min (a, b) + random (Math.abs (a - b) + 1);
```

```
}
MovieClip.prototype.PlayQueue = function (clip)
{
  var orchestra = new Sound (this);
  orchestra.attachSound (clip);
  orchestra.start ();
};
function PlayClips ()
{
  var background = "background" + randomBetween (1, 5);
  var drums = "drum" + randomBetween (1, 5);
  var guitar = "guitar" + randomBetween (1, 5);
  var overlay = "overlay" + randomBetween (1, 5);
  var clips = new Array (background, drums, guitar, overlay);
  for (var i = 0; i < clips.length; i++)
  {
    var mc = createEmptyMovieClip ("SoundHolder" + i, i);
    mc.PlayQueue (clips[i]);
  }
}
PlayClips ();
```

That's a fairly concise piece of code. Preview the movie and skip the code walk-through, or read on for the nitty-gritty details—the choice is yours!

Let's look at the PlayClips function to see how it all fits together. For each of the tracks, we create a variable (e.g. drums) that we fill with one of the linkage identifiers for the sound clips in the library, using the randomBetween function to generate a random number between one and five. We then combine these variables into an array of sound clips:

```
var clips = new Array (background, drums, guitar, overlay);
```

From here, we use a for loop to create an empty movie clip for each element of the array. These clips play the selected sound clips at random. This is accomplished by calling the PlayQueue movie clip method (which we'll examine in a moment) and passing the sound clip linkage identifier as a parameter.

```
for (var i = 0; i < clips.length; i++)
{
  var mc = createEmptyMovieClip ("SoundHolder" + i, i);
  mc.PlayQueue (clips[i]);
}
```

We call the `PlayQueue` method for each of the new movie clips created by the `PlayClips` function. This embeds a sound clip into each of these movie clips, then plays it.

```
MovieClip.prototype.PlayQueue = function (clip)
{
  var orchestra = new Sound (this);
  orchestra.attachSound (clip);
  orchestra.start ();
};
```

Because the sound clips are created in quick succession at runtime, the effect is one of a single composite track with a background, plus drum, guitar, and overlay sections.

6. Save and preview your document.

You may notice that every time you play the movie, you get a different composition. Some work very well, while others sound fairly clunky! It's all about experimentation and seeing what's possible.

Random Track Overlay Effect

This effect is based on the previous "headless" example, but builds on it quite extensively, utilizing the `CheckBox` component, custom event handlers, and providing users with the ability to switch tracks on or off. The user interface is shown in Figure 5.2.

Figure 5.2. This random track overlay effect builds on the previous example.

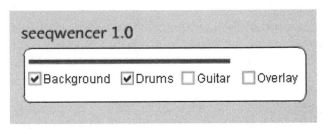

CheckBox incompatibilities

While developing this effect, which uses the CheckBox component, I was perplexed to find that the code I had in place for Flash MX didn't work with Flash MX 2004. I investigated this through the Reference Panel and found that there is no getValue method for the Flash MX 2004 version of the CheckBox component. Additionally, the CheckBox no longer allows for a change event handler.

An engineer friend at Macromedia told me that these features hadn't just been deprecated—they had been removed completely!

The code and steps that follow are for Flash MX, while the changes for the 2004 version are provided as asides. The example provided in the code archive was developed using the Flash MX version of the component.

To modify this effect, locate random-gui.fla in the code archive.

Setting the Scene

1. Create a new Flash document that's 550 pixels wide and 100 pixels high. Modify the frame rate to 24 fps (Modify > Document...).

2. Rename Layer1 as **Actions** and create beneath it three layers named Check-Boxes, Elements, and Background.

3. Select File > Import to Library... and select the following MP3 files in the code archive: Background1.mp3, Background2.mp3, Background3.mp3, Background4.mp3, Background5.mp3, Drum1.mp3, Drum2.mp3, Drum3.mp3, Drum4.mp3, Drum5.mp3, Guitar1.mp3, Guitar2.mp3, Guitar3.mp3, Guitar4.mp3, Guitar5.mp3, Overlay1.mp3, Overlay2.mp3, Overlay3.mp3, Overlay4.mp3, and Overlay5.mp3.

4. Select each of the sound clips within the Library Panel, then right-click and select Linkage.... Check the Export for ActionScript checkbox, accept the provided unique identifier (remove the .mp3 extension if you're using Flash MX 20004), and click OK.

5. From the Components Panel (Window > Development Panels > Components), select Flash UI Components (or just UI Components in Flash MX 2004) and drag four instances of the CheckBox component onto the CheckBoxes layer of the stage. Arrange them from left to right using the Align Panel to set their spacing if necessary (Window > Design Panels > Align).

6. Select each CheckBox component on the stage in turn, from left to right, and apply the instance name and parameters shown in Figure 5.3.

Figure 5.3. The properties for the four CheckBox components are displayed in Flash.

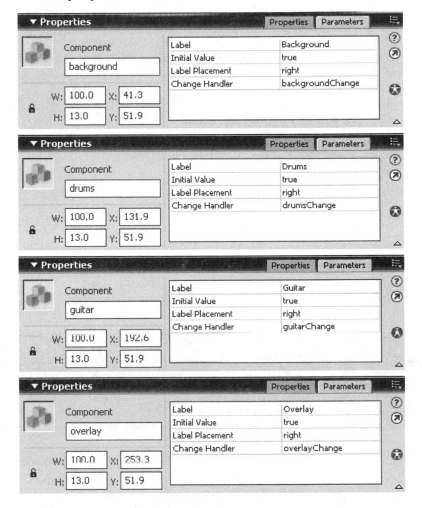

No Change Handler in Flash MX 2004

The Change Handler parameter for each CheckBox is especially import-ant here, as it will be used to mute a track when the corresponding checkbox is unchecked. This parameter doesn't exist in Flash MX 2004, so we'll add some ActionScript later to handle these events in that version.

7. Select the first frame of the Elements layer and insert into it a 270x4 pixel rectangle. Convert this to a movie clip symbol named `Progress`, and name the instance `progress`. This will act as a quick progress bar, indicating the progress of the composition as it plays.

8. Select the first frame of the Background layer and create a frame around the controls. If you're stuck for inspiration, look at Figure 5.2. Once you're happy with the frame, lock this layer.

Now, let's add the code to make the effect work.

Adding the ActionScript

9. With the first frame of the Actions layer selected, add the following code to the Actions Panel:

File: **random-gui.fla**   Actions : 1 (excerpt)

```
function randomBetween (a, b)
{
  return Math.min (a, b) + random (Math.abs (a - b) + 1);
}
function roundNumber (toRound, numDecimals)
{
  return Math.round (toRound * Math.pow (10, numDecimals)) /
      Math.pow (10, numDecimals);
}
MovieClip.prototype.PlayQueue = function (clip)
{
  this.orchestra = new Sound (this);
  this.orchestra.attachSound (clip);
  this.orchestra.start ();
};
function PlayClips ()
{
  var background = "background" + randomBetween (1, 5);
  var drums = "drum" + randomBetween (1, 5);
  var guitar = "guitar" + randomBetween (1, 5);
  var overlay = "overlay" + randomBetween (1, 5);
  var clips = new Array (background, drums, guitar, overlay);
  var mc;
```

```
for (var i = 0; i < clips.length; i++)
{
  mc = createEmptyMovieClip ("SoundHolder" + i, i);
  mc.PlayQueue (clips[i]);
}
mc.onEnterFrame = function ()
{
  _root.progress._xscale = this.orchestra.position /
      this.orchestra.duration * 100;
};
mc.orchestra.onSoundComplete = function ()
{
  stopAllSounds ();
  LoopClips ();
};
}
function LoopClips ()
{
  _root.SoundHolder0.orchestra.start ();
  _root.SoundHolder1.orchestra.start ();
  _root.SoundHolder2.orchestra.start ();
  _root.SoundHolder3.orchestra.start ();
}
PlayClips ();
```

We've used the `randomBetween` and `roundNumber` functions previously in this chapter, so there's no need to cover them again.

The `PlayQueue` method is identical to that used in the previous example, as is the `PlayClips` function, except for a couple of event handlers we added to the last dynamically generated movie clip.

```
mc.onEnterFrame = function ()
{
  _root.progress._xscale = this.orchestra.position /
      this.orchestra.duration * 100;
};
mc.orchestra.onSoundComplete = function ()
{
  stopAllSounds ();
  LoopClips ();
};
```

After the sound object is initialized, the sound clip is attached, and the sound clip has started to play, we dynamically track the position of the last sound object that's created using an `onEnterFrame` event handler attached to the containing movie clip. This event handler controls the width of the progress bar by altering its `_xscale` property. When the sound finishes, the `onSoundComplete` event handler will call the `stopAllSounds` function. Immediately after that, we call `LoopClips` to restart the four tracks we've produced, creating the effect of an infinite loop.

```
function LoopClips ()
{
  _root.SoundHolder0.orchestra.start ();
  _root.SoundHolder1.orchestra.start ();
  _root.SoundHolder2.orchestra.start ();
  _root.SoundHolder3.orchestra.start ();
}
```

So far, so good, right? When the movie is running, we want to dynamically switch the different tracks on or off by clicking the checkboxes on the stage. To this end, each `CheckBox` has its own event handler that controls the volume of the track. Let's add these now.

10. Add the following code below the existing code in the Actions Panel:

File: **random-gui.fla**   Actions : 1 (excerpt)

```
function backgroundChange (background)
{
  if (background.getValue ())
  {
    _root.SoundHolder0.Orchestra.setVolume (100);
  }
  else
  {
    _root.SoundHolder0.Orchestra.setVolume (0);
  }
}
function drumsChange (drums)
{
  if (drums.getValue ())
  {
    _root.SoundHolder1.Orchestra.setVolume (100);
  }
  else
  {
    _root.SoundHolder1.Orchestra.setVolume (0);
  }
}
```

```
function guitarChange (guitar)
{
  if (guitar.getValue ())
  {
    _root.SoundHolder2.Orchestra.setVolume (100);
  }
  else
  {
    _root.SoundHolder2.Orchestra.setVolume (0);
  }
}
function overlayChange (overlay)
{
  if (overlay.getValue ())
  {
    _root.SoundHolder3.Orchestra.setVolume (100);
  }
  else
  {
    _root.SoundHolder3.Orchestra.setVolume (0);
  }
}
```

The names of these functions correspond to the Change Handler parameter values we assigned to each of the CheckBox components when we created them. All these event handlers work the same way.[1] They check whether the CheckBox is checked using the getValue method, then set the volume of the corresponding sound clip to match. The initial state of each CheckBox is true (checked). So, when the checkbox is clicked, its status switches to false, and the volume is set to 0 for that particular Sound object. Clicking it again changes the status to true and the volume to 100. Using the change handlers in this way, we can drop individual tracks out and bring them back in at will.

11. Save your Flash document and preview it.

You're probably listening to a funky composition right now. Click the checkboxes to drop different tracks out and bring them back in. If you don't like the composition, or it's a little too wild for your tastes, preview the movie again to see what the random sequencer comes up with!

---

[1] If you're feeling ambitious, there is room for a little optimization by combining the common functionality of the four handlers into a single function.

Changes for Flash MX 2004

If you're using Flash MX 2004, you'll find that the checkboxes don't work as advertised. That's because the CheckBox component, besides looking better, lacks a Change Handler parameter. As a result, our event handler methods have not been hooked up to the checkboxes. This is a good thing, because these methods use another feature that's missing from the Flash MX 2004 CheckBox component: the getValue method. Let's now make the changes necessary to get the example working in Flash MX 2004.

First, change each of the event handler functions so they check the selected property of the appropriate CheckBox, rather than the getValue method, which no longer exists. For example, adjust this line of the backgroundChange function:

```
if (background.getValue ())
```

Replace it with this line:

```
if (background.selected)
```

Next, set up the event handler functions so they're called when one of the checkboxes is clicked. Add the following code below all the other code in the Actions Panel:

```
var cboxListener = new Object ();
cboxListener.click = function()
{
  backgroundChange (background);
  drumsChange (drums);
  guitarChange (guitar);
  overlayChange (overlay);
};

background.addEventListener ("click", cboxListener);
drums.addEventListener ("click", cboxListener);
guitar.addEventListener ("click", cboxListener);
overlay.addEventListener ("click", cboxListener);
```

This creates a new Object with a single method called click, which is set up as an **event listener** for each of the four CheckBox objects on the stage. When any one of the checkboxes is clicked, the click method is called. In turn, it calls each of our four event handlers to update the volume accordingly.

Watch the file size!

This example contains 20 ten-second clips, weighing in at nearly 3MB in total! This project would be better suited to CD or kiosk deployment than to distribution over the Internet. If the clips were shorter, or if there were fewer of them, it might be possible to distribute the application over the Internet—just be careful with the file size. Don't say I didn't warn you!

Modifications

We can make this effect even more interactive by, for example, directly controlling the properties of the Sound objects. In the following modification, we'll control the volume of the various sound clips with the NumericStepper component, which ships with Flash MX 2004. The interface is shown in Figure 5.4.

Figure 5.4. Add volume control to the dynamic sound clips.

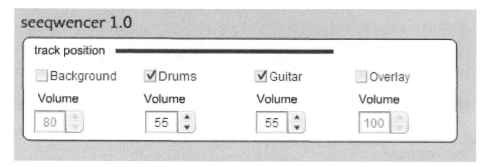

As we'll be adding the Flash MX 2004 NumericStepper component, we'll take advantage of the new CheckBox component that comes with Flash MX 2004, rather than the Flash MX version we used in the previous example.

If you're working with Flash MX, you might as well skip ahead to the next example.

To edit this effect, locate random-volume.fla in the code archive.

Setting the Scene

Building on the previous example, we'll add several pieces of code to accommodate the volume control mechanism, and we'll replace the existing Flash MX CheckBox components with their Flash MX 2004 counterparts. We'll also add the new NumericStepper component to the interface to provide users with volume control.

12. If you're working from the previous example, locate the Flash MX CheckBox components within the CheckBoxes layer, and delete them.

13. Select the first frame of the CheckBoxes layer and drag four instances of the CheckBox component from the UI Components section of the Components Panel, spacing them evenly across the stage. Name these instances, from left to right: backgroundCBox, drumsCBox, guitarCBox, and overlayCBox.

14. For each of the CheckBox instances you just created, change the selected parameter within the Property Inspector to true, so that the checkboxes will be selected by default.

15. Change the label parameter for each of the CheckBox instances. From left to right, they should read: Background, Drums, Guitar, and Overlay.

16. Drag four instances of the NumericStepper component from the UI Components section of the Components Panel into the first frame of the CheckBoxes layer. Align each NumericStepper beneath each of the checkboxes. Name the instances vol1Control, vol2Control, vol3Control, and vol4Control, and set their widths to 50 pixels.

17. For each of the NumericStepper component instances, set the parameters within the Property Inspector as follows:

maximum	100
minimum	0
stepSize	5
value	100

18. Above each of the NumericStepper components, add a static text box containing the text "Volume" to indicate the purpose of the NumericStepper component. The outcome should resemble Figure 5.4.

19. Alter the width and height of the movie and the rounded rectangle frame to accommodate the extra controls we've added.

Now we can add the extra ActionScript needed to accomplish this effect.

Adding the ActionScript

20. Select the first frame of the Actions layer. We'll leave the math and playback functions/methods (randomBetween, roundNumber, PlayQueue, PlayClips,

LoopClips) alone, but replace the remaining code (the checkbox event handlers) with the following:

File: **random-volume.fla**   Actions : 1 (excerpt)

```
var backgroundOff = false;
var drumsOff = false;
var guitarOff = false;
var overlayOff = false;
function backgroundChange ()
{
  if (backgroundCBox.selected)
  {
    backgroundOff = false;
    vol1Control.enabled = true;
  }
  else
  {
    backgroundOff = true;
    vol1Control.enabled = false;
    _root.SoundHolder0.orchestra.setVolume (0);
  }
}
function drumsChange ()
{
  if (drumsCBox.selected)
  {
    drumsOff = false;
    vol2Control.enabled = true;
  }
  else
  {
    drumsOff = true;
    vol2Control.enabled = false;
    _root.SoundHolder1.orchestra.setVolume (0);
  }
}
function guitarChange ()
{
  if (guitarCBox.selected)
  {
    guitarOff = false;
    vol3Control.enabled = true;
  }
  else
  {
    guitarOff = true;
```

```
      vol3Control.enabled = false;
      _root.SoundHolder2.orchestra.setVolume (0);
  }
}
function overlayChange ()
{
  if (overlayCBox.selected)
  {
    overlayOff = false;
    vol4Control.enabled = true;
  }
  else
  {
    overlayOff = true;
    vol4Control.enabled = false;
    _root.SoundHolder3.orchestra.setVolume (0);
  }
}
function setCustomVolume ()
{
  if (!backgroundOff)
  {
    SoundHolder0.orchestra.setVolume (vol1Control.value);
  }
  if (!drumsOff)
  {
    SoundHolder1.orchestra.setVolume (vol2Control.value);
  }
  if (!guitarOff)
  {
    SoundHolder2.orchestra.setVolume (vol3Control.value);
  }
  if (!overlayOff)
  {
    SoundHolder3.orchestra.setVolume (vol4Control.value);
  }
}
var volumeListener = new Object ();
volumeListener.change = function ()
{
  setCustomVolume ();
};
var cboxListener = new Object ();
cboxListener.click = function ()
{
  backgroundChange ();
```

```
   drumsChange ();
   guitarChange ();
   overlayChange ();
   setCustomVolume ();
};
vol1Control.addEventListener ("change", volumeListener);
vol2Control.addEventListener ("change", volumeListener);
vol3Control.addEventListener ("change", volumeListener);
vol4Control.addEventListener ("change", volumeListener);
backgroundCBox.addEventListener ("click", cboxListener);
drumsCBox.addEventListener ("click", cboxListener);
guitarCBox.addEventListener ("click", cboxListener);
overlayCBox.addEventListener ("click", cboxListener);
```

Once again, we have functions to handle the CheckBox changes (backgroundChange, drumsChange, guitarChange, and overlayChange). They all look fairly similar.

```
function backgroundChange ()
{
  if (backgroundCBox.selected)
  {
    backgroundOff = false;
    vol1Control.enabled = true;
  }
  else
  {
    backgroundOff = true;
    vol1Control.enabled = false;
    _root.SoundHolder0.orchestra.setVolume (0);
  }
}
```

These functions detect the current status of the relevant CheckBox by analyzing its selected property. If the CheckBox is selected, we set a variable to false (in this case, the variable is backgroundOff) to indicate that the corresponding clip is not switched off. These four variables are set to false to begin with, since all four sound clips are switched on at the start of the movie. We also enable the associated volume control NumericStepper (vol1Control).

If the CheckBox is *not* selected, we set the variable to true and disable the corresponding NumericStepper component, indicating that the sound clip is switched off. We also set the volume of the related sound clip to zero. This switches the clip off, but allows it to keep playing silently, maintaining its position in case we decide to switch it back on later.

The `setCustomVolume` function sets the volume of each clip to the value specified by its associated `NumericStepper` control, unless the flag variable indicates that it's currently switched off.

```
function setCustomVolume ()
{
  if (!backgroundOff)
  {
    SoundHolder0.orchestra.setVolume (vol1Control.value);
  }
  if (!drumsOff)
  {
    SoundHolder1.orchestra.setVolume (vol2Control.value);
  }
  if (!guitarOff)
  {
    SoundHolder2.orchestra.setVolume (vol3Control.value);
  }
  if (!overlayOff)
  {
    SoundHolder3.orchestra.setVolume (vol4Control.value);
  }
}
```

All that's left is to ensure these functions are called at the appropriate times. A new listener `Object` called `volumeListener` offers a method called `change` that calls the `setCustomVolume` function.

```
var volumeListener = new Object ();
volumeListener.change = function ()
{
  setCustomVolume ();
};
```

By calling the `addEventListener` method from each of the `NumericStepper` components, we have this object handle changes to the volume of our clips:

```
vol1Control.addEventListener ("change", volumeListener);
vol2Control.addEventListener ("change", volumeListener);
vol3Control.addEventListener ("change", volumeListener);
vol4Control.addEventListener ("change", volumeListener);
```

If any of the NumericStepper component values change, the setCustomVolume function is called to handle it.

We've also set up an event listener in a similar manner for the CheckBox components:

```
cboxListener = new Object ();
cboxListener.click = function ()
{
  backgroundChange ();
  drumsChange ();
  guitarChange ();
  overlayChange ();
  setCustomVolume ();
};
...
backgroundCBox.addEventListener ("click", cboxListener);
drumsCBox.addEventListener ("click", cboxListener);
guitarCBox.addEventListener ("click", cboxListener);
overlayCBox.addEventListener ("click", cboxListener);
```

When any one of the checkboxes is clicked, the event handler calls the four functions we defined earlier (switching on or off the correct sound clip) before calling setCustomVolume to correctly set the volume of any clip that has just been switched on.

21. Save your document and export the SWF file to an appropriate location.

IMPORTANT

Don't forget ActionScript 2.0

Components distributed with Flash MX 2004 work internally using features of ActionScript 2.0. If you try to publish a movie that contains such components with Publish settings configured for ActionScript 1.0, the components will not work (they'll look like white rectangles with black borders).

New movies created in Flash MX 2004 default to ActionScript 2.0, so you're okay there. But, if you start from the finished version of the previous example provided in the code archive, you'll need to change the ActionScript version setting for the file. Simply click the background of the movie, then click the Settings... button in the Property Inspector. You can adjust the ActionScript version setting on the Flash tab.

Use the checkboxes to switch on and off some of the tracks; notice how they disable and enable the volume controls we've added. Experiment with the volume controls to set a nice balance between the tracks, and see what masterpieces you can come up with!

You can build on this example to modify any number of sound object properties. Spend a little time with it and see what you can achieve.

XML, MP3, and ID3 Tag Reader

This effect uses the same choir sound clips we used previously in this chapter, but with a slightly different approach. We'll import a playlist from an XML file and load the MP3 files dynamically into Flash. We'll also present song information (including Album, Artist, and Song Title) that's stored within the MP3 in what are called **ID3 tags**, as shown in Figure 5.5.

Figure 5.5. Create a random MP3 player using XML and ID3 data.

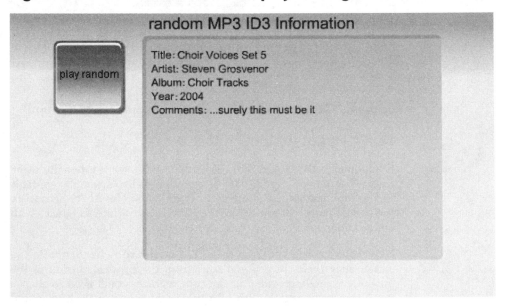

ID3 tag information is referenced differently in Flash MX than in Flash MX 2004, owing to the differences between versions of Flash Player. Macromedia Flash Player 7 supports the latest ID3 v2.2 and v2.4 tags. As the data is stored at the beginning of the MP3 file, this information is referenced immediately upon opening the MP3 stream. On the other hand, Macromedia Flash Player 6 supports only ID3 v1.0 and v1.1 tags, which are stored at the end of the file. On that platform, we must wait until the stream is fully loaded before we can retrieve the ID3 tag information.

We'll initially create an MP3 player for version 6 of the Flash Player, supporting ID3 v1.x tags. Then, we'll modify the effect to take advantage of ID3 v2.x tag support within version 7 of the Flash Player.

To edit this effect, locate `mp3-mx.fla` in the code archive.

It uses several MP3 files: `choir1.mp3`, `choir2.mp3`, `choir3.mp3`, `choir4.mp3`, and `choir5.mp3`. We'll also be needing the XML file that acts as the playlist; it's called `playlist.xml` and can also be found in the code archive.

Setting the Scene

For this project, we need a clickable movie clip that loads a random MP3 file and a dynamic text field that displays the ID3 data from the MP3 file.

1. Create a new Flash document that's 500 pixels wide and 450 pixels high. Accept the default frame rate and click OK.

2. Rename the default layer Actions and add beneath it two new layers named Interface and Background.

3. Select the first frame of the Interface layer and create a movie clip called `PlayRandomButton` containing a button that's approximately 70 pixels high and 70 pixels wide. Name the instance `randomplayer` and move the clip to the left of the stage centre, as shown in Figure 5.5.

We'll use this clip to randomly load an MP3 file and pass the ID3 tag information from the MP3 file into a dynamic text field.

4. Create a new, 320x160 pixel dynamic text field to the right of the button. Name the field `trackID3Info`.

5. In the Property Inspector for the new field, click the Character... button and choose Basic Latin (or All Characters in Flash MX).

This dynamic text field will act as a container that receives the ID3 tag information from the dynamically loaded MP3 files.

Now, for a little window-dressing:

6. Add to the first frame of the Background layer a rectangle that frames the text area you just created.

You can add as many extras as you wish to increase the aesthetics of the interface. Refer to Figure 5.5 for inspiration!

7. Save your work.

8. Locate the files choir1.mp3, choir2.mp3, choir3.mp3, choir4.mp3 and choir5.mp3 from the code archive and move them into the same folder in which you saved the document.

Creating the XML Playlist

We now need to create the XML playlist that references the MP3 files we're planning to load.

 Tip For more information on working with XML, see *Introduction to XML*, by Harry Fuecks[2].

9. Type the following code into a text editor and save it as playlist.xml in the same folder.

File: **playlist.xml**   Actions : 1

```
<?xml version="1.0" encoding="iso-8859-1"?>
<playlist>
  <mp3file track="choir1.mp3"/>
  <mp3file track="choir2.mp3"/>
  <mp3file track="choir3.mp3"/>
  <mp3file track="choir4.mp3"/>
  <mp3file track="choir5.mp3"/>
</playlist>
```

Unlike HTML, which uses a predefined set of tags, XML allows you to create custom data structures. As long as all opening tags have a matching closing tag (or, as in the case of the mp3File tag in this example, they close themselves),

[2] http://www.sitepoint.com/article/930

Flash will import the data structure as an ActionScript XML object, allowing you to manipulate and access the information contained within the file.

This XML file is structurally simple. The playlist tag is the top-level node, and the mp3file tags are its child nodes. These child nodes also contain an attribute called track, which holds the name of the MP3 file we wish to pull into Flash.

Our ActionScript will import this XML file and move through the data structure, populating an array with the names of the MP3 files it contains.

Adding the ActionScript

10. Select the first frame of the Actions layer and add the following code to the Actions Panel:

File: **mp3—mx.fla**   Actions : 1 (excerpt)

```
var tracklist = new Array ();
var mp3List = new XML ();
mp3List.ignoreWhite = true;
mp3List.onLoad = createPlayList;
mp3List.load ("playlist.xml");
function createPlayList (success)
{
  if (!success)
  {
    return;
  }
  var topLevel = null;
  for (i = 0; i <= this.childNodes.length; i++)
  {
    if (this.childNodes[i].nodeValue == null &&
        this.childNodes[i].nodeName == "playlist")
    {
      topLevel = this.childNodes[i];
      break;
    }
  }
  if (topLevel != null)
  {
    for (i = 0; i <= topLevel.childNodes.length; i++)
    {
      if (topLevel.childNodes[i].nodeName == "mp3file")
      {
        var track =
```

```
            topLevel.childNodes[i].attributes["track"];
        _root.tracklist.push (track);
      }
    }
  }
}
}
function randomBetween (a, b)
{
  return Math.min (a, b) + random (Math.abs (a - b) + 1);
}
function playTrack ()
{
  var track = _root.track;
  if (track.getBytesLoaded () == track.getBytesTotal () &&
      track.duration > 0)
  {
    clearInterval (_root.checkLoaded);
    trackID3Info.text = "";
    trackID3Info.text += "Title: " + track.id3.songname +
        newline;
    trackID3Info.text += "Artist: " + track.id3.artist +
        newline;
    trackID3Info.text += "Album: " + track.id3.album +
        newline;
    trackID3Info.text += "Year: " + track.id3.year + newline;
    trackID3Info.text += "Comments: " + track.id3.comment +
        newline;
  }
}
randomplayer.onPress = function ()
{
  stopAllSounds ();
  var trackNo = randomBetween (0, _root.tracklist.length - 1);
  _root.track = new Sound ();
  _root.track.loadSound (_root.tracklist[trackNo], true);
  _root.checkLoaded = setInterval (playTrack, 500);
};
```

Let's break this code into manageable chunks and see what's going on.

First, we create an empty array to contain our list of MP3 tracks.

```
var tracklist = new Array ();
```

Next, we create an XML object called mp3List, and set its ignoreWhite property to true so that line feeds and whitespace aren't parsed as separate nodes.

```
var mp3List = new XML ();
mp3List.ignoreWhite = true;
```

We then set the event handler that will execute when the XML file has loaded (createPlayList) and load the data from playlist.xml.

```
mp3List.onLoad = createPlayList;
mp3List.load ("playlist.xml");
```

Now we define the createPlayList function, which gets called to handle the XML data once it has loaded.

```
function createPlayList (success)
{
  if (!success)
  {
    return;
  }
  var topLevel = null;
  for (i = 0; i <= this.childNodes.length; i++)
  {
    if (this.childNodes[i].nodeValue == null &&
        this.childNodes[i].nodeName == "playlist")
    {
      topLevel = this.childNodes[i];
      break;
    }
  }
}
```

The first thing we do is check whether the XML file loaded successfully, as indicated by the success parameter. If it didn't, we bail out before attempting to process it.

We then enter a for loop based on the number of top-level nodes within the XML object (this). We check these nodes until we find the one that has a null nodeValue, meaning it's a tag (as opposed to a piece of text) and that its name is playlist. This node is stored in a variable named topLevel. We then break out of the for loop.

Next, we enter another for loop, in order to examine its children:

```
  if (topLevel != null)
  {
```

```
    for (i = 0; i <= topLevel.childNodes.length; i++)
    {
      if (topLevel.childNodes[i].nodeName == "mp3file")
      {
        var track = topLevel.childNodes[i].attributes["track"];
```

For each of the child nodes, we check to see if it's an `mp3file` tag, and then populate a variable with the `track` attribute of the tag, which is the name of an MP3 file.

Finally, we populate the `tracklist` array using its `push` method to add the file-name to the start of the array.

```
        _root.tracklist.push (track);
```

That takes care of building the playlist. Now, when the `randomplayer` movie clip is clicked, the following code is brought into play:

```
randomplayer.onPress = function ()
{
  stopAllSounds ();
  var trackNo = randomBetween (0, _root.tracklist.length - 1);
  _root.track = new Sound ();
  _root.track.loadSound (_root.tracklist[trackNo], true);
  _root.checkLoaded = setInterval (playTrack, 500);
};
```

First, we stop all currently running sounds using the `stopAllSounds` function. We then populate a variable called `trackNo` with a random number in order to choose one of the tracks in our `tracklist` array.

We then create a new `Sound` object and load it up with a random MP3 file using the `trackNo` variable we have just populated.

Finally, we use the `setInterval` function to call the `playTrack` function every half-second. We store the interval identifier in a variable called `checkLoaded` in the root of the movie so we can cancel it when appropriate.

Now, all that's left to discuss is the `playTrack` function:

```
function playTrack ()
{
  var track = _root.track;
  if (track.getBytesLoaded () == track.getBytesTotal () &&
      track.duration > 0)
```

```
{
  clearInterval (_root.checkLoaded);
  trackID3Info.text = "";
  trackID3Info.text += "Title: " + track.id3.songname + newline;
  trackID3Info.text += "Artist: " + track.id3.artist + newline;
  trackID3Info.text += "Album: " + track.id3.album + newline;
  trackID3Info.text += "Year: " + track.id3.year + newline;
  trackID3Info.text += "Comments: " + track.id3.comment +
      newline;
}
}
```

Each time this function is called, we check whether the MP3 file has loaded successfully. Once it has, we cancel the interval that is set to call the function every half-second with the `clearInterval` function. We can then populate the `trackID3Info` dynamic text field with the ID3 tag information from the MP3 file.

ID3 v1.x Caveat

As Flash Player 6 and Flash MX support only ID3 v1.0 and v1.1 tags, we have to make sure that the MP3 file is completely loaded before we attempt to pull the ID3 tag information from it. This is essential, as the ID3 tag data is found at the end of the MP3 file.

In Flash MX 2004, which can produce content for Flash Player 7 and supports the ID3 v2.2 and v2.4 tag information located at the beginning of the MP3 file, this information is much more easily accessed. We'll see what this means to Flash developers when we modify this example.

11. Save your document and preview your work.

When the movie loads, the XML file is imported and the `tracklist` array is populated with all the track information from the `playlist.xml` file. Clicking on the `randomplayer` movie clip loads an MP3 file and displays its ID3 tag data in the dynamic text field.

Modifications

As we discussed before, it's much easier to reference ID3 tag data in Flash Player 7. This Player supports v2.2 and v2.4 ID3 tags, which are stored at the beginning of the MP3 file rather than at the end.

Flash MX 2004 only!

As you can only produce Flash Player 7 SWF files using Flash MX 2004, this modification is suitable for Flash MX 2004 only.

To edit this effect, locate `mp3–mx2004.fla` in the code archive.

We need only make a couple of simple modifications to the movie to allow Flash MX 2004 to read ID3 v2.2 and 2.4 tag information.

12. Select the first frame of the Actions layer, then locate and delete the `playTrack` function from the Actions Panel. It's no longer needed!

13. Replace the `onPress` event handler code for the `randomPlayer` movie clip with the following code:

File: **mp3–mx2004.fla**   Actions : 1 (excerpt)

```
randomPlayer.onPress = function ()
{
  stopAllSounds ();
  var trackNo = randomBetween (0, trackInfo.length - 1);
  var track = new Sound ();
  track.onID3 = function ()
  {
    trackID3Info.text = "";
    trackID3Info.text += "Title: " + track.id3.TIT2 + newline;
    trackID3Info.text += "Artist: " + track.id3.TPE1 + newline;
    trackID3Info.text += "Album: " + track.id3.TALB + newline;
    trackID3Info.text += "Year: " + track.id3.TYER + newline;
    trackID3Info.text += "Comments: " + track.id3.COMM +
        newline;
  };
  track.loadSound (tracklist[trackNo], true);
};
```

This code is essentially the same as before, but it uses an event handler to process the ID3 tag information rather than calling a function every half-second to check for it.

After we've created the new Sound object (`track`), we reference a new event handler, called `onID3`, which is available in Flash Player 7. This is invoked when new ID3 data is detected for a loaded MP3 file, which means that we don't need to confirm that the MP3 file has completely loaded before we check for the ID3 tag data. Once the `onID3` event handler is invoked, we can proceed to populate the `trackID3Info` dynamic text field with the ID3 2.0 tags. It's as simple as that!

Tip

ID3 Reference

For a complete listing of supported ID3 tags within Flash MX 2004, search for `Sound.ID3` in the Help Panel.

14. Save and preview your work.

Now, when you click the `randomPlayer` movie clip, the MP3 file starts to play and the ID3 tag data is displayed in the dynamic text field almost instantly. You no longer need to wait for the MP3 file to load completely as you did in the previous example.

Conclusion

Who said that all you can do with sound clips is play them? Certainly not me! I hope that we've covered enough material within this chapter to fuel your desire to create some really interesting sound-based interfaces, experimental effects, and other items.

It's now time to see what we can accomplish using video effects in Flash!

Video Effects

Appropriate, effectively-produced video effects can bring your Flash movies to life. The type of effect you use, and the way you implement it, will of course depend on the type of project you're completing. But, from the subtle use of background video to a full-blown interactive movie, the application of video in Flash can be an interesting and exciting project.

Since the introduction of video support in Flash MX, developers have embraced these new abilities. With the release of Flash MX 2004, the API has been extended to provide developers and designers greater control over the inclusion of video. Here's a list of some of the enhanced video capabilities that are included in the Flash MX 2004 release.

FLV Support

FLV files (Flash videos) can now be played back directly from disk, eliminating the file size and length limitations under which developers previously labored.

Video Import Wizard

A new step-by-step wizard provides control over both the range of an imported movie and color correction on the video.

These features are available only in Flash MX 2004 Professional, and deserve serious consideration when you're deciding which upgrade path to follow:

Professional Application Integration

You can now export video directly to FLV format from your favorite supported video-editing application via the QuickTime FLV Export Plug-In. This saves time when importing your clips into Flash.

Video Quality and Screen Recording

The QuickTime FLV Export Plug-In provides extra control over exported FLV files, including the ability to optimize frame rates and frame sizes.

Streaming Media Components

This suite of components with drag-and-drop functionality lets you add controls to imported video for quick playback manipulation.

Flash MX 2004 provides many options for video integration, allowing you to import video and achieve considerable dynamic control over it. We'll start by looking at the simple process of importing video clips. Later, we'll move on to explore the intricacies of ActionScript-based video control.

When to Use Video in Your Flash Movies

"You know, this could do with some sprucing up."

How often have you thought this about one of your Flash projects? When you do, don't turn to video! Simply adding a flat video to your project for the sake of it, with no forethought or planning, can often detract from the overall impact of your project.

Video, like all the effects we've discussed, needs a little planning. Properly executed, the application of video can be stunning. Even the use of very subtle video—small clips, carefully applied—can bring to life an otherwise flat project, compelling users to interact and become involved with your application. But if you're in any doubt as to whether or not you should include video in your project, don't! Trying to shoehorn content into your Flash movie will likely produce disastrous results, ruining a concept you've worked hard to develop.

If you've concluded that a subtle sprinkling of video through your project will enhance its underlying appeal, the next step is planning. You'll need to decide how, where, and when video will be included. Ask yourself whether video will complement your project's theme, style, and content. Also consider the impact of video upon the project's file size and distribution media. If you're creating an ActionScripted project that's based around video, you probably already have a reasonable idea of how video will fit into your project and the various ways in which your work will be accessed and displayed.

There are several simple tools you can use to facilitate the integration of video into your work:

☐ Use masking to alter the shape and structure of the video window so that it looks less like a conventional "imported video."

☐ Create subtle backgrounds that indicate the video is part of the scenery of your project, rather than an afterthought.

☐ Re-skin existing controls, or create your own control interface, for video clip playback.

As we'll see through this chapter, there are many other techniques you can use to increase the appeal of video in Flash projects, but these basic guidelines represent a good foundation.

Video Inclusion Options

There are two main methods for including video in projects built using Flash MX 2004: embed the video directly into the finished SWF file, or utilize the new FLV (Flash video) technology to deliver steaming video. Both options have pros and cons, and it's important that we're aware of them before we start any projects involving video footage.

Embedded Video

Gone are the days when video was simulated by a movie clip containing a sequence of bitmaps guaranteed to bloat the file size of your movie. Embedding video is now a simple process. With Flash MX, you can directly import it into Flash, place it on the timeline, and access its individual frames. You can then overlay other objects on different layers to produce quite complex and engaging presentations with only a little ActionScript.

Watch the file size!

Depending on the quality, length, and size of the video you're importing, the size of exported SWF files can be very large. If you want to use large video clips in your projects, and you have access to Flash MX 2004 Professional, consider using external FLV files to reduce the file size (see the following section).

A major problem inherent in SWF movies with embedded video is that users have to download all the frames of an embedded video before it begins to play. The new FLV format is progressive; it's based around the QuickTime video format, and allows playback before the entire movie has downloaded.

Other problems with embedding relate to memory saturation and the synchronization of video and audio tracks. Generally speaking, the larger the embedded video, the greater the chance the Flash Player will crash due to memory allocation errors and loss of image and sound synchronization. A loss of synchronization is obviously undesirable under *any* circumstances. But sometimes, it can cause real problems. Imagine, for example, an online training movie in which the visuals stop relating to the oratory overlay.

If you do plan to use embedded video, be aware of these issues. Try to keep the file sizes of any imported video as small as possible while maintaining decent quality, and be aware that end users will not enjoy waiting for your project to display on screen.

FLV

To include lengthy videos effectively in your projects, you should use the FLV file format for delivery. This eliminates restrictions on memory usage. Moreover, FLV files stream video into the Flash Player, so it can begin to play before the transfer from the server is complete. This ability in itself is of great advantage—users no longer have to wait for the movie to load before it begins to play, and developers enjoy greater scope to include large video files without impacting negatively on the user experience.

Finally, with FLV files, the frame rate of the movie you serve to the user is independent of the frame rate of the SWF movie from which it is referenced. If your Flash movie runs at 12 fps and references several external FLV files with differing frame rates, each will play at the frame rate at which it was produced, rather than the frame rate of the final Flash movie.

Given all the advantages of the FLV file format, you may well be thinking that there must be a catch. There don't appear to be any insurmountable disadvantages with the format, though one negative is that FLV files are not accessible via the timeline. Using the embedded video method, developers can control the timeline of the movie, its position, and many other factors with ease. The FLV format does, however, allow you to alter your position within the movie using the new NetStream objects, which we'll discuss shortly.

Capturing Your Movie

Therei are many tools you can use to capture movie clips, from DV cameras to Webcams. Your choice will obviously depend on the medium you'll use to deliver your movie and the audience to which it will be displayed. You can't create a broadcast-quality CD using movies that have been scaled up from 160x200 pixel Webcam captures! When you're capturing clips, remember the following guidelines:

Make the footage reusable.
Shoot the video at a good frame size. You can always scale down; it's more difficult to scale up.

Create movie libraries.
Categorize your content into logically organized groups so that you can quickly repurpose clips for future projects.

Invest in a robust video application.
Applications such as Final Cut Pro and After Effects will quickly pay for themselves. Use them to add creative effects to your movies. In conjunction with the QuickTime FLV Exporter Plug-In that comes with Flash MX 2004 Professional, they allow you to export video directly in FLV format, ready for use within Flash.

Once you've process your movie clips and applied the effects you require, it's time to import them into Flash for positioning and the application of further effects. There's a lot you can do with video in Flash—we'll only have time to scratch the surface here. These first steps will, I hope, pique your interest and inspire you to explore other avenues.

Importing Your Movie

Flash MX 2004 makes working with video much easier, thanks to its new features. The whole process, from importing to publishing, has been overhauled. Flash now provides you the ability to edit the range of frames you're importing. You can create multiple clips, trim the length of the movie, reorder video clips, and more.

Try importing a QuickTime movie (File > Import > Import to Library..., then select the movie you wish to import) and having a play with Flash MX 2004's Video Import Wizard, shown in Figure 6.1.

Figure 6.1. Use the Video Import Wizard to edit video before its imported into Flash.

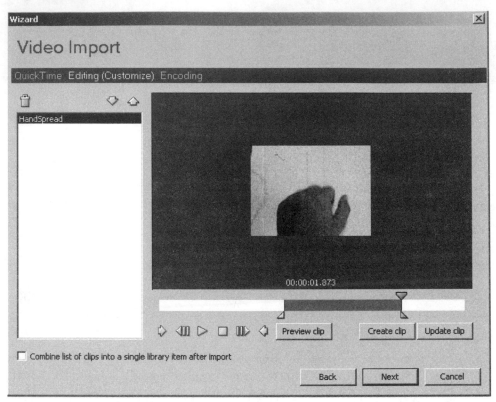

Developers now have the option to edit video before importing it into Flash. This is a huge improvement on Flash MX: you can create an infinite number of smaller video clips from the original master clip.

As you can see in Figure 6.1, by dragging the "in" and "out" points beneath the blue scrubber bar, you can select a small portion of the video clip to import, and confirm that the content is what you need by clicking the Preview Clip button. Clicking the Create Clip button will add the selection to the window on the left of the Video Import panel. You can edit its name by double-clicking the high-lighted clip. Once you're happy with the clip(s) you've created, you can either splice them together into a single clip or import them as individual clips. Simple!

After you've selected the clips you want to import, you're presented with another option screen in which you can choose encoding options for delivering your video to the end user.

Compression Settings

Flash offers several compression profiles. These correspond to different connection speeds, so base your selection on appropriate target audience statistics. Alternatively, you can import clips using a profile you create for yourself that defines video quality, dimensions, cropping, and other settings. To create a profile, select Create New Profile from the Compression Profile drop-down list.

Once you reach the profile creation screen shown in Figure 6.2, select the Bandwidth or Quality options, moving the sliders to suit your needs. A live preview of your movie will display within the preview window.

Figure 6.2. Create custom compression settings.

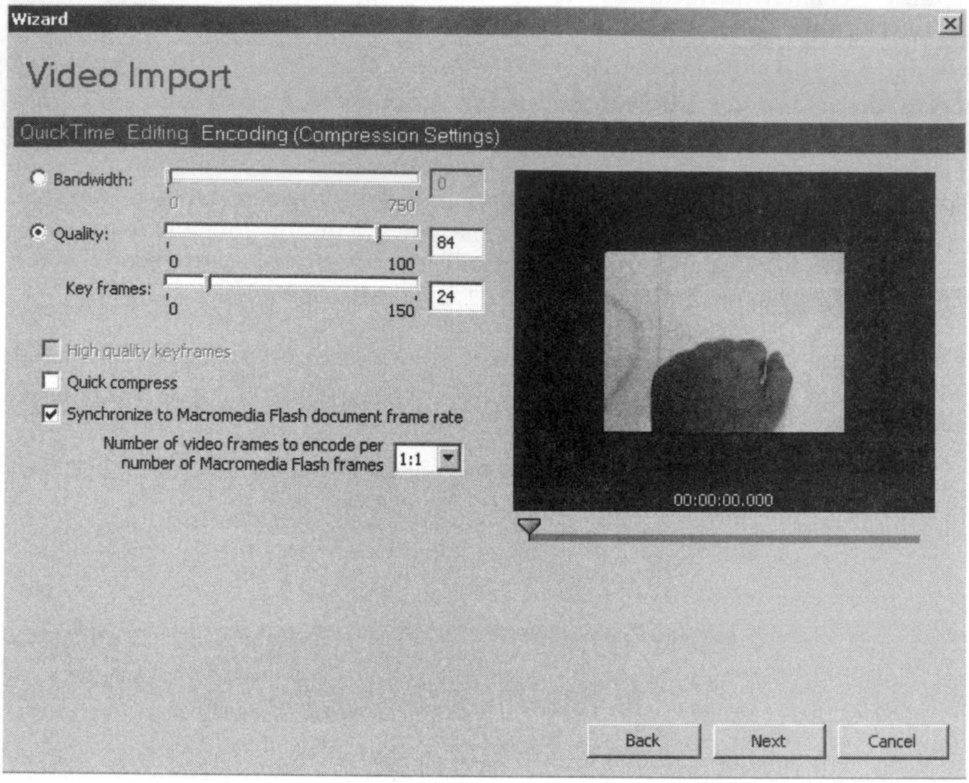

Stop to check the results!

The compression settings you choose in a custom profile can have a large impact on the resulting video quality. After you've selected the values for video bandwidth or quality using the sliders, use the scrubber within the live preview area as you view your clip. Tonal quality and color range, in particular, can be affected by changes in compression.

Once you're satisfied with your settings, click Next to save the new compression profile for future use.

There is one other element of major interest to those importing video for use in Flash: the Advanced settings option available in the Encoding screen.

Advanced Video Import Settings

A variety of advanced options are available within Flash's Advanced Video Import Settings. Explore and experiment with these—especially saturation, hue, brightness, and contrast, all of which are useful for last-minute alterations (see Figure 6.3).

Figure 6.3. Flash offers a variety of video import options in its advanced settings.

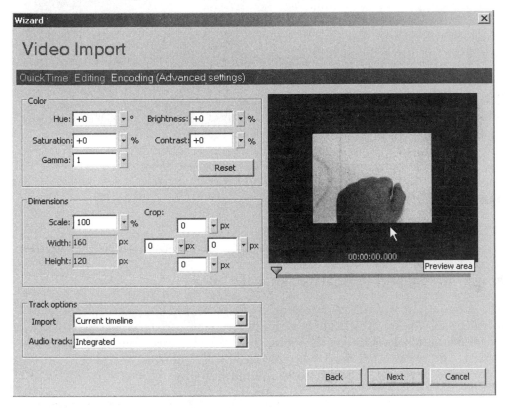

The right tool for the job

Tip

To perform extensive modifications to video footage before importing it into Flash, invest in a quality post-production application such as Adobe After Effects. Not only will such products allow you to perform basic manipulations similar to those provided by the Video Import Wizard within Flash MX

2004, they also include a range of other manipulation techniques. Adobe After Effects is also extensible via free and commercial add-ons.

Track Options

The 2004 release of Flash allows you to select how and where imported video is placed in a document. To manipulate video with ActionScript, you'll probably decide to import the track as a movie clip (select Movie clip from the Import menu under Track options). You can then control the video using the familiar `play` and `stop` movie clip methods, using the other ActionScript methods to determine position within the current clip.

If, on the other hand, you want to export a video to its own SWF file so that you can import it into other projects or dynamically include it via ActionScript, the Current Timeline option is the one you want.

The options on the Audio track menu (Separate, Integrated and None) revolve around the audio component of the clip. This is a major benefit if you require tight control. To import a video clip as a background, and keep the file size to the bare minimum, select None. This will remove the audio track and preserve the video track, reducing the final export size of your video.

Cropping Video Clips

Within the Advanced Settings option of the Encoding panel is an option that alters the dimensions of the clip you're importing. You can select to scale the clip to a percentage of the master clip (very handy if you wish to add lightweight video imagery to your project), or you can crop the video.

The Crop option is useful in trimming excess fat from clips prior to import. It's a real boon when you're dealing with a widescreen format video clip that has letterboxing (black bands) at the top and bottom. To import a video clip in this format, and remove the dead space on the top and bottom of the clip, simply enter values into the top and bottom crop boxes.

This doesn't require guesswork; when you enter crop values, you can preview the result in the preview area. Once you've entered your cropping values, quickly skim through the video with the scrubber at the bottom of the preview area, as shown in Figure 6.4.

Figure 6.4. Crop your video clips before import.

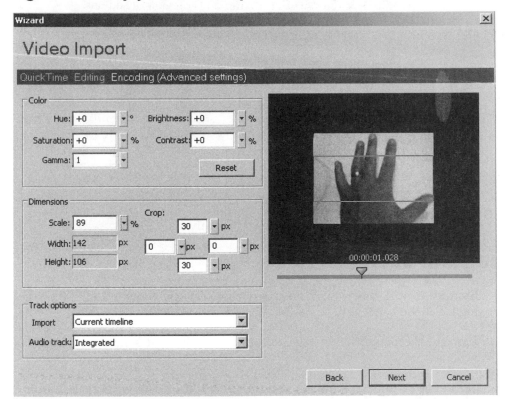

Once you're happy with your settings, click Next to give a name to your custom advanced settings. Click Next again to move to the final screen and select Finish. Your custom compression and advanced settings will be applied, and imported into Flash!

Accessing External FLV Files

As we've already discussed, there are huge benefits to using the external FLV method to implement large video clips in your projects. This method features a lack of restrictions on memory usage, and the advantage that the streamed video will start to play immediately on the user's monitor. In this example, shown in Figure 6.5, we'll see how easy it is to import a QuickTime movie, export it to FLV format, and reference the external file for playback within your project.

Figure 6.5. Access external FLV files within Flash MX 2004.

To edit the effect, locate `flv.fla` in the code archive.

Setting the Scene

1. Start by creating a new Flash document that's 550 pixels wide and 400 pixels high. Set the frame rate to 24 fps.

2. Rename the default layer asVideo and create above it a new layer named Actions.

3. Select File > Import > Import to Library... and locate `wave_away.mov` from the code archive.

4. Select Embed video in Macromedia Flash document and click Next.

5. Select Edit the video first and click Next.

6. Select from the clip the range you wish to import and click Create clip, leaving the default name for the clip as it is. Click Next.

7. Select DSL/Cable 256 kbps from the Compression Profile menu or choose a connection speed that suits your needs.

8. From the Advanced settings drop-down list, select Create new profile.... Under Track Options select Movie clip from the Import menu and None from the Audio Track menu. Click Next. Change the Name for the advanced settings profile to `No sound - movie clip` and click Next. Click Finish.

9. When you're prompted to adjust the length of the timeline, click Yes. The timeline of the movie clip symbol will be extended to the required length.

You have now successfully imported the video clip into the library of your Flash movie; you now need to export it into FLV format.

Tip

Experiment with quality settings

In this example, we've selected a medium bandwidth quality level for the video clip to prove that FLV files are compact and portable. Try importing your video clips with different settings—you may find that you can maintain acceptable quality with even smaller files.

10. Open the Library Panel and select the `wave_away.mov Video` embedded video clip. Right click and select Properties....

11. Click Export... and save the clip as `wave_away.flv` in a directory of your choice.

It's as simple as that! You've successfully imported a large QuickTime movie (5.27MB), converted it into a highly compressed format, and exported it to FLV format. Depending on your exact settings, the file should now weigh in at less than 110KB! That's quite a reduction in size—by anyone's standards.

As we now have the video clip in an external file, we don't need to embed it in our Flash movie. Instead, we'll create a "dummy" movie clip in which we'll load the external video file:

12. In the Library Panel, select and delete both the embedded video clip (`wave_away.mov Video`) and the movie clip symbol that contains it (`wave_away.mov`).

13. Still in the Library Panel, click the options menu (the little icon in the top-right corner) and choose New Video. Rename the video `FLV_001`

14. Create a new movie clip symbol (Insert > New Symbol...) named `Video`, and open it for editing if Flash doesn't do that automatically.

15. Drag an instance of the `FLV_001` embedded video from the library into the `Video` movie clip. Name the instance `FLV_001` and, using the Property Inspector, position it at (0, 0) with a width of 160 and a height of 120.

16. Return to the main stage and drag an instance of the `Video` movie clip into the Video layer, naming it `Video`.

With the video clip successfully exported to FLV format and a movie clip in place ready to play it, you can now add some simple ActionScript to reference and play the FLV file.

Professional video exporting

You can circumvent steps 3-1 by purchasing Flash MX 2004 Professional. That version comes with the QuickTime FLV Export Plug-In, which allows you directly to export video files in FLV format from your post-production application of choice.

Adding the ActionScript

Playing an externally referenced FLV file, requires a `NetConnection` object. This was introduced with the release of Macromedia Flash Communication Server and subsequently added to the Flash MX 2004 API.

17. Select the first frame of the Actions layer and add the following code to the Actions Panel:

File: **flv.fla**　　　　　　　　　　　　　　　　　　　　　　　　　　　　　　Actions : 1

```
var connection = new NetConnection();
connection.connect(null);
var stream = new NetStream(connection);
_root.Video.FLV_001.attachVideo(stream);
stream.play("file://wave_away.flv");
```

18. Save the document and preview your work.

Looking for more code? Sorry, that's it! All you need to reference and play an external FLV file is included in the above listing. Let's take a quick look at what's going on.

The code that creates the necessary connections is remarkably simple. First, we create a `NetConnection` object and establish the local connection.

```
var connection = new NetConnection();
connection.connect(null);
```

We then create a `NetStream` object, passing the `NetConnection` as the parameter, and attach the stream to the blank video object (`FLV_001`) we have embedded in our video clip (`Video`).

```
var stream = new NetStream(connection);
_root.Video.FLV_001.attachVideo(stream);
```

With all the required objects and connections in place, we simply play the stream, telling it where to fetch the video.

```
stream.play("file://wave_away.flv");
```

The URL `file://wave_away.flv` tells Flash to look for the `wave_away.flv` file in the same location as the SWF file. You can also specify a relative path (e.g. `file://video/wave_away.flv`) to load the file from the `video` subdirectory) or an absolute URL beginning with `http://`.

By using some of the built-in components in the 2004 release, you can easily add a few extras to really bring a project to life.

Modifications

Ideas for improving your presentation cam be as simple as adding a subtle background to the movie, or as advanced as harnessing the power of built-in components to give quick visual feedback on the user's progress through the clip.

Adding a Loading Progress Bar

Many users want feedback on the loading progress of Flash movies.

As shown in Figure 6.6, you can use a component in Flash MX 2004 (the `ProgressBar`) to provide this information.

Figure 6.6. Add the `ProgressBar` component in Flash MX 2004.

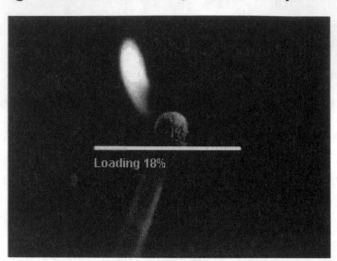

To edit this effect, locate `flv-progress.fla` in the code archive.

First, let's spice this example up by using a larger, more interesting video clip. I've provided the pre-encoded `match_300K.flv` file in the code archive, so all you need to do is adjust your stage layout to make room for the new clip.

19. Select the `Video` movie clip on the stage and double-click it to edit its contents. Select the `FLV_001` video clip instance and alter its dimensions via the Property Inspector to 320x240.

20. Return to the main stage, select the first frame of the Actions layer, and change the name of the file that the stream is told to play.

File: **flv-progress.fla**   Actions : 1 (excerpt)

```
stream.play("file://match_300K.flv");
```

21. Preview your work so far.

The new FLV file displays a burning matchstick for almost a minute. Despite this extensive play length, the clip weighs in at under 2MB and the quality is quite high. Due to its length and size, this clip lends itself perfectly to the streaming external FLV treatment!

22. Open the Components Panel (Window > Development Panels > Components), and expand the UI Components tree.

23. Select the `ProgressBar` component and drag an instance into the video layer, naming it `videoinfo`.

24. Select the `ProgressBar` and edit the parameters for the component to match those shown in Figure 6.7.

Figure 6.7. Edit the parameters for the `ProgressBar` component.

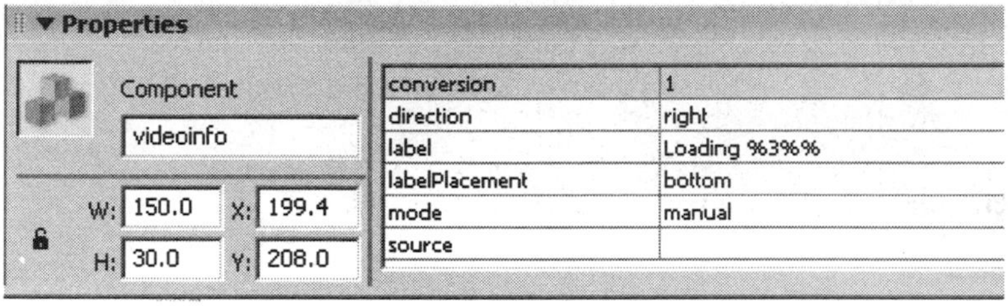

25. In the Actions Panel, add the following code beneath the script you just inserted:

File: **flv-progress.fla**   Actions : 1 (excerpt)

```
_root.Video.onEnterFrame = function ()
{
  if (_root.stream.bytesLoaded < _root.stream.bytesTotal)
  {
    _root.videoinfo.visible = true;
    _root.videoinfo.setProgress (_root.stream.bytesLoaded,
        _root.stream.bytesTotal);
  }
  else
  {
    _root.videoinfo.visible = false;
  }
};
```

Do you remember embedding the video object into the `Video` movie clip earlier? If you look at the above code, you'll see why that was done. To provide constant feedback with the progress bar, you need an `onEnterFrame` event handler, which performs the updates, and an `onEnterFrame` event handler, which calls for a movie clip.

You can determine how much of the movie has been loaded by examining the `bytesLoaded` and `bytesTotal` properties of the `NetStream` object (`stream`). When the former is less than the latter, we know the movie is still downloading, so you display the progress bar (by setting its `visible` property to `true`). The `setProgress` method updates the progress bar, giving it the `bytesLoaded` and `bytesTotal` values as the currently completed and total values it needs respectively.

```
if (_root.stream.bytesLoaded < _root.stream.bytesTotal)
{
  _root.videoinfo.visible = true;
  _root.videoinfo.setProgress (_root.stream.bytesLoaded,
      _root.stream.bytesTotal);
}
```

Once the whole of the movie is loaded, we switch the visibility of the `ProgressBar` to `false`.

```
else
{
  _root.videoinfo.visible = false;
}
```

26. Save your Flash document and preview the movie.

Presto! You've constructed a functioning visual feedback device that shows users how much of the movie has loaded.

Loading too fast?

If you view this example locally, the movie clip may load so fast that the progress bar never even appears.

If you upload the example to your Website, matters will be very different. To quickly see the progress bar in action, you can edit your ActionScript to load the movie clip from SitePoint's Web server:

```
stream.play("http://www.sitepoint.com/books/flashant1/ex
amples/match_300K.flv");
```

As this example has shown, utilizing prepackaged components can save development time, while giving users the feedback they require. Try experimenting with some of the other components that come with Flash MX 2004 and Flash MX 2004 Professional to see what you can come up with.

Adding Control Buttons

Wecan further expand the previous example by adding simple control buttons that take advantage of the NetStream class' capabilities, as shown in Figure 6.8. All these buttons ship with the 2004 release; they're found in Window > Other Panels > Common Libraries > Buttons.

Figure 6.8. Add control buttons for external FLV playback.

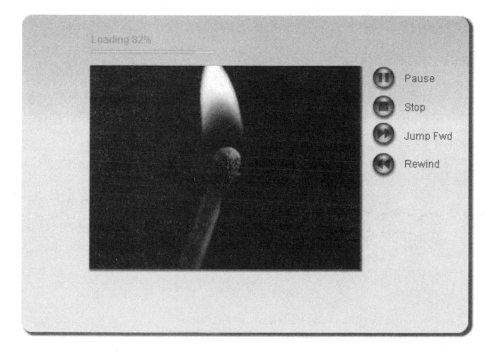

To modify this effect, find flv-control.fla in the code archive.

27. Building on the previous example, create a new layer named Buttons and add above it a layer named Button Labels.

28. Select Window > Other Panels > Common Libraries > Buttons and locate the Playback folder. Drag instances of `gel Pause`, `gel Stop`, `gel Fast Forward`, and `gel Rewind` from the button library onto the Buttons layer.

29. Name the instances of the buttons `pause`, `stop`, `jump_fwd` and `rewind`, respectively.

30. Add some relevant text labels to the right of each button in the Buttons Labels layer, as shown in Figure 6.8.

31. Select the first frame of the Actions layer and replace the existing code with the following:

File: **flv-control.fla**   Actions : 1

```
playFLV ("file://match_300K.flv");
function playFLV (clipname)
{
  _root.connection = new NetConnection ();
  _root.connection.connect (null);
  _root.stream = new NetStream (_root.connection);
  _root.Video.FLV_001.attachVideo (_root.stream);
  _root.stream.play (clipname);
  _root.Video.onEnterFrame = UpdateProgressBar;
}
function UpdateProgressBar ()
{
  if (_root.stream.bytesLoaded < _root.stream.bytesTotal)
  {
    _root.videoinfo.visible = true;
    _root.videoinfo.setProgress (_root.stream.bytesLoaded,
        _root.stream.bytesTotal);
  }
  else
  {
    _root.videoinfo.visible = false;
  }
}
_root.stop.onPress = function ()
{
  _root.stream.close ();
  _root.Video.onEnterFrame = null;
  _root.videoinfo.visible = false;
};
_root.pause.onPress = function ()
{
```

```
  _root.stream.pause ();
};
_root.jump_fwd.onPress = function ()
{
  _root.stream.seek (_root.stream.time + 2);
};
_root.rewind.onPress = function ()
{
  playFLV ("file://match_300K.flv");
};
```

I've encapsulated the code that plays the video clip into a new function called playFLV. This accepts a single parameter—the URL of the FLV file we want to play. The updating of the ProgressBar component is carried out by the UpdateProgressBar function, which is called by playFLV immediately after the movie starts playing.

To start playing the video automatically, playFLV is called on the first line of the script.

The rest of the code handles the four buttons. The Stop button handler calls the close method of the stream object before disconnecting the onEnterFrame event handler that updates the ProgressBar and hiding the bar.

```
_root.stop.onPress = function ()
{
  _root.stream.close ();
  _root.Video.onEnterFrame = null;
  _root.videoinfo.visible = false;
};
```

The Pause button takes advantage of the stream's pause method. Clicking once pauses the video; clicking again starts playback from the point at which the clip was paused.

```
_root.pause.onPress = function ()
{
  _root.stream.pause();
};
```

To jump two seconds forward through the video when a user clicks the Jump Fwd button, we use the stream's seek method and its time property:

```
_root.jump_fwd.onPress = function ()
{
  _root.stream.seek (_root.stream.time + 2);
};
```

The Rewind button restarts the clip from the beginning simply by calling the playFLV function again.

```
_root.rewind.onPress = function ()
{
  playFLV ("file://match_300K.flv");
};
```

32. Save your work and preview it.

Try clicking the various buttons. With a little investigation, you can take advantage of other NetStream features. You can provide more visual feedback about the frames per second, current time, and other information. You can even assign you own buttons or sliders to modify the streaming buffer size.

Random Movie Loader

Tossing a random element into the mix always produces an interesting effect, and video is no exception. With a little sprinkling of ActionScript we can randomly load additional clips.

This example picks up where the previous section left off, adding some extra feedback to show the user the current clip position in seconds, and loading one of three random external FLV files: a burning matchstick, a waterfall scene, and a lightning scene. Once the random movie has been loaded, we'll let the user select a movie from a ComboBox component that we'll add to the stage, as shown in Figure 6.9.

Figure 6.9. Add control buttons for external FLV playback.

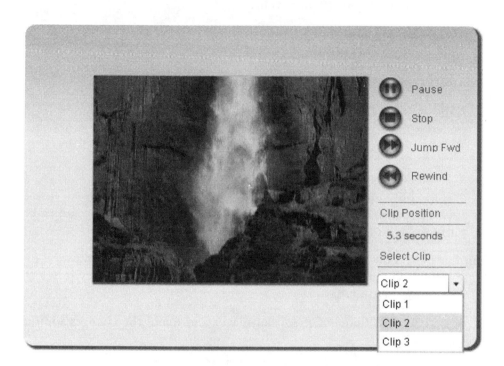

To edit this effect, locate `flv-random.fla` in the code archive.

33. Building on the previous example, add a new dynamic text field to the Buttons layer. Select the text box and change the instance name to `clipPosition`. Click Character... in the Property Inspector and select Basic Latin as the range of characters to include. Click OK.

34. Insert into the Button Labels layer a relevant heading for the dynamic text field (for inspiration, refer to Figure 6.9).

35. Drag an instance of the `ComboBox` component from the UI Components section of the Components Panel into the first frame of the Buttons layer. Place it below the dynamic text field you just added, naming it `selectClip`.

36. In the Property Inspector for the ComboBox component, edit the data para-meter by adding the following values:

```
file://match_300K.flv
file://waterfall.flv
file://lightning.flv
```

37. Edit the labels parameter by adding the following values:

```
Clip 1
Clip 2
Clip 3
```

38. Add a heading (e.g. Select Clip) just above the ComboBox, to indicate its purpose.

You now have a ComboBox that stores a list of the available clips and their loca-tions. Now, add the code that references these options when they're selected while the movie is running.

39. Select the first frame of the Actions layer and make the changes/additions shown in bold:

File: **flv-random.fla**   Actions : 1

```
function playFLV (clipname)
{
  _root.connection = new NetConnection ();
  _root.connection.connect (null);
  _root.stream = new NetStream (_root.connection);
  _root.Video.FLV_001.attachVideo (_root.stream);
  _root.stream.play (clipname);
  _root.Video.onEnterFrame = UpdateProgressBar;
}
function UpdateProgressBar ()
{
  if (_root.stream.bytesLoaded < _root.stream.bytesTotal)
  {
    _root.videoinfo.visible = true;
    _root.videoinfo.setProgress (_root.stream.bytesLoaded,
        _root.stream.bytesTotal);
  }
  else
  {
```

```
    _root.videoinfo.visible = false;
  }
  _root.clipPosition.text =
      roundNumber (_root.stream.time, 1) + " seconds";
}
function playRandomClip ()
{
  selectClip.selectedIndex = randomBetween (0,
      selectClip.length - 1);
  _root.selectListener.change ();
}
_root.stop.onPress = function ()
{
  _root.stream.close ();
  _root.Video.onEnterFrame = null;
  _root.videoinfo.visible = false;
};
_root.pause.onPress = function ()
{
  _root.stream.pause ();
};
_root.jump_fwd.onPress = function ()
{
  _root.stream.seek (_root.stream.time + 2);
};
_root.rewind.onPress = function ()
{
  playFLV (selectClip.selectedItem.data);
};
function roundNumber (toRound, numDecimals)
{
  return Math.round (toRound * Math.pow (10, numDecimals)) /
      Math.pow (10, numDecimals);
}
function randomBetween (a, b)
{
  return Math.min (a, b) + random (Math.abs (a - b) + 1);
}
var selectListener = new Object ();
selectListener.change = function ()
{
  _root.stream.close();
  playFLV (selectClip.selectedItem.data);
};
selectClip.addEventListener ("change", selectListener);
playRandomClip ();
```

We've made several modifications to the code. One plays a random video clip. Another displays within the user interface the number of seconds elapsed in the clip. A third lets the user select the movie clip to play from the drop-down list.

First, we added the following code to the `UpdateProgressBar` function:

```
_root.clipPosition.text = roundNumber (_root.stream.time, 1) +
    " seconds";
```

This code populates the dynamic text field we created earlier with the number of seconds that have elapsed in the current video clip. It uses our trusty `roundNumber` function, which is declared later in the code.

We then introduce a new function, `playRandomClip`, which chooses a random item in the `selectClip` drop-down list by setting its `selectedIndex` property to a random number between zero (the first item in the list) and the number of items it contains minus one (the last item in the list). For this, we use the `randomBetween` function, also declared later. Once a random selection has been made, the function calls the `change` method of the `Object` responsible for handling changes to the list selection.

Whenever the user makes a new selection from the drop-down list, we want to respond by playing the associated movie clip. The following code sets up an `Object` with a `change` method as an event listener that will do just that:

```
var selectListener = new Object ();
selectListener.change = function ()
{
  _root.stream.close();
  playFLV (selectClip.selectedItem.data);
};
selectClip.addEventListener ("change", selectListener);
```

When the user selects a clip from the list, the handler first stops the streaming of the current clip (since we don't want to keep downloading a movie we are no longer playing), then calls `playFLV`, passing it the data value associated with the currently selected item in the menu (the URL of the selected movie).

The last line of code simply calls the `playRandomClip` function, which selects a random item from the menu and then triggers the event handler to play the movie.

40. Save and preview the Flash document.

We now have a pretty nifty external FLV interface and random loader, which provides users the ability to select different clips from an easy-to-use drop-down menu. To expand the number of clips available, simply modify the `ComboBox` component to reflect the new additions. The ActionScript code needs no modification, since it gets everything it needs from that component.

Creating a Video Wall

In this effect, we'll take a single embedded video clip and create a video wall effect using scripted duplication and a smattering of randomness. The result, shown in Figure 6.10, is easy to modify and shows what can be achieved with a little inventiveness.

Figure 6.10. Create a video wall effect.

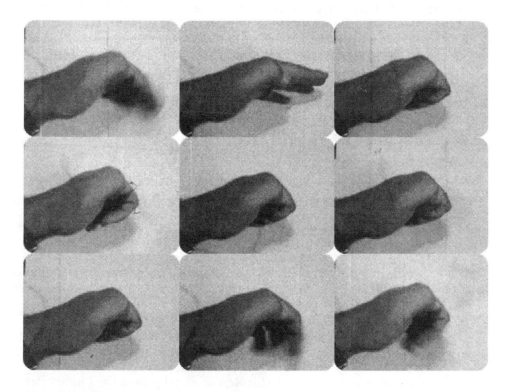

To edit this great effect, grab `videowall.fla` from the code archive.

The background mask used for this effect (`Video_Wall_Background.png`) can also be found in the code archive.

Setting the Scene

1. Start by creating a new Flash document that's 550 pixels wide and 400 pixels high. Set the frame rate to 24 fps.

2. Rename the default layer Video and create above it a new layer named Mask. Add another layer, named Actions, above the Mask layer.

3. Select File > Import > Import to Library... and locate `wave_away.flv` in the code archive.

4. Create a new movie clip symbol (Insert > New Symbol...) and name it `waving_hand`. Drag an instance of the `Wave_Away` video object from the Library Panel into the newly created movie clip. If you're prompted, allow Flash to add the necessary frames to play the whole video. Position the video at (0, 0) and resize it so that its dimensions are 160x120 pixels.

    ### Scale first to save file size

    For the purposes of this example, you can simply resize the video object after you've imported it into Flash. But since we're only displaying our video clips at a resolution of 160x120 pixels, it doesn't make sense to have users download a 320x240 pixel video clip!

    To deploy this effect on the Web, it would make sense to go back and re-import the original video file, scaling it down to 160x120 pixels as it's converted to FLV format. You can use the Advanced settings in the Video Import Wizard to do this.

5. Select the `waving_hand` movie clip symbol in the Library Panel, then right-click and select Linkage.... Select the Export for ActionScript checkbox and set the identifier to `waving_hand`. Click OK.

6. Create another new movie clip symbol (Insert > New Symbol...) and name it `videobox`. Leave this symbol empty and return to the main stage.

7. Drag an instance of the (empty) `videobox` movie clip from the Library Panel into the first frame of the Video layer and name the instance `videobox`. Position it at (10, 10).

This clip will house all of the dynamically created clips that will make up the video wall. Why create an empty movie clip like this rather than use the `createEmptyMovieClip` method? Well, creating it ahead of time makes it easier to apply a mask layer to it. We could apply the mask using ActionScript as well, but writing the necessary code is a tedious process compared to just setting it up on the stage.

8. Select File > Import > Import to Library... and locate `Video_Wall_Back-ground.png` in the code archive.

9. Drag an instance of the background image from the Library Panel into the first frame of the Mask layer, placing it at (10, 10).

10. Right-click the Mask layer and select Mask.

Adding the ActionScript

Now, we'll add the script that makes the effect happen.

11. Select the first frame of the Actions layer and add the following code:

File: **videowall.fla**   Actions : 1

```
function randomBetween (a, b)
{
  return Math.min (a, b) + random (Math.abs (a - b) + 1);
}
var rows = 3;
var columns = 3;
var clipwidth = 160;
var clipheight = 120;
var layer = 0;
for (i = 0; i < rows; i++)
{
  for (j = 0; j < columns; j++)
  {
    var mc = videobox.attachMovie ("waving_hand", "video" +
        i + j, layer++);
    mc._y = i * clipheight;
    mc._x = j * clipwidth;
    mc.gotoAndPlay (randomBetween (1, mc._totalframes));
  }
}
```

This code is pretty simple to follow. We set some basic parameters for the movie, including the number of columns and rows, the height and width of the movie clip in question, and a variable to keep track of the stacking order of the video clips.

We then use nested `for` loops to work through the columns and rows using the variables we set earlier.

```
for (i = 0; i < rows; i++)
{
  for (j = 0; j < columns; j++)
  {
```

Within the loops, we use the `attachMovie` method to attach instances of the `waving_hand` movie clip symbol to the (initially empty) `videobox` movie clip. We use the two loop variables, `i` and `j`, along with the width and height of the movie clip to set the placement of each video in the video wall.

```
    var mc = videobox.attachMovie ("waving_hand", "video" + i + j,
        layer++);
    mc._y = i * clipheight;
    mc._x = j * clipwidth;
```

Now, let's add a touch of randomness. We start the video clips playing from a random frame number, using the `_totalframes` property of the movie clip to obtain the total number of frames in the clip and the `randomBetween` function to pick one at random.

```
    mc.gotoAndPlay (randomBetween (1, mc._totalframes));
```

12. Save the document and preview your work.

It looks like there are nine different video clips on the stage, but the Flash movie is really playing just the one—with a smattering of randomness. The effect is easy to modify, so try experimenting with the settings, or use these examples as starting points for your own projects.

Modifications

We can add some extra video clips to make the video wall more interesting, as shown in Figure 6.11.

Figure 6.11. Create a video wall effect with multiple random video clips.

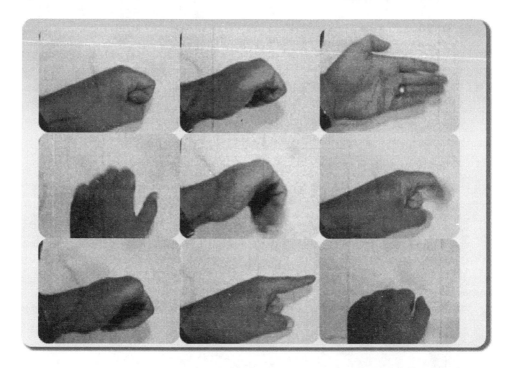

To edit this effect, locate `videowall-random.fla` in the code archive. The source video files you'll need are `wave_away.flv`, `point.flv`, `show.flv` and `spread.flv`.

13. Referencing the guidelines from the previous example, import the following clips from the code archive into the Library Panel:

   ❏ `point.flv`

   ❏ `show.flv`

   ❏ `spread.flv`

14. Create three new movie clips (Insert > New Symbol...) and name them as follows:

   ❏ `pointing_hand`

☐ showing_hand

☐ spreading_hand

15. Into each of these, embed the corresponding video clip, positioning it at (0, 0) and resizing it to 160x120 pixels.

16. Select the first new movie clip within the Library Panel, then right-click and select Linkage.... Select the Export for ActionScript checkbox and accept the default identifier value. Click OK. Repeat this process for the other movie clips.

17. Select the first frame of the Actions layer and make the changes shown in bold below to the code in the Actions Panel:

File: **videowall-random.fla**   Actions : 1

```
var clips = new Array ('pointing_hand', 'showing_hand',
    'spreading_hand', 'waving_hand');
MovieClip.prototype.ControlPlayback = function ()
{
  this.onRollOver = function ()
  {
    this.stop ();
  };
  this.onRollOut = function ()
  {
    this.play ();
  };
};
function randomBetween (a, b)
{
  return Math.min (a, b) + random (Math.abs (a - b) + 1);
}
var rows = 3;
var columns = 3;
var clipwidth = 160;
var clipheight = 120;
var layer = 0;
for (i = 0; i < rows; i++)
{
  for (j = 0; j < columns; j++)
  {
    var mc = videobox.attachMovie (clips[randomBetween (0,
        clips.length - 1)], "video" + i + j, layer++);
```

```
    mc._y = i * clipheight;
    mc._x = j * clipwidth;
    mc.gotoAndPlay (randomBetween (1, mc._totalframes));
    mc.ControlPlayback ();
  }
}
```

There are some rather nice touches within the code (if I do say so myself), so let's take a closer look.

We start by declaring an array that contains a list of the linkage IDs for the four movie clips. The code that creates the movie clips for the video wall now uses randomBetween to select a random clip from this array for each position in the video wall.

For each of the dynamically created movie clips, we also call the ControlPlayback method to stop playback when the cursor is hovered over the clip and start it again when the cursor moves away. It's not necessary to add this functionality—the example will work fine without it—but it does add a little more interest to the effect.

18. Save and preview your work.

The additions of the extra random video clips and user responsiveness make for an interesting effect. I'm sure you'll find a few cool ways to integrate this effect into future video projects of your own.

Creating a Video Scrubber Device

This is a great little effect that lets users control the playback of a video clip, while at the same time providing feedback on their progress through the clip.

As you can see in Figure 6.12, we'll use a custom slider component to control the playback of the clip. I've this simple component so that we don't need to spend five or six pages discussing how to create a slider control.

Figure 6.12. Use components to enhance video interaction.

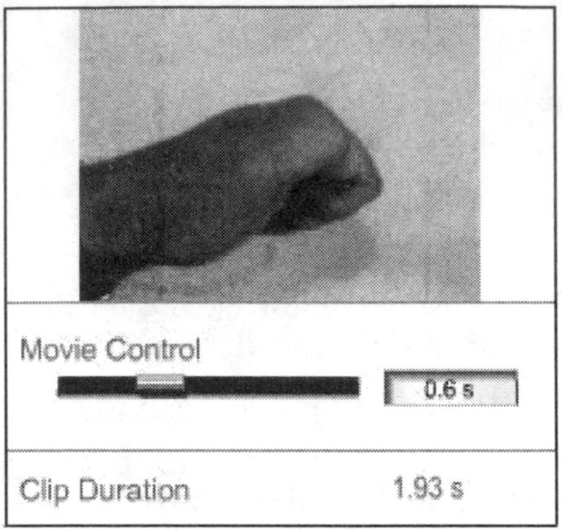

We'll use the `Scrubber` component and set up event handlers to produce the desired effect. There are several other slider components available on the Web—you might want to experiment with them when you have a spare moment.

One that sticks in my mind comes with Macromedia DevNet Volume III, as part of a set called Flash UI Components Set 5. This is a commercial extension package that comes with several other timesaving components.

For this example, the custom `Scrubber` component accompanying this book is more than enough.

The finished effect is saved as `video-scrubber.fla` in the code archive.

Setting the Scene

First, we need to locate the FLA that contains the component we'll use in this effect, then add the necessary video clip and supporting graphics to the stage:

1. Locate `scrubber.fla` in the code archive and open it with either Flash MX or Flash MX 2004. This file contains a ready-made slider component, which will be the starting point for this example. Note that the frame rate of this movie has been set to 15 fps.

2. Add four layers above the Components layer, naming them Text, Video, Frame, and Actions.

3. Select File > Import > Import to Library... and locate `wave_away.flv` in the code archive. Click OK.

4. Create a new movie clip symbol (Insert > New Symbol...) and name it `VideoHolder`.

5. Drag an instance of the `wave_away` video object from the Library Panel into the `VideoHolder` movie clip, positioning it at (0, 0). Resize the video object to 160x120 pixels, and name the instance `video`.

6. Return to the main stage and drag an instance of the `VideoHolder` movie clip from the Library Panel into the first frame of the Video layer, naming it `VideoHolder`.

7. Select the `Scrubber` component in the Components layer and name the instance `slider`. Position the component below the video clip.

8. Select the Text layer and create a dynamic text field aligned with the one in the `Scrubber` component. Name the instance `clipduration`. With the text area selected, click Character... in the Property Inspector, choose Basic Latin, and click OK.

9. Add some static text above the slider and next to the dynamic text field to tell users what these tools are. These labels should read `Movie Control` and `Clip Duration`, respectively.

10. Select the first frame of the Frame layer and drag out a rectangle with a single-point black stroke to enclose your video and controls, as shown in Figure 6.12.

That's all we need to do to set the scene; let's get on with the ActionScript!

Adding the ActionScript

The `Scrubber` component includes several built-in methods and properties for the retrieval of information relating to the scrubber bar's position and its minimum and maximum values. A method is also available for setting the text in the text area to the right of the slider. We'll see these in action when we start adding the ActionScript to control the playback of the imported video clip.

Let's take a look at the methods and properties that are available through the Scrubber component.

setVal

Parameters
setting

Returns
Nothing

Description
This sets the value of the scrubber, controlling the horizontal position of the scrubber bar.

Example
The following code sets the scrubber to display a value of 50:

```
myScrubber.setVal(50);
```

The exact position of the scrubber bar that results from this will depend on the minimum and maximum values assigned to the scrubber. If they were zero and 100, respectively, this would move the scrubber bar halfway along the track.

setMinValue

Parameters
min

Returns
Nothing

Description
This sets the minimum value of the scrubber. When the scrubber's value is equal to this value, the scrubber bar will be at the left edge of the track. The default minimum value is zero.

Example
The following code sets the scrubber's minimum value to 50:

```
myScrubber.setMinValue(50);
```

Following this call, the scrubber will not allow you to set values below 50. (Attempting to do so will simply set the scrubber value to 50.)

setMaxValue

Parameters
max

Returns
Nothing

Description
This sets the maximum value of the scrubber. When the scrubber's value is equal to this value, the scrubber bar will be at the right edge of the track. The default maximum value is 100.

Example
The following code sets the scrubber's maximum value to 150:

```
myScrubber.setMinValue(150);
```

Following this call, the scrubber will not allow you to set values above 150. (Attempting to do so will simply set the scrubber value to 150.)

pushData

Parameters
dataToPush

Returns
Nothing

Description
Sets the text to be displayed in the text area to the right of the slider.

Example
The following code will render the text "1.5 s" in the text box to the right of the slider:

```
myScrubber.pushData("1.5 s");
```

getMinValue

Parameters
None

Returns
This returns the minimum value that the scrubber will accept.

Description
This method lets you obtain the minimum value, as set by `setMinValue`.

Example
The following code stores the minimum value for the instance of the `Scrubber` component into a variable named `minVal`:

```
var minVal = myScrubber.getMinValue();
```

getMaxValue

Parameters
None

Returns
This returns the maximum value that the scrubber will accept.

Description
This method lets you obtain the maximum value, as set by `setMaxValue`.

Example
The following code stores the maximum value for the instance of the `Scrubber` component into a variable named `maxVal`:

```
var maxVal = myScrubber.getMaxValue();
```

getVal

Parameters
None

Returns
This returns the value currently assigned to the scrubber.

Description

The value returned by this function can come from two places, because the scrubber can have values assigned to it in two ways. The first, most obvious way is the setVal method. However, users can overwrite values assigned with that method by dragging the scrubber bar.

Example

The following code stores the current value of the scrubber bar in a variable named myVal:

```
var myVal = myScrubber.getVal();
```

Knowing the methods and properties for the Scrubber component, you should feel at ease adding ActionScript to control the movie clip.

11. Select the first frame of the Actions layer and add the following code to the Actions Panel:

File: **video-scrubber.fla**   Actions : 1

```
var scrubbing = false;
_global.frameRate = 15;
this.onLoad = function () {
  slider.setMinValue (0);
  slider.setMaxValue (VideoHolder._totalframes);
  slider.setVal (0);
  var duration = VideoHolder._totalframes / frameRate;
  clipduration.text = roundNumber (duration, 2) + " s";
}
function roundNumber (toRound, numDecimals)
{
  return Math.round (toRound * Math.pow (10, numDecimals)) /
      Math.pow (10, numDecimals);
}
this.onEnterFrame = function ()
{
  if (!this.scrubbing)
  {
    // Set slider from video
    slider.setVal (VideoHolder._currentframe);
  }
  else
  {
```

```
    // Set video from slider
     VideoHolder.gotoAndStop(Math.floor(slider.getVal()));
   }
   var position = (VideoHolder._currentframe - 1) / frameRate;
   slider.pushData (roundNumber (position, 2) + " s");
};
slider.onMouseDown = function ()
{
  _root.scrubbing = true;
  _root.VideoHolder.stop();
};
slider.onMouseUp = function ()
{
  _root.scrubbing = false;
  _root.VideoHolder.play();
};
```

Let's see how this all fits together.

First, we set a couple of variables for the movie:

```
var scrubbing = false;
_global.frameRate = 15;
```

The first variable, scrubbing, tracks whether the user has seized control of the movie by dragging the scrubber bar. When this is true, the movie will track the location specified by the scrubber bar. When it's false, the movie will play normally. We want to start with the movie playing normally, so this variable starts out false.

The second variable, frameRate, is declared globally, and is set to match the frame rate of the movie. Since Flash may not display the movie at the assigned frame rate on slower PCs, ActionScript does not provide a way to read the frame rate of the movie. But without the frame rate, we have no way of converting the number of frames in the video clip (to which we *do* have access) to a duration in seconds. We therefore use this variable as the basis for that calculation (approximate as it may be).

The remainder of the initial setup takes place in an onLoad event handler. We do this because we use methods of the Scrubber control, which are not available until the component has fully loaded (including execution of the ActionScript it contains).

```
this.onLoad = function () {
  slider.setMinValue (O);
  slider.setMaxValue (VideoHolder._totalframes);
  slider.setVal (O);
  var duration = VideoHolder._totalframes / frameRate;
  clipduration.text = roundNumber (duration, 2) + " s";
}
```

The code sets up the minimum, maximum, and initial values of the Scrubber control. The duration of the video clip is then calculated based on the number of frames of the VideoHolder movie clip, and is written to the clipduration dynamic text field we created earlier.

We then use the onEnterFrame event handler of the main movie to link the Scrubber control with the video clip.

```
this.onEnterFrame = function ()
{
  if (!this.scrubbing)
  {
    // Set slider from video
    slider.setVal (VideoHolder._currentframe);
  }
  else
  {
    // Set video from slider
    VideoHolder.gotoAndStop(Math.floor(slider.getVal()));
  }
  var position = (VideoHolder._currentframe - 1) / frameRate;
  slider.pushData (roundNumber (position, 2) + " s");
};
```

As I explained above, the scrubbing variable determines how the video clip and the Scrubber control work in relation to each other. If the user isn't dragging the Scrubber, we set the value of the Scrubber to the current frame of the movie clip, which is playing normally. If the user is dragging the Scrubber, we move the video clip to the frame specified by the Scrubber, using Math.floor to round the value down to an integer. In either case, we update the position displayed by the text box in the Scrubber using the pushData method.

onEnterFrame and stopped movie clips

Can you see why we haven't used the onEnterFrame event handler of the VideoHolder movie clip to perform these updates? The reason is that when the user takes control of the video clip by dragging the scrubber bar, the

VideoHolder movie clip is stopped (note the use of gotoAndStop in the above code). When that happens, the clip's onEnterFrame event handler is no longer called for each frame, so updates cease. If you *really* need to keep the main movie's onEnterFrame event handler free for some other purpose, you can enclose VideoHolder inside another movie clip.

Last comes the ActionScript that controls what happens when we detect that the cursor has grabbed the scrubber bar.

```
slider.onMouseDown = function ()
{
  _root.scrubbing = true;
  _root.VideoHolder.stop();
};
slider.onMouseUp = function ()
{
  _root.scrubbing = false;
  _root.VideoHolder.play();
};
```

When the mouse is clicked and held down on the Scrubber control, we set the scrubbing variable to true and stop the video clip so that its position can be controlled by the onEnterFrame event handler. When the mouse is released, we set scrubbing back to false and play the video clip from its current position.

12. Save and preview the document.

If you play with the Scrubber control, you can effectively scrub around the video clip. Release the Scrubber control, and the movie keeps playing from the position you scrubbed to.

Scrubbing or scratching?

Although we used this slider device for video, there's certainly no reason why you can't use it to shuffle through audio information. See if you can expand on some of the examples in Chapter 5 using the Scrubber component.

We could have achieved this result using a Scrubber control created from scratch, but we've saved a lot of time using a ready-made component.

Subtle Use of Video

This effect looks like full motion video, yet the exported SWF weighs only 20KB. Instead of imported video, it uses several frames of a video cropped and overlaid onto a single background image that's a full-size frame from the video clip. This clever trickery allows for animated effects that actually look like video, as in Figure 6.13, but at a fraction of the cost in terms of bandwidth and CPU usage.

Figure 6.13. Clever use of video can create subtle effects in Flash.

Why, you may ask, does the file contain an animation of a running faucet? Within the video clip that formed the basis for this effect there is a limited amount of movement—only the water coming out of the tap is actually moving. We can isolate the moving elements of the video clip at specific keyframes, as shown in Figure 6.14, and export these static elements as a series of images, producing a lightweight effect that has the same impact as a full-blown video.

Figure 6.14. Isolate moving elements from a video clip to produce lightweight animations.

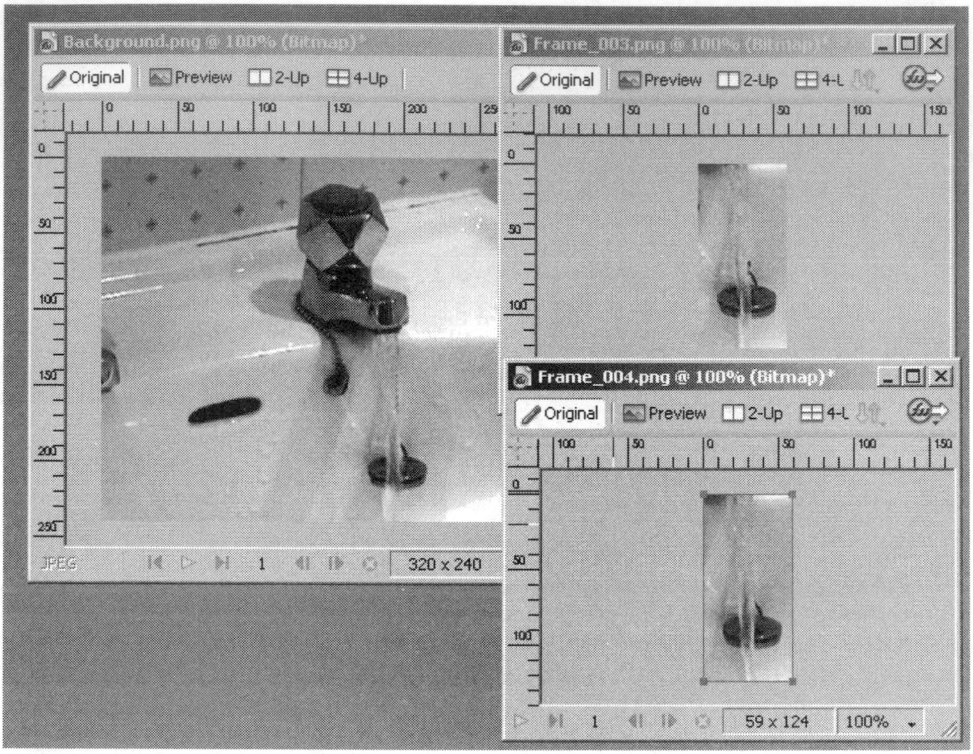

The same is true for any scene in which there is a single item that has a limited amount of movement. For example, a tree moving in the wind or a rotating wheel would be other prime candidates for this technique. This type of animation eliminates the need to import a video clip. A series of static images is simply added to a movie clip within Flash.

To edit this effect, locate `SubtleVideo.fla` in the code archive.

Export an SWF from the `SubtleVideo.fla` file, and view the resulting movie. It's quite astonishing that the file size is so small, yet the animation is so effective. If you were to import a clip of the running tap and export it as an SWF, the file size would be much larger.

Tip

Detail may lurk in the shadows

When extracting static imagery from a video clip, remember to take into account any shadows or light that may be cast or reflected. Capturing these extra artifacts will result in a more realistic effect.

Setting the Scene

1. Create a new Flash Document that's 600 pixels wide and 300 pixels high. Accept the default frame rate, and click OK.

2. Rename the default layer as Background and add a layer above it named Water_Animation.

3. Locate `SubtleSource.zip` in the code archive and extract it to a location of your choice.

These files form the basis for this effect, comprising a single, full-frame background layer and three sub-frames for the water animation.

4. Select File > Import > Import to Library.... Locate the extracted files and, with all the files selected, click Open.

5. Select the first frame of the Background layer and drag an instance of the `Background` graphic to the center of the stage.

6. Create a new movie clip (Insert > New Symbol...). Name the symbol `Water_Animation`.

7. With the first frame of the movie clip selected, add three keyframes (Insert > Timeline > Keyframe).

8. Select the first keyframe and drag an instance of `Frame_002` from the Library Panel into the keyframe. Alter the position of the graphic to (0, 0).

9. Repeat the previous step, inserting `Frame_003` and `Frame_004` into the second and third keyframes respectively.

If you use the timeline scrubber to view the three frames now, you'll see what we're hoping to achieve with the effect.

10. Navigate to the Water_Animation layer created in step 2 and drag an instance of the `Water_Animation` movie clip into the first frame.

11. Position the `Water_Animation` movie clip instance over the background so that it fits perfectly.

 Tip

See-through water!

Once you've selected the movie clip instance, temporarily reduce the clip's Alpha property with the Property Inspector to help you position the clip as accurately as possible over the background image.

12. Save the document and preview your work.

This effect looks so realistic, yet it uses only three cropped frames from the original video clip and a single full frame that serves as the background.

Although it's not a true video-based effect, this example shows how you can use video effectively in your Flash projects to bring them to life with a minimum of effort and hassle.

Conclusion

This chapter has been a rollercoaster ride through what can be accomplished using video in Flash. We've covered numerous topics, from large external streaming videos to smaller embedded clips and frame extraction methods. We've taken advantage of some of the handy components available for Flash MX 2004, but there are many more. See what you can accomplish with the techniques and effects we've explored in this chapter and experiment with different methods of presenting video. Soon, you'll be creating amazing presentations and video projects in Flash!

7

Flash Forms

Forms are among the most common ways for users to interact with Web applications. When you think of Web forms, the first thing that springs to mind is likely to be HTML forms. This type of forms has been around for many years; nearly all Internet users have filled out an online form at one time or another. HTML-based forms have progressed from the days when they displayed only plain text. Today, forms are much more complicated, with drop-down lists triggering changes in the way the form works, or the data that's displayed to visitors, or in some other way personalizing the user experience. Now, you can mimic, and even improve on that functionality using the new features available in Flash MX 2004 and, in particular, Flash MX 2004 Professional.

A good Web form is easy to use and applies validation techniques to ensure that only well-formed data is submitted. In this chapter, we'll explore a range of new components and methodologies for creating Web-based Flash forms that enhance the user experience and establish a foundation for interfacing with external data sources.

Creating Flash-based applications that mirror the functionality of standard HTML forms has become easier with the 2004 release. The "Screen" based development environment (available only in the Professoinal version) is analogous to Microsoft Visual Studio. It uses a series of screens and forms to build form- and screen-based applications, as shown in Figure 7.1. Special transition effects are also available for navigation between screens and forms.

Figure 7.1. The Flash Form Applications Screen Outline Pane is included in Flash MX 2004 Professional.

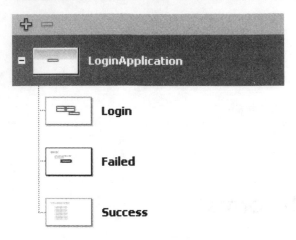

We'll focus on the user interface components that are available from the UI Components section of the Components Panel in Flash MX 2004 and Flash MX 2004 Professional. Let's take a quick look at what's available.

Table 7.1. User Interface Components Available Within Flash MX, Flash MX 2004, and Flash MX 2004 Professional

UI Component	Description	MX	MX 2004	MX 2004 Pro
Alert	Displays information that we define in response to an event	No	No	Yes
Button	Provides a simple button that can trigger an event	Yes	Yes	Yes
Checkbox	Offers a selection that can be toggled on or off	Yes	Yes	Yes
ComboBox	Allows single selection from a drop-down list	Yes	Yes	Yes
DataGrid	Creates data-rich displays within applications by retrieving information from external sources	No	No	Yes
DateChooser	Allows the user to select a date from a calendar display	No	No	Yes
DateField	Allows the user to select a date from a popup calendar, which then populates its in-built text box	No	No	Yes
Label	Similar to a text box, but allows for easy labeling of items on the stage	No	Yes	Yes
List	A scrollable multi-selection device that can include media items such as graphics or movie clips	Yes	Yes	Yes
NumericStepper	Displays a list of numbers that you can step through	No	Yes	Yes
RadioButton	Offers one of a number of mutually-exclusive options for selection	Yes	Yes	Yes
TextArea	A multiline text field component	No	Yes	Yes
TextInput	A highly configurable, single line text field component	No	Yes	Yes

UI Component	Description	MX	MX 2004	MX 2004 Pro
Scrollbar	A scrollbar that can be attached to a ScrollPane and other elements within Flash MX	Yes	No	No
ScrollPane	A configurable pane that can contain other elements and to which you can attach a scrollbar	Yes	Yes	Yes

Other components are available and I'd recommend that you look through them at your leisure. Those outlined in Table 7.1 are the ones you're most likely to employ.

Creating Usable Flash Forms

Before discussing any examples, we need to review the requirements for creating these applications, including the need to plan ahead to save development time.

Form Function

There are several questions to consider when planning forms, whether in HTML or Flash. First, "What is the function of the form?" Also, "What information do I need?" The form's objectives will dictate the controls that will be required in its development.

In creating a registration form, you might add several controls: input boxes for name and address, checkboxes and radio buttons for questions you may need to ask the user, drop-down menus for responses that involve multiple choices—the list goes on. A login form, on the other hand, usually requires no more than user name and password fields, and is therefore much simpler to design.

The information your form collects will determine how many user input controls it should contain, but there are some simple rules of thumb that can make the design process a little easier.

Gathering Information
Think first about the questions you need to ask. If you don't need the data, don't ask the questions; longer forms are less likely to be completed.

Layout and Question Grouping

Use color-coding to unite groups of questions into clearly separate sections. For example, a user contact information section might contain address, telephone, and email address fields. This will help the user to move swiftly through your form.

Provide Instructions

When necessary, provide instructions to help the user complete the form. Don't write an essay—keep it short, sharp, and comprehensible.

Required Information

Required form fields should be clearly marked. Consider which information will be required and which will be optional.

In a form has required fields, consider also the client- and server-side validation implications.

Data Validation

The task of validating data is important in any form. Validation might be used to ensure that required fields are not left empty.

There are two main types of validation, each of which has its pros and cons.

Client-side validation

Client-side validation involves functions executed on the client machine to check the validity of form content before it's sent to a server. Examples include checking that a submitted email address actually has all the requirements of a valid address (including the "@" and "." symbols), and that the required number of characters has been entered into a password field.

Server-side validation

Server-side validation is typically used for more complicated validation tasks, such as checking that a user exists within a database or confirming the validity of a credit card number.

For most applications, the best formula is a mixture of appropriate client- and server-side validation techniques. Server-side validation is outside the scope of this book, but we will cover some basic client-side validation using ActionScript.

Form Basics: A Simple Login Form

In this example, we'll create the login form shown in Figure 7.2 with Flash MX 2004 Professional. We'll include client-side validation, using the built-in `Alert` and `TextInput` components.

Figure 7.2. Use Flash MX Professional 2004 to create form-based applications.

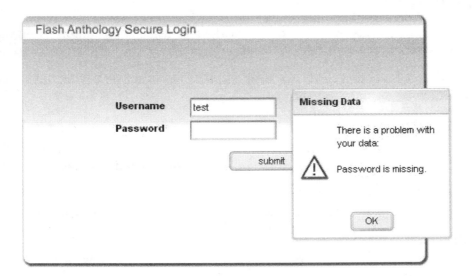

The methodology used in Flash MX 2004 Professional to build forms is quite different from that found in previous versions.

From a development perspective, it's extremely easy. You simply create a new form application, then create a series of screens and forms that can contain many items—it's almost like having multiple timelines at your disposal. Navigation around the screens is achieved by means of the Screen Outline Pane, which allows you to view or hide screens as you need them.

To edit this effect, locate `login.fla` in the code archive.

Setting the Scene

1. Create a new Flash Form Application. Select File > New... then select Flash Form Application. Set the stage size to 468x290 pixels.

2. Within the Screen Outline Pane, click on the application screen and, in the Property Inspector, rename the application LoginApplication. Rename form1 as Login.

Now, two screens are available: LoginApplication and Login.

3. Select the LoginApplication screen from the Screen Outline Pane, open the Timeline Pane if it isn't already visible, and rename the default layer as Background. Add another layer above this, naming it Actions.

As in previous examples, the Actions layer will hold all the ActionScript, while the Background layer holds a global background that will be available to all the other forms and screens within the application.

4. Select the Login screen from the Screen Outline Pane, and rename the default layer as Text. Add another layer above this, naming it Text Boxes.

The Text layer will hold the text labels, while the Text Boxes layer will hold the components on the Login screen.

Now it's time for some fun! We have a large number of components at our disposal, so let's add a few to the Login screen.

5. Select the Text Boxes layer of the Login screen and drag an instance of the TextInput component from the Components Panel into the first frame. Name the instance username.

6. Drag another instance of the TextInput component from the Components Panel into the same layer, this time naming it password.

7. Select the username instance and, from the Component Inspector, alter the settings to match those in Figure 7.3.

Figure 7.3. Edit the parameters for the username TextInput component through the Component Inspector.

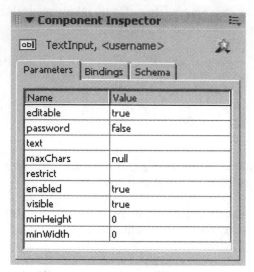

 Tip

Switch On the Component Inspector

If the Component Inspector Panel is not shown, select Window > Development Panels > Component Inspector to display it.

8. Select the **password** instance of the **TextInput** component and, from the Component Inspector, alter the settings to match those in Figure 7.4.

Figure 7.4. Edit the parameters for the password `TextInput` component via the Component Inspector.

Name	Value
editable	true
password	true
text	
maxChars	null
restrict	
enabled	true
visible	true
minHeight	0
minWidth	0

Component Inspector
TextInput, <password>
Parameters | Bindings | Schema

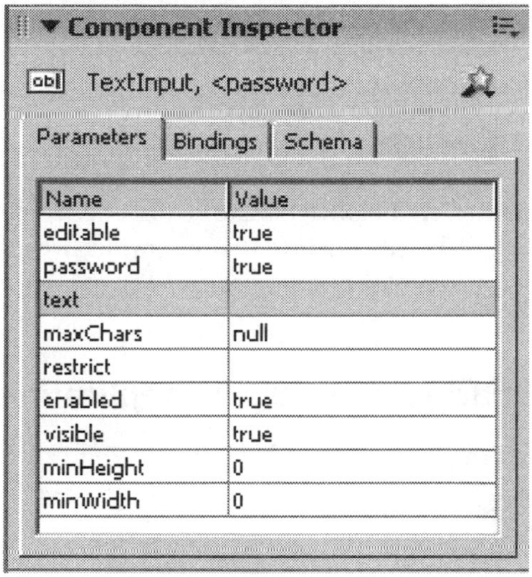

Hiding Passwords

As the password parameter of the **password** instance is set to **true**, characters will be masked as the user types into this field.

9. Select the Text layer in the Login screen and drag an instance of the **Label** component from the Components Panel, aligning it next to the **username** **TextInput** component. Select the **Label** component and edit its parameters from the Component Inspector as follows:

   Html true

   Text Username

10. Select the Text layer within the Login screen, drag another instance of the **Label** component from the Components Panel, and align it next to the **password TextInput** component. Select the **Label** component and edit its parameters from the Component Inspector as follows:

    Html true

Text   `<b>Password</b>`

11. Select the Text Boxes layer in the Login screen and drag an instance of the Button component into the first frame, naming it `submit`.

12. Navigate back to the LoginApplication screen through the Screen Outline Pane and add an appropriate background.

You can either create the background in Flash MX 2004, or use a vector-based application such as Fireworks MX 2004. For this example, I created the image shown in Figure 7.5 to act as a global background for the application.

Figure 7.5. Create a global background for the application.

We've created the screens to hold the application; now we need to indicate which are the required fields.

We'll add a component that's available only in the Professional version of Flash: the `Alert` component.Later, we'll add the ActionScript necessary to provide a visual prompt to users.

Flash MX 2004 Users Take Note!

While the `Alert` component is only available in Flash MX 2004 Professional, it is possible to mimic the effect in the standard version using a custom movie clip with dynamic text fields to which you can pass error messages. The clip's `_visible` property could be set to `true` or `false`, depending upon whether or not a section of the client-side validation fails.

13. Drag an instance of the `Alert` component onto the stage from the Components Panel, then delete it.

Why have we just deleted the `Alert` component? Well, we don't want it on the stage at all times; we need it only when we want to trigger it with ActionScript. Although we remove it from the stage, it remains in the library, and we can call it with ActionScript when we need it.

We can then create a custom icon that sits inside the Alert window (as shown in Figure 7.6). To do this, we'll create within the library a movie clip with a linkage identifier, and reference it with ActionScript later.

Figure 7.6. Create a custom icon for the `Alert` component.

14. Create a new movie clip symbol (Insert > New Symbol...). Name the symbol `problem` and draw an icon to symbolize an error (see Figure 7.6, for example). For the code archive example, I produced a standard alert icon using Fireworks MX 2004 and imported it into the `problem` clip.

15. Select the `problem` clip from the Library Panel, then right-click and select Linkage.... Select the Export for ActionScript checkbox and accept the default identifier option (`problem`). Click OK.

Now that we've created a linkage identifier for the custom icon, we can instantiate it via ActionScript at any time.

We've now laid all the groundwork for our application. We just need to add the ActionScript that will make it work.

Adding the ActionScript

All the components we've used so far have been off-the-shelf components. They're well-written and offer numerous methods for setting and retrieving values, and for setting custom styles.

Now it's time to add the ActionScript that will validate the entries within the TextInput components and display the alert if there's a problem.

16. Navigate back to the LoginApplication screen using the Screen Outline Pane and select the first frame of the Actions layer. Add the following code to the Actions Panel:

File: **login.fla**   LoginApplication : Actions : 1

```
import mx.controls.Alert;
Alert.okLabel = "OK";
_root.LoginApplication.Login.submit.onPress = function ()
{
  var dataError = new Array ();
  if (this._parent.username.text.length == 0)
  {
    dataError[dataError.length] = "Username";
  }
  if (this._parent.password.text.length == 0)
  {
    dataError[dataError.length] = "Password";
  }
  if (dataError.length > 0)
  {
    var error = "There is a problem with your data:\n\n" +
        dataError[0];
    for (i = 1; i < dataError.length; i++)
    {
      error += ", " + dataError[i];
    }
    if (dataError.length > 1)
    {
      error += " are missing.";
```

```
      }
    else
    {
      error += " is missing.";
    }
    Alert.show (error, "Missing Data", Alert.OK, this, null,
        "problem");
  }
};
```

Let's see how the code fits together.

First of all, we **import** the `mx.controls.Alert` class provided by the `Alert` component in the library:

```
import mx.controls.Alert;
```

Now, don't freak out: this isn't as scary as it looks. All the components provided with Flash MX 2004 can be accessed and used as classes by ActionScript code, rather than placed on the stage at design time. In this case, we want to use the `Alert` component, but its **fully-qualified class name**, `mx.controls.Alert`, is a little ungainly. To use its abbreviated class name, `Alert`, we must import it into our current script.

When we show an alert, we can have a number of buttons in the box (e.g., Yes, No, Cancel). In this example, the alert will have only a single button: OK. We can customize the label of this button by setting the `okLabel` property of the `Alert` class.

```
Alert.okLabel = "OK";
```

To handle the form validation, we create an `onPress` event handler for the `submit` button.

```
_root.LoginApplication.Login.submit.onPress = function ()
{
```

As you can see from this line, each of the screens in the Screen Outline Pane behaves like a movie clip when it comes to the ActionScript. The `submit` button resides within the `Login` screen, which is nested within the `LoginApplication` screen, which is in the `_root` of the movie.

The `onPress` event handler contains all the client-side validation code, which triggers the appearance of the alert if any of the requirements for a valid submission are not met.

There are a number of ways to write form validation code. We'll use an array to store a list of the fields that are in error, and then present the list to the user.

```
var dataError = new Array();
```

In this case, we simply want to check that both fields contain a value.

```
if (this._parent.username.text.length == 0)
{
  dataError[dataError.length] = "Username";
}
if (this._parent.password.text.length == 0)
{
  dataError[dataError.length] = "Password";
}
```

If either field doesn't contain a value (i.e. the `length` of its `text` property is zero), we add its name to the end of the `dataError` array.

After performing these checks, if the `dataError` array is not empty, we build an error message using the names of the fields stored in the array.

```
if (dataError.length > 0)
{
  var error = "There is a problem with your data:\n\n" +
    dataError[0];
  for (i = 1; i < dataError.length; i++)
  {
    error += ", " + dataError[i];
  }
  if (dataError.length > 1)
  {
    error += " are missing.";
  }
  else
  {
    error += " is missing.";
  }
}
```

This code begins by creating the start of the error message, including the first field that was in error. The `for` loop then adds any remaining fields, separating them with commas. Finally, one of two endings is used to complete the message, depending on how many fields were in error.

The error message is then displayed using an alert, which we accomplish with the `Alert` class's `show` method:

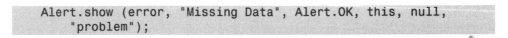

```
Alert.show (error, "Missing Data", Alert.OK, this, null,
    "problem");
```

The parameters for this method are as follows:

❑ the message

❑ the title

❑ the button(s) to be displayed

❑ the control or movie clip over which the alert should be centered

❑ the object that will be notified when the user clicks a button to close the alert (In this case, we provide none.)

❑ the linkage name of the icon to appear in the alert box

For greater detail on the parameters and their values, refer to the Using Components section of the Flash MX 2004 MX Professional help.

17. Save and preview your work.

Figure 7.7. Conditional alert information is provided through the Alert component and custom control script.

If users forget to enter a user name or password, or both, they're presented with a custom alert that informs them of the error, as shown in Figure 7.7.

If users fill in both fields and press the Submit button, no error is produced. The data passes the client-side validation and is sent to the server for confirmation that the user name and password are legitimate.

We'll investigate server-side validation later in this chapter. First, let's see what simple modifications we can make to enhance the look and feel of the form.

Modification: Adding a Focus Glow

We can modify the styles of the `TextInput` components and create a custom glow that sits behind the component that's in focus within the `TextInput` component, as shown in Figure 7.8.

To edit this effect, locate `login-styles.fla` in the code archive.

Figure 7.8. Simple style modifications can enhance the look and feel of the application.

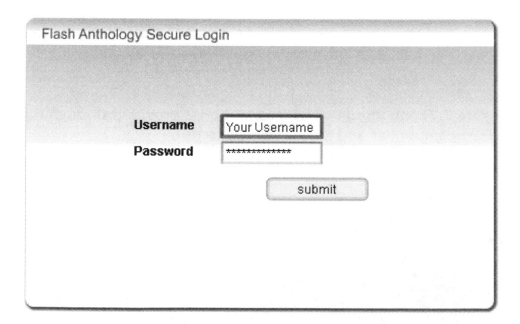

This example builds on the previous one.

18. Select the Login screen and create below the Text layer a new layer named Highlights.

19. Create a new movie clip symbol (Insert > New Symbol.... Name it highlight and click OK.

20. With the `highlight` symbol open for editing, select the rectangle tool and create a 100x22 pixel rectangle with a red fill color at (0, 0). Don't use a stroke.

21. Select the rectangle, click Modify > Shape > Soften Fill Edges... and enter the following settings:

Distance	4 px
Number of steps	4
Direction	Expand

22. Drag and select the rectangle and its softened edges, grouping them together (**Ctrl-G** on Windows, **Command-G** on Mac).

23. Drag an instance of the `highlight` movie clip from the Library Panel into the Highlights layer of the Login screen, positioning it directly beneath the username `TextInput` component. Name it `usernamehigh`.

24. Repeat the previous step so that a second instance sits beneath the password `TextInput` component. Name it `passwordhigh`.

Now that we've created the clips for the glow, we're ready to add the ActionScript that will switch them on or off dynamically, based on which of the `TextInput` areas has focus.

25. Add the following code to the Actions Panel below the last line of existing code:

File: **login-styles.fla**   LoginApplication : Actions : 1 (excerpt)
```
_root.LoginApplication.Login.passwordhigh._visible = false;
_root.LoginApplication.Login.usernamehigh._visible = false;
_root.LoginApplication.Login.username.onSetFocus = function ()
{
```

```
  this.setStyle ("highlightColor", "red");
  this.setStyle ("shadowColor", "red");
  this.setStyle ("shadowCapColor", "red");
  _root.LoginApplication.Login.usernamehigh._visible = true;
};
_root.LoginApplication.Login.username.onKillFocus = function ()
{
  this.setStyle ("highlightColor", "white");
  this.setStyle ("shadowColor", "white");
  this.setStyle ("shadowCapColor", "white");
  _root.LoginApplication.Login.usernamehigh._visible = false;
};
_root.LoginApplication.Login.password.onSetFocus = function ()
{
  this.setStyle ("highlightColor", "red");
  this.setStyle ("shadowColor", "red");
  this.setStyle ("shadowCapColor", "red");
  _root.LoginApplication.Login.passwordhigh._visible = true;
};
_root.LoginApplication.Login.password.onKillFocus = function ()
{
  this.setStyle ("highlightColor", "white");
  this.setStyle ("shadowColor", "white");
  this.setStyle ("shadowCapColor", "white");
  _root.LoginApplication.Login.passwordhigh._visible = false;
};
```

We begin by setting the highlights to be invisible, because the application starts with neither field in focus.

Next, we use onSetFocus and onKillFocus event handlers for each field to detect whether or not the TextInput component has focus. Whenever one of the fields gains focus, its onSetFocus event handler will be called; losing focus will trigger its onKillFocus event handler.

When the username TextInput component gains focus, we alter the style of the object to give it a red highlight by modifying the inner style of the component. We also switch on the visibility of the highlight movie clip.

```
this.setStyle ("highlightColor", "red");
this.setStyle ("shadowColor", "red");
this.setStyle ("shadowCapColor", "red");
_root.LoginApplication.Login.usernamehigh._visible = true;
```

When the component loses focus, we adjust the style to a white highlight and hide the highlight movie clip.

```
this.setStyle("highlightColor", "white");
this.setStyle("shadowColor", "white");
this.setStyle("shadowCapColor", "white");
_root.LoginApplication.Login.usernamehigh._visible = false;
```

26. Save and preview your work.

It's a simple modification, but one that provides that extra feedback to the user. Try playing with the various style values (documented in the Using Components section of Flash Help) to see what other effects you can create.

Handling Form Data

The next example, shown in Figure 7.9, expands on the first by submitting the form contents for server-side validation.

Figure 7.9. Use screens to develop a simple rich Internet application.

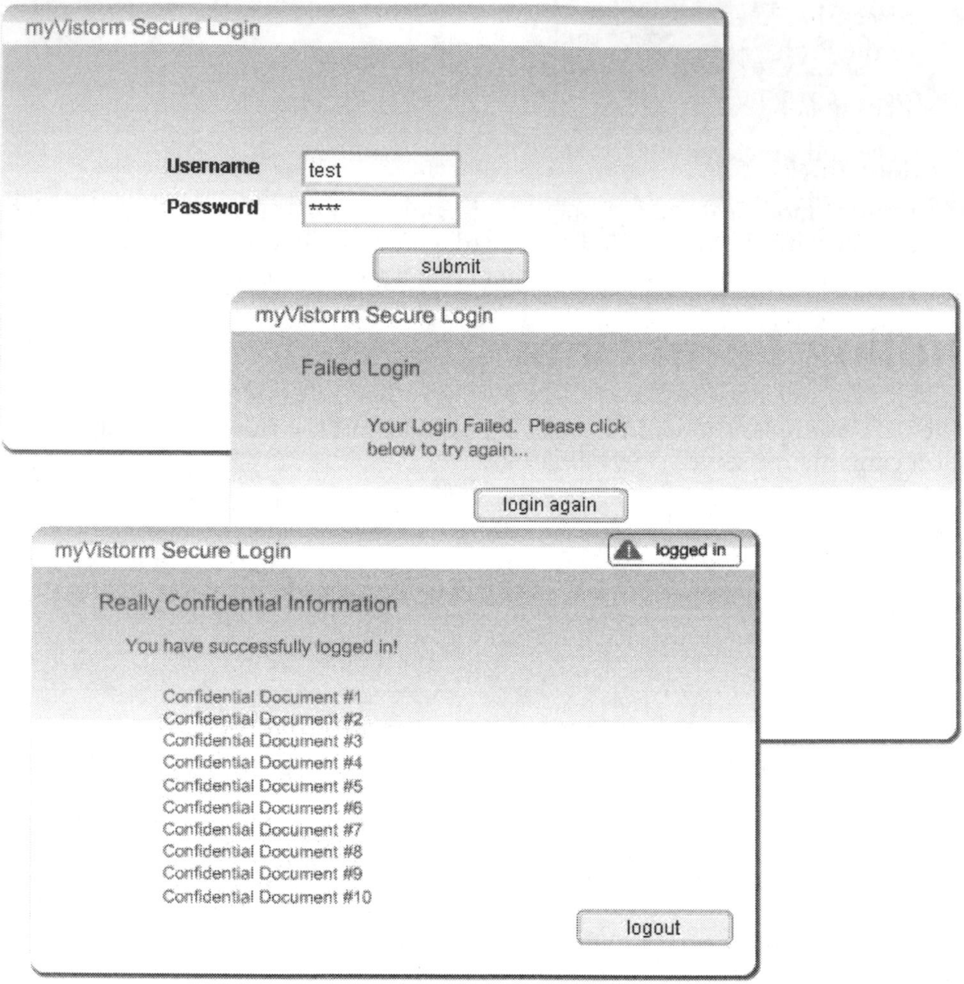

To modify this effect, locate login-handle.fla in the code archive.

Setting the Scene

Start with the finished file from the previous example, without the modifications to add "glowing" highlights (login.fla in the code archive).

1. In the Screen Outline Pane, add two more screens directly below the Login screen. Name these Failed and Success.

2. Select the Failed screen in the Screen Outline Pane. On the Parameters page of the Property Inspector, set the visible property for the screen to false.

3. Repeat step 2 with the Success screen, setting its visible property to false.

We'll use these screens after validation to redirect users to the appropriate location, depending on whether or not their login was successful. We've set them to be hidden at first and revealed later using ActionScript.

4. Right-click the Success screen in the Screen Outline Pane and choose Insert Nested Screen. Rename the new screen as SecureContent.

This nested screen will host the secure content that the application is designed to protect.

5. Select the Failed screen from the Screen Outline Pane and rename the default layer in the timeline as Text. Repeat this for the Success screen.

6. Select the Failed screen and add some content to indicate that the user has failed to log in. Drag an instance of the `Button` component from the UI Components section of the Components Panel into the first frame of the Text layer. Name it `login` and change the label to read `login again`.

Later, we'll reference this button from the root of the application, returning users to the login screen so they can try to log in again.

7. Select the Success screen and drag an instance of the `Button` component from the UI Components section of the Components Panel into the first frame of the Text layer. Name it `logout` and change the label to `logout`.

Now, we need to create a small graphic that will sit in the top-right corner of the main LoginApplication screen and tell users whether or not they're logged in.

8. Create a new movie clip symbol named `loggedin` and insert an appropriate graphic to indicate that users are logged in. The graphic used in Figure 7.10 can be found in the code archive—it's named `loggedin.png`.

Figure 7.10. Create a simple graphic to represent the login status of users.

9. Select the LoginApplication screen and create a new layer named LoggedIn. Drag an instance of the new movie clip into the first frame and name it `loggedin`. Position the graphic as shown in Figure 7.10.

You may be wondering, "Why not just place it in the top-right corner of the success screen?" The reason is simple: once the user is logged in, we want this graphic to be visible on all screens of the application. Rather than duplicate it for every screen, we can simply add it to the top-level screen and use ActionScript to show/hide it on cue. This gives us one less thing to do if we decide to add more screens to the application in future.

Now all we need is some super-secret content to protect with this elaborate system of screens and components.

10. Click File > New... and select Flash Document to create a new Flash movie. Adjust the stage size to match the main application: 468x290 pixels.

11. Add to the stage some content that represents the secure information.

12. Save and publish the movie as `secure.swf`. Place it in the same directory as the main application.

Alternatively, you can use the `secure.fla` file provided in the code archive.

It's time to add the ActionScript that will tie the application together.

Adding the ActionScript

We need to add ActionScript to allow the posting of data that we've validated on the client side. The data will be posted to a server-side application that will check whether the credentials provided (user name and password) are valid or not.

There is quite a lot of code, but don't feel overwhelmed. As always, we'll walk through it step by step so you understand exactly what's going on. Ready? Let's get started.

13. Returning to the main application file, select the first frame of the Actions layer within the LoginApplication screen. Replace the existing script in the Actions Panel with that shown below (new code is shown in bold).

File: **login-handle.fla**   LoginApplication : Actions : 1

```
import mx.controls.Alert;
Alert.okLabel = "OK";
_root.loggedIn = false;
checkLogin ();
_root.LoginApplication.Login.submit.onPress = function ()
{
  var dataError = new Array ();
  if (this._parent.username.text.length == 0)
  {
    dataError[dataError.length] = "Username";
  }
  if (this._parent.password.text.length == 0)
  {
    dataError[dataError.length] = "Password";
  }
  if (dataError.length > 0)
  {
    var error = "There is a problem with your data:\n\n" +
        dataError[0];
    for (i = 1; i < dataError.length; i++)
    {
      error += ", " + dataError[i];
    }
    if (dataError.length > 1)
    {
      error += " are missing.";
    }
    else
    {
      error += " is missing.";
    }
    Alert.show (error, "Missing Data", Alert.OK, this, null,
        "problem");
  }
  else
  {
```

```
      var loadInformation = new LoadVars ();
      loadInformation.username = this._parent.username.text;
      loadInformation.pass = this._parent.password.text;
      loadInformation.onLoad = validateuser;
      loadInformation.sendAndLoad ('login.php', loadInformation,
          "POST");
  }
};
function validateuser ()
{
  if (this.validate == "success")
  {
    _root.loggedIn = true;
    _root.LoginApplication.Success.SecureContent.contentPath =
        'secure.php';
    _root.LoginApplication.Login.visible = false;
    _root.LoginApplication.Success.visible = true;
  }
  else
  {
    _root.LoginApplication.Login.visible = false;
    _root.LoginApplication.Failed.visible = true;
  }
  checkLogin ();
}
_root.LoginApplication.Failed.login.onPress = function ()
{
  _root.LoginApplication.Login.visible = true;
  _root.LoginApplication.Failed.visible = false;
};
_root.LoginApplication.Success.logout.onPress = function ()
{
  var loadInformation = new LoadVars ();
  loadInformation.sendAndLoad ('logout.php', loadInformation,
      "POST");

  _root.loggedIn = false;
  _root.LoginApplication.Success.SecureContent.contentPath =
      null;
  checkLogin ();
  _root.LoginApplication.Login.visible = true;
  _root.LoginApplication.Success.visible = false;
};
function checkLogin ()
{
```

```
  _root.LoginApplication.loggedin._visible = _root.loggedIn;
}
```

Let's examine the code step by step.

We set a variable (`loggedIn`) that tracks whether or not the user is logged in and then calls `checkLogin`, a function that updates the visibility of the `loggedin` graphic based on that variable.

```
_root.loggedIn = false;
checkLogin();
```

Next, we extend the event handler for the submit button on the login form so that if validation is successful, the credentials provided by the user are sent to the server:

```
else
{
  var loadInformation = new LoadVars ();
  loadInformation.username = this._parent.username.text;
  loadInformation.pass = this._parent.password.text;
  loadInformation.onLoad = validateuser;
  loadInformation.sendAndLoad ('login.php', loadInformation,
      "POST");
}
```

ActionScript includes a class called `LoadVars`, which allows us to submit a request to a server-side script and receive a response, all without leaving the Flash movie. First we create an object of that class (`loadInformation`), then we add variables to it for the user name and password entered by the user. We give it an `onLoad` event handler to handle the response it will send back, and finally we send the request with the `sendAndLoad` method. In calling this method, we pass the relative or absolute URL we wish to load (`login.php`, in this example), the `LoadVars` object where we wish to store the server response, and the type of server request we wish to make (`POST` in this case).

Although we'll write a simple server-side login script (`login.php`) to complete this example, its details are largely beyond the scope of this book. In broad terms, the script receives the user name and password and checks them against a list or database of authorized users. If the credentials are valid, the script notes that the user is logged in and grants requests for protected resources. It then sends back this response:

```
validate=success
```

If, on the other hand, the credentials don't match any of the authorized users for the site, the script should send back this response:

```
validate=failed
```

Both of these responses create a variable named `validate` in the `loadInformation` object, which our `onLoad` event handler can then check to see if the login attempt was successful. That event handler is the `validateuser` function.

```
function validateuser ()
{
  _root.LoginApplication.Login.visible = false;
  if (this.validate == "success")
  {
    _root.loggedIn = true;
    _root.LoginApplication.Success.SecureContent.contentPath =
        'secure.php';
    _root.LoginApplication.Success.visible = true;
  }
  else
  {
    _root.LoginApplication.Failed.visible = true;
  }
  checkLogin ();
}
```

The first thing this function does is hide the login form by setting the Login screen's `visible` property to `false`. Whether the login attempt was successful or not, we want to show something new to the user at this stage, so it makes sense to start by tucking the form away for now.

Since `validateuser` is being called as an event handler for the `loadInformation` object, it can refer to that object as `this`. `this.validate`, then, contains the response from the server: `success` or `failed`. In the case of the former, it sets the `loggedIn` variable to `true` to indicate that the user is now logged in. It then sets the `contentPath` property of the SecureContent page, which you'll remember we left empty earlier when we set up all the screens.

Setting the `contentPath` property instructs Flash to load new content for that page from the URL specified. In this code, we've told it to request the `secure.php` file from the same location where it obtained the main movie. Once again, we'll set up a very simple script to allow us to test this application. For now, this script sends back the protected content only if the user is on record as being logged in.

Always ask the server!

You may be thinking "What, ask the server *again*? We already *know* the user is logged in!" We're in the middle of handling that, aren't we?"

Well sure, but the server doesn't know that. All the server knows is that you're asking for a piece of protected content. If we simply allowed the Flash movie to directly load the protected content once the user had logged in, there would be nothing preventing someone from just typing the URL of that protected content into their browser and downloading it without ever logging in.

To keep secure content secure, the server must confirm that the request is coming from a user who is logged in. That's why we don't place the protected content on the SecureContent page in our main application—the main application file is being sent to users who haven't logged in! A clever hacker would have a very good chance of breaking into the SWF file and gaining access to the protected content, since SWF files are designed to be small and efficient—not hacker-proof.

In short, the *server* must keep track of which users are logged in and decide whether or not to honour requests for secure content.

If all goes well, the server will respond to the request by sending the `secure.swf` file, which Flash will load into the SecureContent page. To make it visible, the function shows the Success screen (by setting its `visible` property to `true`), which contains SecureContent as a nested screen.

If, however, the server responds to the login attempt by sending back `validate=failed`, the function will show the Failed page instead.

Finally, we call the `checkLogin` function to switch on the graphic showing that the user is logged in, if appropriate.

OK, that takes care of getting the user logged in and displaying the protected content, but what about logging the user out when they're done? And what about letting them take another shot at logging in if they didn't get their credentials right the first time? The buttons that reside in the Success and Failed screens both send the user back to the Login screen for these respective reasons. The event handler for the `login` button on the Failed screen is quite straightforward, hiding the Failed page and showing the Login page.

```
_root.LoginApplication.Failed.login.onPress = function ()
{
  _root.LoginApplication.Login.visible = true;
```

```
  _root.LoginApplication.Failed.visible = false;
};
```

The `logout` button, on the other hand, has a bit more work to do.

```
_root.LoginApplication.Success.logout.onPress = function ()
{
  var loadInformation = new LoadVars ();
  loadInformation.sendAndLoad ('logout.php', loadInformation,
      "POST");

  _root.loggedIn = false;
  _root.LoginApplication.Success.SecureContent.contentPath = null;
  checkLogin ();
  _root.LoginApplication.Login.visible = true;
  _root.LoginApplication.Success.visible = false;
};
```

The first thing this event handler does is notify the server that the user is logging out. This ensures that the server won't grant any more requests for protected content until the user (or some other user) logs in again. We don't need to send any variables to the server to log out; we simply create a `LoadVars` object and instruct it to request `logout.php`, a server-side script that marks the current user as being logged out.

Having notified the server of what's happening, we set the `loggedIn` variable to `false` to reflect the user's logged-out status. For good measure, we also set the `contentPath` of the SecureContent page to `null`, unloading the secure content from the movie. Finally, we call `checkLogin` to hide the graphic that indicates the user is logged in.

With all the housekeeping done, we hide the Success screen and show the Login screen so other users can log in.

All that's left is to implement the `checkLogin` function we've called at various times in the code above:

```
function checkLogin ()
{
  _root.LoginApplication.loggedin._visible = _root.loggedIn;
}
```

As you can see, this simply shows or hides the `loggedin` graphic depending on the value of the `loggedIn` variable.

14. Save the document.

That takes care of the ActionScript, but there's still the server-side component to consider. As I've said, the details of a server-side authentication system are beyond the scope of this book, but for the sake of completeness, I'll offer some very basic script written in PHP that will allow you to test this example in action. Since the server-side script is completely independent of Flash, you can choose another server-side language, such as ColdFusion, Java, or ASP.NET, if you prefer.

There are three server-side scripts involved in this example. I included each of these in the code above:

login.php	Authenticates the user by checking the user name and password provided. Marks the user as logged in on the server.
secure.php	Sends secured Flash content if the user is marked as logged in on the server.
logout.php	Marks the user as logged out on the server.

Here's the PHP code for a very basic implementation of `login.php`:

File: **login.php**

```php
<?php
session_start();
if ($_REQUEST['username'] == 'test' &&
    $_REQUEST['pass'] == 'test')
{
  echo 'validate=success';
  $_SESSION['flashanttestlogin'] = TRUE;
}
else
{
  echo 'validate=failed';
  $_SESSION['flashanttestlogin'] = FALSE;
}
?>
```

note

Hard-Coded Credentials

I've hard-coded the correct user name and password (both 'test'), but normally you'd attempt to find the values submitted by the user in a database or other list of acceptable credentials.

Here's `secure.php`:

File: **secure.php**

```php
<?php
session_start();
if (isset($_SESSION['flashanttestlogin']) &&
    $_SESSION['flashanttestlogin'])
{
  header('content-type: application/x-shockwave-flash');
  header('content-length: ' . filesize('secure.swf'));
  @readfile('secure.swf');
}
?>
```

IMPORTANT

Protect the Secure File

This sample script reads and sends to the browser the contents of the file `secure.swf` in the current directory. In a practical application, you'll want to protect this file by configuring your server to deny access to it, or by placing it in a directory that is not publicly accessible. However you do it, make sure that Web browsers cannot simply request the file directly and thus bypass the security of the application.

Finally, here's `logout.php`:

```php
<?php
session_start();
unset($_SESSION['flashanttestlogin']);
?>
```

Not up on server-side scripting? Don't feel like going to such lengths just to test this example? That's okay. I've put these scripts on the book's Website so you can try the example without having to write your own scripts. Simply modify the ActionScript in the example to point to these URLs:

http://www.sitepoint.com/books/flashant1/examples/login.php
http://www.sitepoint.com/books/flashant1/examples/secure.php
http://www.sitepoint.com/books/flashant1/examples/logout.php

15. Save the document(s) and preview the movie in Flash.

When you enter 'test' as both your username and password, you should log in successfully and gain access to the protected information. Entering any other user name and password combination will send you to the Failed screen, where you can click the button to attempt to log in again.

Using this example as a basis, you can add screens to your members' area to create a scalable login solution with many pages!

Snazzy Forms: Creating a Simple Navigation System from Form Components

What is a snazzy form? Well, it's a form that's interesting, engaging, and fun to work with. There are so many things we can do with forms that it's mind-boggling. Basically, anything that involves a form object can be classified as a form, even if it doesn't post information anywhere. You'll no doubt understand this if you've ever worked with HTML jump menus—forms that send you off to another area of a Website when you make a selection from a drop-down list.

In this example, we'll use the `ComboBox` component to create a small navigation system that takes you to different screens of a Flash MX 2004 Professional application.

Figure 7.11. Use the `ComboBox` component to create a form-based navigation system.

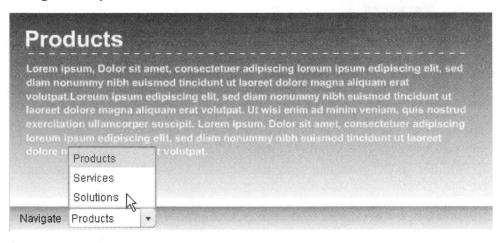

To edit this effect, locate `jump.fla` in the code archive.

Setting the Scene

1. Create a new Flash Form Application. Select File > New..., then select Flash Form Application. Resize the document to 550x250 pixels.

2. Within the Screen Outline Pane, click on the uppermost screen and, through the Property Inspector, rename it as SectionJumper. Rename form1 as Section1. Add two new screens named Section2 and Section3.

3. Select the SectionJumper screen from the Screen Outline Pane and add the layers shown in Figure 7.12.

Figure 7.12. Create the layers for the ScreenJumper application.

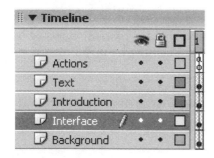

4. Select each screen from the Screen Outline Pane and rename Layer1 as Text. Add a further layer below, naming it Background.

5. Select the SectionJumper screen and add a 550x30 rectangle to the first frame of the Background layer. Position the rectangle to sit at the bottom of the screen. Set the fill color of the rectangle to a color of your choice (in this example, I've chosen a dark to light gray gradient). This will form the background for the ComboBox component.

6. Add a background to your application and position it at (0, 0). Copy and paste the background into the Background layer of each child screen, altering the color to reflect the content of the different areas (Figure 7.13).

Figure 7.13. Change the color of the background to reflect different areas.

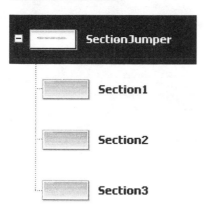

7. Select each of the child screens and insert relevant text to reflect the content of the different areas. In this example, I added the following headings: Products, Services, Solutions. I've also added "lorem ipsum" dummy text to fill the content areas.

8. Drag an instance of the `ComboBox` component from the UI Components of the Component Panel and place in the first frame of the Interface layer of the SectionJumper screen. Position it in the lower-left corner of the screen and add to the Text layer a text label to describe its purpose. See Figure 7.11 for inspiration.

9. Name the instance of the `ComboBox` component `jumper` and, from the Component Inspector, change the settings to those shown in Figure 7.14.

Figure 7.14. Modify the `ComboBox` component values for the navigation item.

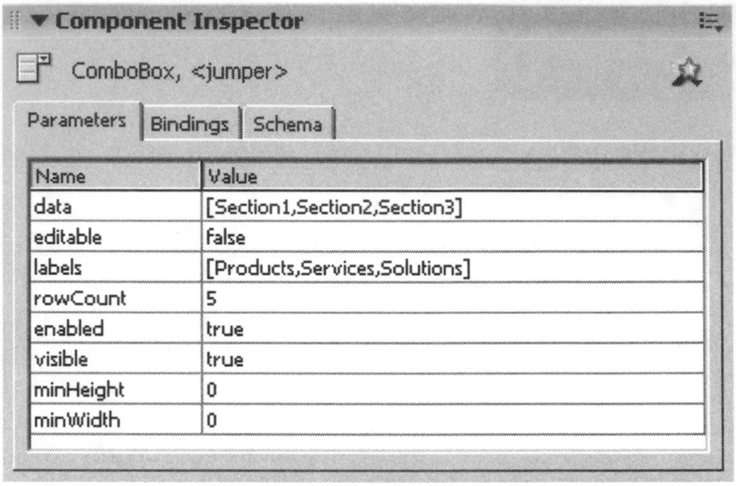

Now that we've added the labels for the `ComboBox` component, we can use an ActionScript handler to change our location.

Adding the ActionScript

The following code is quite compact. It allows navigation through the screens based on the item selected in the `ComboBox` component by setting up an event listener and adding it to the `ComboBox` component.

10. Select the first frame of the Actions layer in the SectionJumper screen and add the following code:

```
SectionJump (-1);
function SectionJump (whereTo)
{
  _root.SectionJumper.Section1.visible = (whereTo == 0);
  _root.SectionJumper.Section2.visible = (whereTo == 1);
  _root.SectionJumper.Section3.visible = (whereTo == 2);
}
var sectionjumper = new Object ();
sectionjumper.change = function (changeEvent)
```

File: **jump.fla**   SectionJumper : Actions : 1

```
{
  SectionJump (changeEvent.target.selectedIndex);
};
jumper.addEventListener ("change", sectionjumper);
```

The SectionJump function hides and shows screens. When passed a value of zero, it shows the first screen; passed a value of one, it shows the second screen, and so on. In this case, we pass it a value of -1, so none of our screens is visible initially (except the root screen, SectionJumper, of course).

Next we create a new Object called sectionjumper and assign to it a method called change. This method handles the events triggered whenever a selection is made from the drop-down menu. It receives a parameter (changeEvent) that contains information about the event, such as a reference to the ComboBox, from which we can obtain the index of the newly-selected list item (changeEvent.target.selectedIndex). This is passed to the SectionJump function to set the visibility of the screens accordingly.

11. Save the document and preview your work.

Using components that are both powerful and simple to use, along with a sprinkling of ActionScript and some thoughtful planning, we've created a simple navigation system. This solution is easily expanded through the addition of extra screens. Experiment to see how easy these modifications can be.

Intricate Forms and Form Validation

In this example, we'll create the Flash registration form shown in Figure 7.15. You've likely seen this type of form a thousand times on the Internet in HTML format.

Figure 7.15. Create rich Flash-based forms.

To edit the effect, locate `intricate.fla` in the code archive.

Setting the Scene

This example pulls together many of the new components offered in Flash MX 2004 Professional, including pop-ups, alerts, a whole host of user interface components, and some nifty form validation techniques. We'll integrate the login example we saw earlier to produce a well-rounded form.

There's a lot of ground to cover in this example, so we'd better get moving!

1. Open a new Flash document with the default size (550x400 pixels) and frame rate (12 fps) settings. Create the layer structure shown in Figure 7.15.

Figure 7.16. Create the layers for the Flash form application.

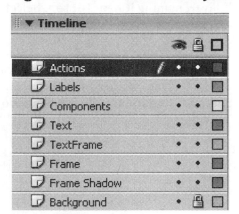

In the next few steps, we'll set the scene and create the background for the form application. If you prefer, you can jump straight to step 5 to start adding the components.

2. Within the Background layer, add an appropriate background image/pattern.

3. Place a 293x260 pixel container rectangle within the Frame layer to outline the form controls.

4. Copy and paste the rectangle object into the Frame Shadow layer, choose a dark fill color, and select Modify > Shape > Soften Fill Edges... with the default settings. Finally, select all the objects on the Frame Shadow layer and group them together (**Ctrl-G** on Windows, **Command-G** on Mac).

5. Add the graphics you need to the Frame layer. For instance, you might add the heading shown in Figure 7.16.

6. Drag three instances of the `TextInput` component from the Components Panel to the first frame of the Components layer. Stack them vertically on the stage, naming them `firstname`, `lastname`, and `email`.

7. Drag three instances of the `Label` component from the Components Panel to the first frame of the Labels layer. Use the Component Inspector to set the text parameter of each to display an appropriate label for the three form fields. `First Name`, `Surname`, and `Email` will do nicely.

8. Drag an instance of the `CheckBox` component from the Components Panel to the first frame of the Components layer, naming it `newsletter`. Select the component and change the label parameter within the Component Inspector to `Receive Newsletter?`.

9. Drag an instance of the `ComboBox` component from the Components Panel to the first frame of the Components layer, and name the instance `interestareas`. Change the data and labels parameters in the Component Inspector to contain the following entries:

    ❏ `Flash ActionScript`

    ❏ `Flash Game Design`

    ❏ `Flash Experimental`

    ❏ `Fireworks Extensibility`

10. Drag an instance of the `Label` component from the Components Panel into the first frame of the Labels layer. Align it next to the `ComboBox` component and set its text parameter to `Interest Areas`.

11. Drag an instance of the `TextArea` component from the Components Panel to the first frame of the Components layer, naming it `comments`.

12. Drag an instance of the `Label` component from the Components Panel into the first frame of the Labels layer. Align it next to the `TextArea` component and set its text parameter to `Comments`.

Next, we'll create a series of help buttons that we'll reference later with Action-Script. These buttons will throw alerts to tell the user what information they should enter. I realize this is more or less self-explanatory, but some of us need all the help we can get!

13. Create a new button symbol (Insert > New Symbol...) containing a new 15x15 pixel button icon that indicates "help" functionality. Name it `HelpPopup`. In Figure 7.16, I've used a simple square gray button displaying a question mark, but you can use the symbol of your choice.

14. Drag five instances of the `HelpPopup` button from the Library Panel to the first frame of the Components layer. Align them to the right of each text component on the stage, as shown in Figure 7.16. Name them, from the top

down: `firstname`, `lastname`, `email`, `interestareas`, and `comments` (the same instance names as the corresponding fields).

15. Select the five button instances you just created and create a movie clip symbol out of them (Modify > Convert to Symbol...). Name the symbol `HelpContainer` and name the instance `helper`. Grouping the buttons in this way makes it easier to move them around and switch them on or off through ActionScript.

16. Create a new button symbol (Insert > New Symbol...) called `ShowHelp` to indicate that the help system can be switched on or off. Place an instance named `showhelp` in the top right-hand corner of the interface, in the first frame of the Text layer.

We'll use this last button to switch the visibility of the `helper` movie clip on or off in accordance with the user's choice.

17. Create a new button symbol named `Submitter` and add appropriate content to indicate that it's a submit button. Drag an instance of the button into the first frame of the Text layer and name it `Submitter`.

We'll use the `Submitter` button to validate the contents of the form. It will confirm that the user has entered valid content into the first name, last name, and email address fields. If the data passes muster, users are sent to another screen and thanked for their submission.

Unlike the previous couple of examples, we're not dealing with a Flash MX 2004 Professional Form Application here, so we don't have the luxury of just creating a new screen for the "thank you" page. Instead, we'll create a new set of frames on the timeline for this purpose:

18. We need to add an extra frame to each of the Actions, Text, TextFrame, Frame, Frame Shadow, and Background layers. To do this, select frame 2 of each layer, then select Insert > Timeline > Keyframe. Once users enter their details successfully, they'll be passed to this frame, which will display a "thank you for registering" message.

19. Select the second frame of the Text layer and add a new multiline dynamic text field with an instance name of `thankyou`. For this object, select Uppercase, Lowercase, and Numerals from the Character Options window (click Character... in the Property Inspector), then click OK.

This dynamic text field will contain a personalized "thank you" message containing the first name of the newly registered user.

20. Alter the title text as needed, as shown in Figure 7.17.

Figure 7.17. Create a post-registration "thank you" screen.

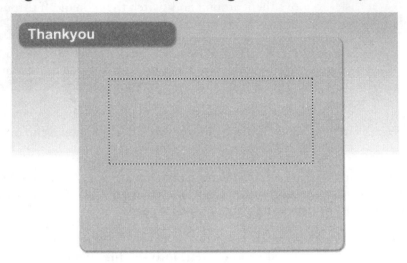

21. Drag instances of the `Window` and `Alert` components to the stage from the UI Components section of the Components Panel, then delete them.

It's okay, I haven't gone mad. We just don't want them to appear on the screen when the movie loads. Having created and deleted these instances, we've added the components to the library and can now reference them as required through ActionScript.

22. Create a new movie clip symbol (Insert > New Symbol...). Name it `problem` and add an icon to symbolize an error (see Figure 7.6 earlier in this chapter for an example icon).

23. Select the `problem` symbol from the Library Panel, then right-click and select Linkage.... Check the Export for ActionScript checkbox, accept the default identifier, and click OK.

24. Create a new movie clip symbol (Insert > New Symbol...). Name it `help` and add an icon that symbolizes helpful information.

25. Select the `help` movie clip from the Library Panel, then right-click and select Linkage.... Select the Export for ActionScript checkbox, accept the default identifier, and click OK.

Now that we've created linkage identifiers for our custom "problem" and "help" icons, we can include them later with ActionScript when we instantiate help and problem alerts in our movie.

26. Create a new 200x200 pixel movie clip symbol (Insert > New Symbol...) named `TeaserContent` and add some garish text, as shown in Figure 7.18.

Figure 7.18. Create the pop-up content for the `Window` component.

27. Right-click the new symbol in the Library Panel and select Linkage.... Select the Export for ActionScript checkbox, accept the default identifier and click OK.

This will provide the content that appears in the `Window` component we'll call as soon as the movie loads, presenting users with a pop-up that encourages them to register. That's right—Flash can have annoying pop-up windows, too!

Phew! It took a lot of work to set the scene for this application and make sure we have all the movie clips, buttons, and components in place before we slot in the ActionScript. Let's do that now.

Adding the ActionScript

I hope you're in the mood for ActionScript, because there's a lot of code in this example, including validation routines and functions that control every aspect of the application.

28. Select the first frame of the Actions layer and add the following code within the Actions Panel:

File: **intricate.fla**   Actions : 1

```
import mx.controls.Alert;
import mx.containers.Window;
import mx.managers.PopUpManager;
stop ();
showTeaser ();
function showTeaser ()
{
  var teaser = PopUpManager.createPopUp (_root, Window, true,
      {title:"Register Now!!", contentPath:"TeaserContent",
      closeButton:true});
  teaser.move (200, 50);
  teaser.setSize (200, 230);
  var teaserListener = new Object ();
  teaserListener.click = function (clickEvent)
  {
    clickEvent.target.deletePopUp ();
  };
  teaser.addEventListener ("click", teaserListener);
}
function showHelpWindow (whichWindow)
{
  var message;
  switch (whichWindow)
  {
  case "firstname" :
    message = "Your First Name";
    break;
  case "surname" :
    message = "Your Last Name";
    break;
```

```
  case "email" :
    message = "Your email address";
    break;
  case "interestareas" :
    message = "Your Interests";
    break;
  case "comments" :
    message = "Any Comments?";
    break;
  default :
    return;
  }
  Alert.show (message, "Help Information", Alert.OK, this,
      null, "help");
}
_root.helper.firstname.onPress = function ()
{
  showHelpWindow ("firstname");
};
_root.helper.lastname.onPress = function ()
{
  showHelpWindow ("surname");
};
_root.helper.email.onPress = function ()
{
  showHelpWindow ("email");
};
_root.helper.interestareas.onPress = function ()
{
  showHelpWindow ("interestareas");
};
_root.helper.comments.onPress = function ()
{
  showHelpWindow ("comments");
};
_root.showhelp.onPress = function ()
{
  _root.helper._visible = !_root.helper._visible;
};
_root.Submitter.onPress = function ()
{
  if (validateForm ())
  {
    saveDetails ();
  }
};
```

```
function validateForm ()
{
  var dataError = new Array ();
  if (_root.firstname.text.length == 0)
  {
    dataError[dataError.length] = "First name";
  }
  if (_root.lastname.text.length == 0)
  {
    dataError[dataError.length] = "Surname";
  }
  if (!ValidEmail (_root.email.text))
  {
    dataError[dataError.length] = "Email";
  }
  if (dataError.length > 0)
  {
    var error = "The following fields have missing or " +
        "invalid data:\n\n" + dataError[0];
    for (i = 1; i < dataError.length; i++)
    {
      error += ", " + dataError[i];
    }
    error += ".";
    Alert.show (error, "Missing Data", Alert.OK, this, null,
        "problem");
    return false;
  }
  return true;
}
function ValidEmail (str)
{
  var str = str.toLowerCase ();
  var parts = str.split ("@");
  if (parts.length != 2)
  {
    return false;
  }
  var domain = parts[1].split (".");
  var ext = domain.pop ();
  if (ext.length < 2)
  {
    return false;
  }
  if (domain[0].length < 2)
  {
```

```
      return false;
    }
    return true;
}
function saveDetails ()
{
    var so = SharedObject.getLocal ("userform");
    so.data["firstname"] = _root.firstname.text;
    so.flush ();
    gotoAndStop (2);
}
```

Some of this code will be familiar from an earlier example in this chapter, so we won't cover old ground again. However, this form is more comprehensive than the last, so let's have a closer look at what's happening.

First, we import the classes for the **Alert** component, the **Window** component, and the **PopupManager**. We need these classes to create alerts when information is detected as missing from the form, and to open the window that appears when the movie loads. We then stop the movie, to keep it at the first frame.

```
import mx.controls.Alert;
import mx.containers.Window;
import mx.managers.PopUpManager;
stop ();
```

Next, we display the pop-up advertisement by calling the **showTeaser** function. This creates a simple window with the title "Register Now!!" that displays an instance of the **TeaserContent** movie clip symbol we created earlier, as shown in Figure 7.19.

```
showTeaser ();
function showTeaser ()
{
  var teaser = PopUpManager.createPopUp (_root, Window, true,
      {title:"Register Now!!", contentPath:"TeaserContent",
      closeButton:true});
  teaser.move (200, 50);
  teaser.setSize (200, 230);
  var teaserListener = new Object ();
  teaserListener.click = function (clickEvent)
  {
    clickEvent.target.deletePopUp ();
  };
```

```
    teaser.addEventListener ("click", teaserListener);
}
```

You can create basic `Window` objects like this using the following code:

```
teaser = PopUpManager.createPopUp (_root, Window, true);
```

In this case, as we wanted our window to have a title, content, and a close button, we added a fourth parameter that specified these options. The remaining code in the `showTeaser` function centers the window on the user's screen, resets its size to accommodate the movie clip we created for the window content, and sets up an event handler to destroy the window when the user clicks the close button.

Figure 7.19. The `Window` component is triggered once the movie has loaded.

Next, we have the `showHelpWindow` function, which is triggered by the multiple Help buttons we created earlier. When one of these buttons is pressed, we pass to showHelpWindow the instance name of the associated field. The function uses this to choose the appropriate help message and display it in an alert.

```
function showHelpWindow (whichWindow)
{
  var message;
  switch (whichWindow)
  {
  case "firstname" :
    message = "Your First Name";
    break;
  case "surname" :
    message = "Your Last Name";
    break;
  case "email" :
    message = "Your email address";
    break;
  case "interestareas" :
    message = "Your Interests";
    break;
  case "comments" :
    message = "Any Comments?";
    break;
  default :
    return;
  }
  Alert.show (message, "Help Information", Alert.OK, this, null,
      "help");
}
```

The function is called from each of the buttons like so:

```
_root.helper.firstname.onPress = function ()
{
  showHelpWindow ("firstname");
};
```

Clicking the button at the top-right of the interface toggles the visibility of the help system. We can do this by toggling the visibility of the helper movie clip that contains the help buttons:

```
_root.showhelp.onPress = function ()
{
  _root.helper._visible = !_root.helper._visible;
};
```

When the submit button is pressed, the client-side validation routine, validateForm, is triggered. It checks the required fields—first name, last name, and email—for information. If it returns true, we save the details by calling saveDetails, which we'll look at in a moment.

```
_root.Submitter.onPress = function ()
{
  if (validateForm ())
  {
    saveDetails ();
  }
};
```

validateForm works as form validation did in our previous examples, with one twist: another function is called to validate the email address.

```
if (!ValidEmail (_root.email.text))
{
  dataError[dataError.length] = "Email";
}
```

I won't bother explaining the details of how ValidEmail works—it's standard JavaScript. It returns true if the email address it is given looks valid, false if not.

In this example, the saveDetails function merely saves the user name entered to a Local Shared Object:

```
function saveDetails ()
{
  var so = SharedObject.getLocal ("userform");
  so.data["firstname"] = _root.firstname.text;
  so.flush ();
  gotoAndStop (2);
}
```

A **Local Shared Object** in Flash is much like a cookie in the world of JavaScript or server-side scripting. The data stored in a Shared Object is saved on the user's computer in a small text file and later can be retrieved by this or another Flash movie from the same site. Storing the user name to a Shared Object could, for example, permit you to display personalized messages in other Flash movies. We'll look more closely at Local Shared Objects in Chapter 8.

In this case, we're using a Shared Object as convenient storage for the user name value, which we'll retrieve and use in the second frame of the timeline. Because we need the user name value later in the same movie, we call the flush method to ensure that the data is written immediately, rather than allowing Flash to defer writing it until the movie is unloaded.

In the real world, we might save all the form fields to the Shared Object, using them later to personalize the application interface. Alternatively, we might submit them to a server-side script for processing, as we did in the previous example.

Once the data is saved in the Shared Object, the user is sent to frame two. All that remains is to add the extra code that populates the dynamic text field on frame two of the timeline with the "thank you" message:

29. Select the second frame of the Actions Layer and enter the following code to the Actions Panel:

File: **intricate.fla**   Actions : 2

```
var so = SharedObject.getLocal ("userform");
_root.thankyou.text = "Thank you "+ so.data["firstname"] +
    " for registering";
```

30. Save and preview your work.

Experiment with the form—see what happens when you overlook fields or enter content in an incorrect format. When you pass the client-side validation successfully, you'll be presented with the "thank you" message.

This example can easily be modified to insert the user data into databases, send email, and grow into a pleasing dynamic application. For help with that, you'll have to wait until the next chapter.

Creating a Scripted Questionnaire

Our final example explores the use of a few more built-in components—in particular, the RadioButton component. In Flash MX 2004, the RadioButton component has been rewritten, putting more methods, properties, and events at our disposal.

In this example, we'll create the questionnaire shown in Figure 7.20. We'll populate the RadioButton component dynamically from an array to produce a series of questions with multiple answers.

As users answer the questions, the results will be pushed into an array and, once collated, displayed back to them. We won't process the output—I'll leave that to you.

Figure 7.20. Use ActionScript and simple Flash components to create a questionnaire.

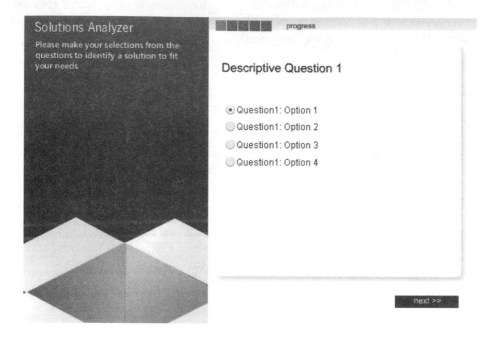

To edit this effect, locate `questions.fla` in the code archive.

Setting the Scene

We'll start by creating several layers to hold different parts of the interface and the application. If you want jump in and start adding the components and ActionScript without an interface, skip Steps 4 through 6.

1. Create a new Flash document that's 600 pixels wide and 400 pixels high. Accept the default frame rate and click OK.

2.   Add the layers illustrated in Figure 7.21. For each, move to frame 2 and select Insert > Timeline > Frame or hit **F5**.

Figure 7.21. Add the necessary layers to the questionnaire application.

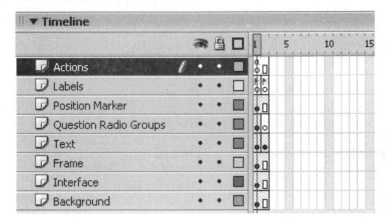

Window Dressing

The Background, Interface and Frame layers hold the static interface elements. They serve to separate the purely graphical parts of the application from the active components, text, and ActionScript.

3.   For the Labels, Question Radio Groups and Text layers, move to frame 2 and select Insert > Timeline > Keyframe. The content in these layers will differ between frames 1 and 2.

4.   Select the first frame of the Labels layer and name it `Introduction` through the Property Inspector. Select the second frame and name it `End`.

We'll use the End label to navigate to this frame when users have completed the questionnaire. It's neater than using frame numbers, as we did in the previous example.

We now need to add the graphics that provide purpose and visual appeal. Skip to step 1 if you want to get the example working and worry about how it looks later.

5. Select the first frame of the Background layer, add an appropriate background to the application, and lock the layer. As you can see in Figure 7.20, I added a simple rectangle with a gradient that graduates from a light gray to white.

6. Select the first frame of the Interface layer and add a 200x400 pixel rectangle to split the movie in two. In Figure 7.20, I gave it a green gradient fill. Move the rectangle to (0, 0) and lock the layer.

7. Add instructional text to tell visitors how to use the application, as shown in Figure 7.20.

8. Select the first frame of the Frame layer and add a 300x300 pixel rectangle colored to your liking (see Figure 7.20 for ideas). This rectangle will serve as a frame for the `RadioButton` components. Place it at (250, 40).

Now that we've designed the interface, we can add all the necessary components.

9. Select the first frame of the Text layer and add a dynamic text field that's approximately 300 pixels wide to the right of the stage. If you added the framing rectangle in step 4, position the text box to sit within the frame, near the top.

10. Select the dynamic text field and change the instance name to **header**. Choose a suitable font (Arial is usually good) and change the font size to 16-point. Click the Character... button in the Property Inspector and select UpperCase, Lowercase, and Numerals.

This text box will display the questions we'll supply dynamically using Action-Script. Now, we need to add to the second frame a static text box that will display when all the questions have been answered.

11. Select the second frame of the Text layer and add a static text box in the same position as the one we added in Step 1. Add this text to the text box: Thank You for Your Answers.

 Tip

Make an Exact Copy

It's easy to copy the dynamic text field from the first frame into the second. Select the box in the first frame, and click Edit > Copy. Move to the second frame, and click Edit > Paste in Place. Change the field type from Dynamic Text to Static Text in the Property Inspector, keeping precisely the same position.

12. In the second frame of the Text layer, add another static text box below the one you just created. Include text to indicate to the user that the question-naire is complete, as shown in Figure 7.22.

Figure 7.22. Add to the second frame the text you want to display on the conclusion screen.

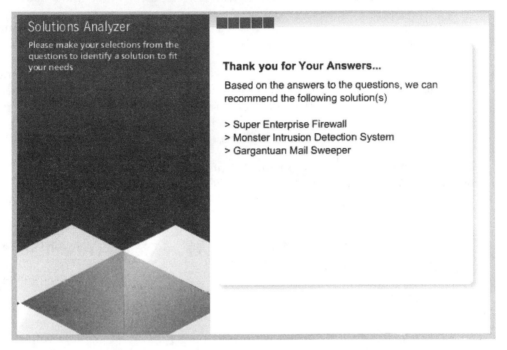

No Actual Processing Here

In Figure 7.22, the static text suggests that the application has processed the user's answers and suggested a solution. This isn't the case for this simplified example. With a little extra code, however, you could easily extend the application to parse the answers and display appropriate suggestions.

Now, you can add the interactive elements, including the button that allows users to move to the next question and a position marking device to indicate users' progress through the application:

13. Create a new movie clip symbol (Insert > New Symbol...) named `NextQuestion` that contains a button users will click to go to the next question. As you can see in Figure 7.20, I used a simple red rectangle with the text "next>>".

14. Drag an instance of the `NextQuestion` movie clip from the Library Panel into the first frame of the Question Radio Groups layer, and name it `question`.

15. Create a new movie clip symbol (Insert > New Symbol...) named `markerbutton` containing a 14x14 pixel rectangle with no stroke and a solid fill color (I chose `#339900`).

16. Drag five instances of `markerbutton` from the Library Panel into the first frame of the Position Marker layer. Arrange the clips in a row at the top of the stage, leaving a single-pixel space between them. Name them, from left to right: `marker1`, `marker2`, `marker3`, `marker4`, and `marker5`.

Using ActionScript, we'll highlight one of these markers at a time. The movie clips `marker1` through `marker4` correspond to the four questions in the questionnaire, as shown in Figure 7.23. `marker5` will be highlighted when the questionnaire is complete.

Figure 7.23. Add the `Position Marker` movie clips to indicate the position of questions.

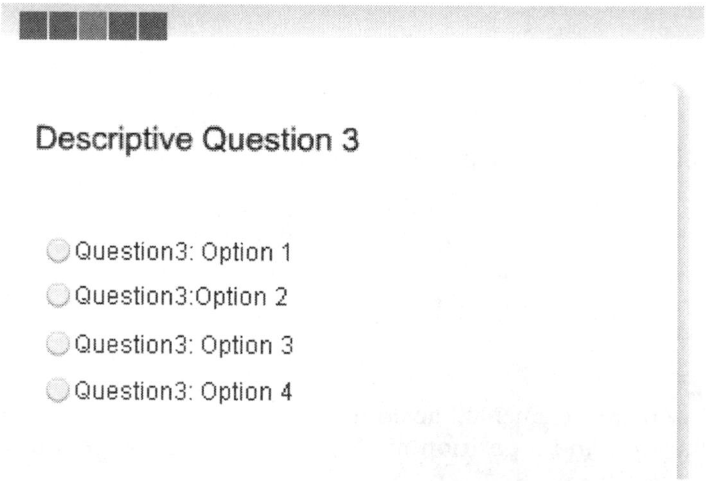

You can now add the `RadioButton` components to the stage.

17. Drag four instances of the `RadioButton` component from the UI Components section of the Components Panel into the first frame of the Question Radio Groups layer. Position them so they're left-aligned, as shown in Figure 7.23. Make sure they're wide enough to hold a variety of answers (I set them to a width of 200 pixels).

18. From the top down, name the instances `option1`, `option2`, `option3`, and `option4`.

    You don't need to insert any parameters with the Property or Component Inspector at the moment—these will be added programmatically through ActionScript later.

That's it! We've included all the necessary interface elements and components. Now, we'll need to add the ActionScript to bring the effect to life.

Adding the ActionScript

Because so much of this application is dynamic, a number of functions are required to make it work.

19. Select the first frame of the Actions layer and add the following code to the Actions Panel:

File: **questions.fla**   Actions : 1

```
var step = 1;
var questions = [
  "Descriptive Question 1", "Descriptive Question 2",
  "Descriptive Question 3", "Descriptive Question 4"];
var choices = [
  [
    "Question1: Option 1", "Question1: Option 2",
    "Question1: Option 3", "Question1: Option 4"],
  [
    "Question2: Option 1", "Question2: Option 2",
    "Question2: Option 3", "Question2: Option 4"],
  [
    "Question3: Option 1", "Question3:Option 2",
    "Question3: Option 3", "Question3: Option 4"],
  [
    "Question4: Option 1", "Question4: Option 2",
    "Question4: Option 3", "Question4: Option 4"]];
var answers = new Array ();
question.onPress = function ()
```

```
{
  if (step <= questions.length && saveSelection (step))
  {
    step++;
  }
  if (step > questions.length)
  {
    trace (answers);
    hideControls ();
    gotoAndStop ("end");
  }
  else
  {
    populateRadios (step);
  }
  highlightMarker (step);
};
function saveSelection (step)
{
  if (_root["Question" + step].selectedData == undefined)
  {
    return false;
  }
  else
  {
    answers.push (_root["Question" + step].selectedData);
    return true;
  }
}
function populateRadios (step)
{
  _root.header.text = questions[step - 1];
  option1.groupName = option2.groupName = option3.groupName =
    option4.groupName = "Question" + step;
  option1.label = option1.data = choices[step - 1][0];
  option2.label = option2.data = choices[step - 1][1];
  option3.label = option3.data = choices[step - 1][2];
  option4.label = option4.data = choices[step - 1][3];
  option1.selected = false;
  option2.selected = false;
  option3.selected = false;
  option4.selected = false;
}
function highlightMarker (step)
{
  var highlightColor = new Color ("marker" + step);
```

```
highlightColor.setRGB (0x33CC00);
if (step > 1)
{
  var normalColor = new Color ("marker" + (step - 1));
  normalColor.setRGB (0x339900);
}
}
function hideControls ()
{
  question._visible = false;
  option1._visible = false;
  option2._visible = false;
  option3._visible = false;
  option4._visible = false;
}
populateRadios (step);
highlightMarker (step);
stop ();
```

We start by initializing a global counter variable, step, to keep track of which question the user is currently answering. We also set up arrays for the list of questions, the available answers, and the actual answers the user chooses.

```
var step = 1;
var questions = [
  "Descriptive Question 1", "Descriptive Question 2",
  "Descriptive Question 3", "Descriptive Question 4"];
var choices = [
  [
    "Question1: Option 1", "Question1: Option 2",
    "Question1: Option 3", "Question1: Option 4"],
  [
    "Question2: Option 1", "Question2: Option 2",
    "Question2: Option 3", "Question2: Option 4"],
  [
    "Question3: Option 1", "Question3:Option 2",
    "Question3: Option 3", "Question3: Option 4"],
  [
    "Question4: Option 1", "Question4: Option 2",
    "Question4: Option 3", "Question4: Option 4"]];
var answers = new Array ();
```

A comma-separated list of values is a shortcut that creates an array containing those values. With this in mind, you can see that the choices variable actually contains an **array of arrays**, each containing the answers available for a particular question.

Looking at the bottom of the script, you'll see that three functions are called when the movie starts:

```
populateRadios (step);
highlightMarker (step);
stop ();
```

Let's look at each of these. `populateRadios` appears daunting, but this function is actually fairly simple:

```
function populateRadios (step)
{
  _root.header.text = questions[step - 1];
  option1.groupName = option2.groupName = option3.groupName =
    option4.groupName = "Question" + step;
  option1.label = option1.data = choices[step - 1][0];
  option2.label = option2.data = choices[step - 1][1];
  option3.label = option3.data = choices[step - 1][2];
  option4.label = option4.data = choices[step - 1][3];
  option1.selected = false;
  option2.selected = false;
  option3.selected = false;
  option4.selected = false;
}
```

This function sets up the interface so users can answer a particular question, the number of which (1 to 4) is passed as a parameter. The first thing it does is set the text of the `header` field to the question taken from the `questions` array.

It then sets all four radio buttons (`option1` to `option 4`) to have the same `groupName`: `Question`*n*, where *n* is the question number. This ensures that users can select only one of the four options and provides a known name that we can use to fetch the selected value later.

The function then sets the `label` and `data` properties of each radio button to a choice for the current question taken from the `choices` array.

Finally, it ensures that all four of the radio buttons are deselected, forcing users to make a choice.

The next function called at startup is `highlightMarker`.

```
function highlightMarker (step)
{
  var highlightColor = new Color ("marker" + step);
  highlightColor.setRGB (0x33CC00);
  if (step > 1)
  {
    var normalColor = new Color ("marker" + (step - 1));
    normalColor.setRGB (0x339900);
  }
}
```

This function updates the markerbutton instances at the top of the stage to reflect the user's progress through the questionnaire. When called, it takes a parameter that indicates the current step (1 to 4 for the questions, or 5 for the final screen). It creates a Color object for the markerbutton that corresponds to the current step, and sets its color to a lighter shade (#33CC00). As users are required to proceed forward through the steps, the application simply restores the previous step's markerbutton to ensure that one step at a time is highlighted.

The third and final function called at startup, stop, is a built-in Flash function. As you can probably guess, this function stops the movie from playing, preventing it from proceeding on its own to the second frame.

We've covered what happens as soon as the movie is loaded; now let's see what occurs when the next >> button is pressed. This is handled with the onPress event handler.

```
question.onPress = function ()
{
  if (step <= questions.length && saveSelection (step))
  {
    step++;
  }
  if (step > questions.length)
  {
    trace (answers);
    hideControls ();
    gotoAndStop ("end");
  }
  else
  {
    populateRadios (step);
  }
  highlightMarker (step);
};
```

The first `if` statement checks to see if the users are currently viewing a question and, if so, attempts to save the selected answers by calling `saveSelection`. It returns true if an answer was selected and saved, and false if no answer was selected. In the former case, the `step` variable is incremented to reflect the fact that users are being moved to the next question.

The function then checks whether or not users have answered all the questions, which is indicated by the `step` variable being larger than the number of questions in the `questions` array. When that occurs, we print out the `answers` array with ActionScript's `trace` function, call `hideControls` (which we'll discuss in a moment) to hide the controls that aren't needed once the questionnaire is complete, and advance the movie to the second frame (labeled end) with `gotoAndStop`.

If more questions remain, we simply call `populateRadios` to update the question text and radio buttons for the new question. In both cases, we finish up by calling `highlightMarker` to update the `markerbuttons`.

As I mentioned, `saveSelection`'s job is to store answers to the current question in the `answers` array.

```
function saveSelection (step)
{
  if (_root["Question" + step].selectedData == undefined)
  {
    return false;
  }
  else
  {
    answers.push (_root["Question" + step].selectedData);
    return true;
  }
}
```

As you'll recall, the`populateRadios` function assigned a group name of `Questionn` to the radio buttons, where *n* is the number of the question currently being answered. `saveSelection` can now retrieve the value selected from the radio buttons as `_root["Question" + step].selectedData`. If users haven't made a selection, this will be `undefined` and will return `false`. Otherwise, the value is added to the end of the `answers` array, using the `push` method supported by ActionScript arrays, before returning `true`.

All that's left is the `hidecontrols` function, which hides the form controls once users have completed the questionnaire.

```
function hidecontrols ()
{
  question._visible = false;
  option1._visible = false;
  option2._visible = false;
  option3._visible = false;
  option4._visible = false;
}
```

20. Save the document and preview your work.

Notice that users click the next>> button without having selected an option, nothing happens. The application waits for an option to be selected. Selected should pop up in the output window, looking something like this:

```
Question1: Option 2,Question2: Option 2,Question3: Option 3,
Question4: Option 3
```

The next chapter will inspire you with ideas for using the data you've collected here.

Conclusion

I'll bet you didn't think you could create such powerful applications in Flash. To be honest, this latest release astonished me; it's now incredibly easy to create forms that are much richer than standard HTML applications. This allows developers to focus on making forms look better, rather than waste time laboring over huge chunks of code that carry out mundane routines.

Form creation is a breeze in the 2004 release, so take time to explore the whole set of components, technologies, and methods at your disposal. It's quite an arsenal—see what you can achieve!

8

External Data

Chapter 7 introduced the basics of working with external data sources for the purposes of server-side validation. To make your applications truly rich, Macromedia has made it relatively easy to populate sections of Flash applications with dynamic data from external sources. For example, you might use `ComboBox`es populated with data from databases or XML, or build dynamic applications for registration and login purposes, as we did in Chapter 7.

In this chapter, we'll explore a variety of methods for including and referencing external data. We'll see how this methodology can be applied, and gain experience with local connection objects, Local Shared Objects, the `LoadVars` class, and the `XML` class.

Setting Variables Outside of Flash: A Breadcrumb Header

In the last chapter, we used a `LoadVars` object for server-side validation. In this example, we'll see another way to introduce dynamic values: by setting them in the `object` tag that loads a movie.

While supplying values in the HTML code that loads a movie is potentially useful, it's even better to supply them in a server-side script that dynamically generates the HTML. This opens up all sorts of possibilities, like pulling dynamic values out of a database and feeding them to a movie for display.

Before we get carried away (after all, this isn't a book on server-side scripting), let's review a simple example of these elements in action. As shown in Figure 8.1, we'll create a simple server-side script in PHP (use another language, if you like) that controls the background color and text of a page header. This header indicates a user's current location within the site, commonly known as breadcrumb navigation.

Figure 8.1. Set variables outside Flash.

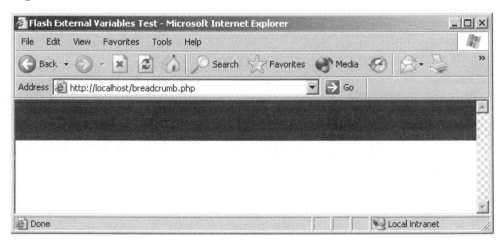

To modify the finished effect, simply grab `breadcrumb.fla` and `breadcrumb.php` from the code archive.

Setting the Scene

Let's start by creating the layout. We'll create a few nested items within movie clips so we can control them later using ActionScript.

1. Create a new Flash document with a width of 550 pixels and a height of 50 pixels.

2. Rename the default layer as Background and add two further layers above it, named Text and Actions.

3. Select the first frame of the Text layer, add a static text field, and type in the following: `You are currently in:`. Select the static text field and turn it into a movie clip symbol (Modify > Convert To Symbol...) named `headerText`. Name the instance of the movie clip on the stage `headerTextMC`.

4. Beneath this static text field, create a dynamic text field that fits most of the movie length, as shown in Figure 8.2, and name it `breadcrumbText`.

Figure 8.2. Create the text objects for the static and dynamic data.

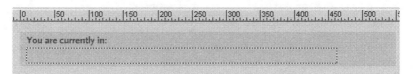

5. With the `breadcrumbText` field selected, click Character... in the Property Inspector and select Basic Latin. Click OK.

6. With the same field selected, choose Modify > Convert To Symbol... to create a movie clip symbol named `breadcrumbText`. Name the movie clip instance on the stage `breadcrumbTextMC`.

7. Select the first frame of the Background layer, create a new 550x50 rectangle and position it at (0, 0) to fill the stage. The fill color you use doesn't matter; we'll use ActionScript later to dynamically reflect the color scheme of the site.

8. Select the new rectangle and convert it to a movie clip symbol (Modify > Convert To Symbol...) named `breadcrumbBackground`. Name the instance on the stage `breadcrumbBackgroundMC`.

9. Save and publish your movie to a location of your choice.

Now, we'll add the scripts that will create the variables we'll pass to the movie.

Adding the Script

As noted earlier, this isn't a book on server-side scripting. That said, this example requires a server-side script to fully demonstrate the power of passing dynamic values to a Flash movie. We'll therefore review a PHP script that produces the desired effect. Feel free to use another language (e.g. ColdFusion, ASP.NET, Java, etc.).

10. Open a code editor. Notepad (on Windows) or TextEdit (on Mac) will work just fine, as will Macromedia Dreamweaver.

11. Type in the following code and save the file as breadcrumb.php.

File: **breadcrumb.php**

```php
<?php
// In practical applications, these variables could come
// from a database or other dynamic source
$navCrumbs = '/Home/Products/Super-Dooper Products';
$navColor = 'b50000';
?>
<!DOCTYPE html PUBLIC "-//W3C//DTD XHTML 1.0 Strict//EN"
    "http://www.w3.org/TR/xhtml1/DTD/xhtml1-strict.dtd">
<html xmlns="http://www.w3.org/1999/xhtml">
<head>
<title>Flash External Variables Test</title>
<meta http-equiv="Content-Type"
    content="text/html; charset=iso-8859-1" />
<style type="text/css">
<!--
body {
  margin: 0;
}
#breadcrumbdiv {
  background-color: <?php echo '#' . $navColor; ?>;
  width: 100%;
  height: 50px;
}
-->
</style>
</head>
<body>
<div id="breadcrumbdiv">
  <object type="application/x-shockwave-flash"
      name="breadcrumb" width="550" height="50" id="breadcrumb"
      data="breadcrumb.swf?breadcrumb=<?php
      echo urlencode($navCrumbs); ?>&breadcrumbColor=<?php
      echo urlencode('0x' . $navColor); ?>">
    <param name="movie"
        value="breadcrumb.swf?breadcrumb=<?php
        echo urlencode($navCrumbs); ?>&breadcrumbColor=<?php
        echo urlencode('0x' . $navColor); ?>" />
```

```
      <param name="quality" value="high" />
    </object>
  </div>
  </body>
  </html>
```

That's a sizeable chunk of code, but most of it's standard HTML and CSS. We have a `div` tag (`id="breadcrumbdiv"`) that contains our Flash movie. Some CSS code in the header ensures that this block spans the width of the page.

The PHP code is highlighted in bold.

At the top of the page, we declare two PHP variables, `$navCrumbs` and `$navColor`:

```
<?php
// In practical applications, these variables could come
// from a database or other dynamic source
$navCrumbs = '/Home/Products/Super-Dooper Products';
$navColor = 'b50000';
?>
```

`$navCrumbs` controls the "bread crumb" text. In this example, I've hard-coded the string, but it could be pulled from a database or XML file and processed before being passed to Flash. The `$navColor` variable controls the background color of both the Flash movie and the `div` block that contains it. Since ActionScript requires colors in the form *0xRRGGBB* and CSS requires them in the form *#RRGGBB*, this variable takes the form *RRGGBB* (b50000, a dark red, in this case), from which we can produce both forms as needed.

The next piece of PHP code outputs this color value as the `background-color` property in the CSS rule for the `breadcrumbdiv` tag:

```
#breadcrumbdiv {
  background-color: <?php echo '#' . $navColor; ?>;
  width: 100%;
  height: 50px;
}
```

Finally, we embed the movie using the `object` tag familiar to all Flash designers. Some PHP code serves to complicate matters a little, however:

```
<object type="application/x-shockwave-flash"
    name="breadcrumb" width="550" height="50" id="breadcrumb"
    data="breadcrumb.swf?breadcrumb=<?php
```

```
        echo urlencode($navCrumbs); ?>&breadcrumbColor=<?php
        echo urlencode('Ox' . $navColor); ?>">
    <param name="movie"
        value="breadcrumb.swf?breadcrumb=<?php
        echo urlencode($navCrumbs); ?>&breadcrumbColor=<?php
        echo urlencode('Ox' . $navColor); ?>" />
    <param name="quality" value="high" />
</object>
```

As you can see (if you squint a little), we don't simply specify the filename of the movie (breadcrumb.swf) in the data attribute of the object tag and in the value attribute of the param name="movie" tag. Instead, we've included a **query string**—a question mark followed by a list of variable names and values.

The query string specifies two variables:

breadcrumb   This specifies the text to appear in the movie. The PHP outputs the $navCrumbs variable, encoded to appear in a URL query string via PHP's urlencode function.

breadcrumbColor   This specifies the background color for the movie as a Flash color code (0x*RRGGBB*). The PHP outputs the $navColor variable with the appropriate prefix, encoded to appear in a URL query string.

The Flash Plug-in looks for variables like this in the movie's query string, and creates matching ActionScript variables in the root of the timeline. Now, we'll add the ActionScript that reads and applies these variables.

12. Back in Flash, add the following code to the first frame of the Actions layer within the Actions Panel:

File: **breadcrumb.fla**   Actions : 1
```
MovieClip.prototype.fadeMe = function (targetAlpha, smoothness)
{
  this.targetAlpha = targetAlpha;
  this.smoothness = smoothness;
  this._alpha = O;
  this.onEnterFrame = function ()
  {
    if (this._alpha < this.targetAlpha)
    {
      var alphaStep = Math.ceil((targetAlpha - this._alpha) /
```

```
             this.smoothness);
          this._alpha += alphaStep;
        }
        else
        {
          this.onEnterFrame = null;
        }
    };
};
function setBreadcrumb (bcText)
{
  breadcrumbTextMC.breadcrumbText.text = bcText;
}
function setBackgroundColor (color)
{
  var bgColor = new Color (breadcrumbBackgroundMC);
  bgColor.setRGB (color);
}
setBreadcrumb (breadcrumb);
setBackgroundColor (breadcrumbColor);
headerTextMC.fadeMe (100, 8);
breadcrumbTextMC.fadeMe (100, 12);
```

By now, most of this code should be familiar to you. The `fadeMe` method, which we add to the `MovieClip` class, takes a target opacity percentage (`targetAlpha`) and a `smoothness` value and fades the clip from transparent to the target opacity. We use this to fade in the two text movie clips at startup:

```
headerTextMC.fadeMe (100, 8);
breadcrumbTextMC.fadeMe (100, 12);
```

Two functions then make the adjustments dictated by the two variables that were received from the HTML generated by the server-side script.

```
function setBreadcrumb (bcText)
{
  breadcrumbTextMC.breadcrumbText.text = bcText;
}
function setBackgroundColor (color)
{
  var bgColor = new Color (breadcrumbBackgroundMC);
  bgColor.setRGB (color);
}
```

`setBreadcrumb` sets the text that appears in the dynamic text field within the `breadcrumbTextMC` movie clip, while `setBackgroundColor` sets the color of the rectangle in `breadcrumbBackgroundMC`.

As I mentioned above, the two variables passed in the query string of the movie's URL, `breadcrumb` and `breadcrumbColor`, are available as ActionScript variables in the root of the movie. Applying the desired customizations is a simple matter of calling the two functions and passing them the respective variables.

```
setBreadcrumb (breadcrumb);
setBackgroundColor (breadcrumbColor);
```

13. Save the movie and publish it as `breadcrumb.swf`.

14. Place the movie and the server-side script (`breadcrumb.php`) on a PHP-enabled Web server, then load `breadcrumb.php` in your browser to see the effect.

No PHP? No Problem!

Don't have a PHP-enabled server? Server-side scripting not your game? You can view this example online at:

http://www.sitepoint.com/books/flashant1/examples/breadcrumb.php

That's all there is to passing external information into Flash.

Inter-Movie Communications

You might assume that Figure 8.3 depicts a single SWF file embedded in a Web page. The figure actually shows *two* SWF files talking to each other via a `LocalConnection` object.

Figure 8.3. Flash provides for inter-movie communication within Web-based environments.

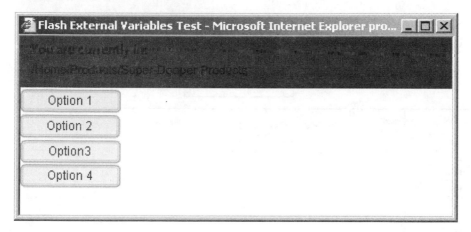

When a menu option in the second SWF file is clicked, it broadcasts information to the first SWF file, which then carries out a function. In this case, it displays an arbitrary message within a dynamic text field.

It's not difficult to use a true mixture of Flash and traditional technologies in your Web applications; the possibilities are limited only by your imagination. For example, you could create a video playback mechanism using two SWF files, where one SWF controls the playback of video within the other.

Let's take a closer look at the example in Figure 8.3 now. This example builds on the previous project to show how easily we can extend an application's functionality using inter-movie communication.

To edit this effect, locate the page header (`breadcrumb-caption.fla`) and the menu of option buttons (`menu.fla`) in the code archive.

Setting the Scene

Before we start, let's review what we're trying to achieve. In essence, we'll use the `LocalConnection` object to facilitate communication between two SWF files. One file (the menu) will broadcast information to the other (the page header) when any of the buttons in the menu is pressed. The menu file will send a different message for each button. This will be placed within a dynamic text field in the header movie, showing which button was pressed. I've distilled the workings of this example into the simple diagram in Figure 8.4.

Figure 8.4. Use a `LocalConnection` object to facilitate communication between SWF files.

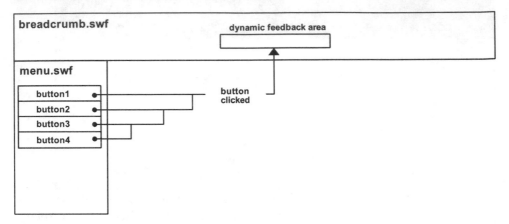

Now that we understand what we're aiming for, it's time to set the scene for both the menu and breadcrumb movies.

Creating the Breadcrumb

If you didn't complete the previous example, grab `breadcrumb.fla` from the code archive and open it to use as a starting point.

1. Create a new dynamic text field within the first frame of the Text layer, naming the instance `menuConnection`. Click Character... and select Basic Latin. Move the dynamic text field to the coordinates (350, 23), approximately. This field will be populated at runtime when options are selected from the menu movie.

2. Save this movie as `breadcrumb-caption.fla`.

Creating the Menu

Now that we've created the page header, it's time to create the menu. We'll create a simple menu system using Flash's built-in `Button` component, but make the menu more aesthetically pleasing if you like.

3. Create a new Flash document with a width and height of 100 pixels, and accept the default frame rate.

4. Rename the default layer as Text and add a further layer above it, named Actions.

5. Drag four `Button` component instances from the UI Components section of the Components Panel into the first frame of the Text layer. From top to bottom, name the instances `button1` through `button4`.

6. Select all the button instances and, from the Property Inspector, give them appropriate labels, e.g. `Option 1` through `Option 4`.

7. Save this Flash movie as `menu.fla`.

Now, we'll add the ActionScript to get these Flash movies talking!

Adding the ActionScript

The first chunk of ActionScript allows the page header movie to process information received through the `LocalConnection` object.

8. Open the `breadcrumb-caption.fla` file and, with the first frame of the Actions layer selected, add the following to the existing ActionScript code:

File: **breadcrumb-caption.fla**   Actions : 1 (excerpt)

```
var menuLocal = new LocalConnection ();
menuLocal.onPress = function (messageToPass)
{
    _root.menuConnection.text = messageToPass;
};
menuLocal.connect ("menuTunnel");
```

In this code, an instance of `LocalConnection` is created within the `menuLocal` variable.

```
var menuLocal = new LocalConnection ();
```

We then add an `onPress` method to this object, taking a string that's passed in (`messageToPass`), and populating the dynamic text field with this value:

```
menuLocal.onPress = function (messageToPass)
{
```

```
  _root.menuConnection.text = messageToPass;
};
```

Finally, we connect the instance of LocalConnection in menuLocal to a connection named menuTunnel, which serves to link the two SWF files.

```
menuLocal.connect ("menuTunnel");
```

9.   Save and publish the Flash movie. Name the file breadcrumb.swf.

We're done with the receiver movie. Let's now consider the menu that broadcasts the information to be displayed.

10. Open the menu file and, with the first frame of the Actions layer selected, add the following code:

File: **menu.fla**   Actions : 1

```
var menuLocal = new LocalConnection ();
button1.onPress = function ()
{
  menuLocal.send ("menuTunnel", "onPress",
      "Option 1 selected");
}
button2.onPress = function ()
{
  menuLocal.send ("menuTunnel", "onPress",
      "Option 2 selected");
}
button3.onPress = function ()
{
  menuLocal.send ("menuTunnel", "onPress",
      "Option 3 selected");
}
button4.onPress = function ()
{
  menuLocal.send ("menuTunnel", "onPress",
      "Option 4 selected");
}
```

Again, we create an instance of the LocalConnection object:

```
var menuLocal = new LocalConnection ();
```

We then set up an onPress event handler for each of the buttons, which calls the send method of the LocalConnection object we just created:

```
button1.onPress = function ()
{
  menuLocal.send ("menuTunnel", "onPress", "Option 1 selected");
};
```

Utilizing the `menuTunnel` connection and the `onPress` method, we send a different message as each button is pressed.

11. Save and publish your Flash movie and name the file `menu.swf`.

We now need to embed these files into a Web page so we can see how they talk to one another.

Updating the Web page

Embedding two Flash movies into a single page so that they may communicate via `LocalConnection` is simple.

12. Open the Web page you created to display `breadcrumb.swf` in the previous example (or use `breadcrumb.php` from the code archive).

13. Add the necessary code to display `menu.swf` in the page. For our sample PHP script, the new code is shown in bold below:

File: **breadcrumb-caption.php**
```php
<?php
// In a practical applications, these variables could come
// from a database or other dynamic source
$navCrumbs = '/Home/Products/Super-Dooper Products';
$navColor = 'b50000';
?>
<!DOCTYPE html PUBLIC "-//W3C//DTD XHTML 1.0 Strict//EN"
    "http://www.w3.org/TR/xhtml1/DTD/xhtml1-strict.dtd">
<html xmlns="http://www.w3.org/1999/xhtml">
<head>
<title>Flash External Variables Test</title>
<meta http-equiv="Content-Type"
    content="text/html; charset=iso-8859-1" />
<style type="text/css">
<!--
body {
  margin: 0;
}
#breadcrumbdiv {
  background-color: <?php echo '#' . $navColor; ?>;
```

```
    width: 100%;
    height: 50px;
}
#menudiv {
  float: left;
  width: 100px;
  height: 100px;
}
-->
</style>
</head>
<body>
<div id="breadcrumbdiv">
  <object type="application/x-shockwave-flash"
      name="breadcrumb" width="550" height="50" id="breadcrumb"
      data="breadcrumb.swf?breadcrumb=<?php
      echo urlencode($navCrumbs); ?>&breadcrumbColor=<?php
      echo urlencode('Ox' . $navColor); ?>">
    <param name="movie" value="breadcrumb.swf?breadcrumb=<?php
      echo urlencode($navCrumbs); ?>&breadcrumbColor=<?php
      echo urlencode('Ox' . $navColor); ?>" />
    <param name="quality" value="high" />
  </object>
</div>
<div id="menudiv">
  <object type="application/x-shockwave-flash"
      name="breadcrumb" width="100" height="100" id="menu"
      data="menu.swf">
    <param name="movie" value="menu.swf" />
    <param name="quality" value="high" />
  </object>
</div>
</body>
</html>
```

14. Save the updated page, upload it to your Web server, and view it in your browser.

Here's One I Prepared Earlier...

Once again, if you don't have the server-side know-how for this example, you can save yourself the headaches and view it online at:

http://www.sitepoint.com/books/flashant1/examples/breadcrumb-caption.php

When you click a link in the menu, a message is sent to the `breadcrumb.swf` file to tell it which option has been selected.

This cool effect is handy if you don't want to create a full-page Flash application, yet you need separate components that can talk to each other dynamically. The `LocalConnection` class can be used in countless applications. Here are a few examples.

❏ HTML pop-up windows containing Flash movies that control and update information in a Flash movie on the main page

❏ Devices that control the playback of video within a separate Flash movie

❏ Navigation systems containing components that interact with each other

Experiment to see how you can apply this technique to your own projects. I'm sure you have some ideas brewing already!

Creating a Simple Blog Reader Application

Many Web developers have asked, "How can I link data from a database to Flash?" The methodology behind hooking up the data is relatively simple once you understand the process.

One of the easiest ways to bring content from an external database into Flash is to use the `sendAndLoad` method of a `LoadVars` object, as we did in Chapter 7. Another approach involves retrieving XML data from the server using the `XML` class. We did this way back in Chapter 5, with our MP3 player example.

In this example, shown in Figure 8.5, we'll use the XML technique to fetch from a database news items that match the date selected by a user.

Figure 8.5. The News Sweeper application integrates data from SQL Server 2000.

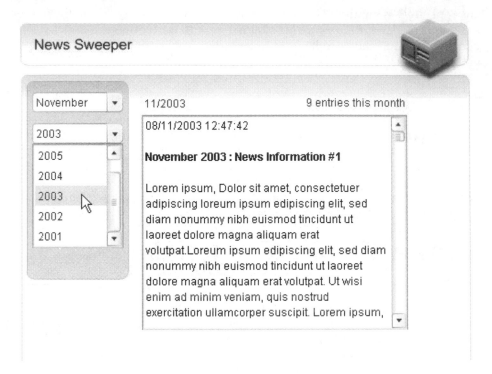

We'll use two `ComboBox` components to pass two parameters—a month and a year—to a server-side script. The script will use those variables to assemble a database query in Structured Query Language (SQL), and retrieve a set of records from the database. The script will format the records into an XML document, which it will return to the Flash movie. The movie will parse the data and display it to the user.

To edit the finished solution, locate `blog.fla` in the code archive.

Setting the Scene

Let's start by building the application space. We'll add extra components and code as we go along.

1. Start by creating a new Flash document that's 500 pixels wide and 400 pixels high, accepting the default frame rate.

2. Rename the default layer as Actions and add three layers below it, naming them Misc, Text and Background.

3. Add a background. I used simple gradient backgrounds with rounded corners to frame the header, content, and control elements. For inspiration, refer to Figure 8.5.

4. Select the first frame of the Text layer and drag two instances of the `ComboBox` component from the UI Components section of the Components Panel onto the stage. Name them `month` and `year` respectively, placing `month` above `year`.

We don't need to populate these `ComboBoxes`; we'll achieve this programmatically through ActionScript in just a moment.

5. Select the first frame of the Text layer and drag an instance of the `TextArea` component from the UI Components section of the Components Panel onto the stage. Name the instance `myBlogContent` and position it as shown in Figure 8.5. Select the `TextArea` component and, in the Component Inspector, edit the html parameter to set it to true.

6. Drag two instances of the `Label` component from the UI Components section of the Component Panel to the stage. Align one instance with left side of the top edge of the `TextArea` component and the other with its the right side. Name the instances `myBlogDate` and `numberOfResults`, respectively.

7. With the `numberOfResults` component selected, set the autoSize parameter in the Component Inspector to right.

`myBlogDate` will display the date of the information retrieved from the server. `numberOfResults` will display the number of entries received.

8. For ideas to further enhance the interface, refer to Figure 8.5.

9. Save the document.

We can now add the ActionScript to make this project work. Before doing that, however, we must first consider the format of the XML data that we expect to receive from the server.

The Server-Side Script

Since this isn't a book on server-side scripting, much less on database-driven Web development, we won't look at the code of the script. In case you don't have the necessary expertise to write your own script for this example, I've set one up for you at this URL:

http://www.sitepoint.com/books/flashant1/examples/blog.php

This script expects to be requested with two variables: month and year. month should contain the number of the month that the user wishes to view (1 to 12), while year should contain the year (e.g. 2004).

The script will return an XML document in this format:

```
<?xml version="1.0" encoding="iso-8859-1"?>
<blog>
  <entry>
    <datetime>12/11/2004 17:02:15</datetime>
    <title>November 2004: News Information #1</title>
    <content>
      Lorem ipsum dolor sit amet, consectetuer adipiscing elit.
      Proin consectetuer placerat ligula. In ut sem. Pellentesque
      sed ipsum eu tortor vestibulum fringilla. Integer quis
      felis eu purus mollis malesuada.
    </content>
  </entry>
  <entry>
    <datetime>28/11/2004 12:47:42</datetime>
    <title>December 2004: News Information #2</title>
    <content>
      Quisque tempor. Curabitur dignissim odio non ligula. Cras
      vestibulum, nisl a accumsan laoreet, tortor felis accumsan
      purus, placerat fermentum urna dolor non felis. Suspendisse
      tristique mattis lectus.
    </content>
  </entry>
</blog>
```

To see this in action, simply type into your browser's address bar the URL of the script above, adding the necessary variables as a query string. For example, this URL should return the XML document above:

http://www.sitepoint.com/books/flashant1/examples/blog.php?month=11&year=2004

Adding the ActionScript

We can now add the code that sends variables to, and receives data from, the server-side script that queries the database.

10. Select the first frame of the Action layer and add the following code to the Actions Panel:

File: **blog.fla**   Actions : 1

```
this.onLoad = GrabData;
var now = new Date ();

year.addItem ("Select a Year", "0");
year.addItem ("2005", "2005");
year.addItem ("2004", "2004");
year.addItem ("2003", "2003");
year.addItem ("2002", "2002");
year.addItem ("2001", "2001");
var currentYear = now.getFullYear ();
for (i = 0; i < year.length; i++)
{
  if (year.getItemAt (i).data == currentYear)
  {
    year.setSelectedIndex (i);
    break;
  }
}
year.change = function ()
{
  if (year.selectedIndex > 0)
  {
    _root.myBlogDate.text = "Requesting Data";
    GrabData ();
  }
};
year.addEventListener ("change", year);

month.addItem ("Select a Month", "0");
month.addItem ("January", "1");
month.addItem ("February", "2");
month.addItem ("March", "3");
month.addItem ("April", "4");
month.addItem ("May", "5");
month.addItem ("June", "6");
month.addItem ("July", "7");
```

```
month.addItem ("August", "8");
month.addItem ("September", "9");
month.addItem ("October", "10");
month.addItem ("November", "11");
month.addItem ("December", "12");
month.setSelectedIndex (now.getMonth () + 1);
month.change = function ()
{
  if (month.selectedIndex > 0)
  {
    _root.myBlogDate.text = "Requesting Data";
    GrabData ();
  }
};
month.addEventListener ("change", month);

function GrabData ()
{
  _root.curMonth = month.value;
  _root.curYear = year.value;
  var xml = new XML ();
  xml.ignoreWhite = true;
  xml.onLoad = showMonthInfo;
  xml.load ('http://www.sitepoint.com/books/flashant1/' +
      examples/blog.php?month=' + _root.curMonth +
      '&year=' + _root.curYear);
}
function showMonthInfo (success)
{
  _root.myBlogDate.text = _root.curMonth + "/" + _root.curYear;
  _root.myBlogContent.text = "";
  if (!success || this.childNodes[0].nodeName != "blog")
  {
    _root.numberOfResults.text = "Error retrieving results.";
    return;
  }
  var blog = this.childNodes[0];
  _root.numberOfResults.text = blog.childNodes.length +
      " entries this month";
  for (i = 0; i < blog.childNodes.length; i++)
  {
    if (blog.childNodes[i].nodeName == "entry")
    {
      var entry = blog.childNodes[i];
      for (j = 0; j < entry.childNodes.length; j++)
      {
```

```
  if (entry.childNodes[j].nodeName == "datetime")
  {
    _root.myBlogContent.text +=
        entry.childNodes[j].firstChild.nodeValue +
        "<br />";
  }
  else if (entry.childNodes[j].nodeName == "title")
  {
    _root.myBlogContent.text += "<b>" +
        entry.childNodes[j].firstChild.nodeValue +
        "</b><br /><br />";
  }
  else if (entry.childNodes[j].nodeName == "content")
  {
    _root.myBlogContent.text +=
        entry.childNodes[j].firstChild.nodeValue +
        "<br /><br />";
  }
      }
    }
  }
}
```

There's a lot of code in this example. Let's talk through it step by step.

The very first line sets up the `GetData` function so that it will be called once the entire movie has loaded:

```
this.onLoad = GetData;
```

We'll see what this function does momentarily.

This is followed by a lengthy, but simple piece of code that populates the year and month drop-downs with values, selects the values that correspond to the current date, and sets up event handlers that will respond to user selections. Here's the code for the year drop-down:

```
year.addItem ("Select a Year", "0");
year.addItem ("2005", "2005");
year.addItem ("2004", "2004");
year.addItem ("2003", "2003");
year.addItem ("2002", "2002");
year.addItem ("2001", "2001");
var currentYear = now.getFullYear ();
for (i = 0; i < year.length; i++)
```

```
{
  if (year.getItemAt (i).data == currentYear)
  {
    year.setSelectedIndex (i);
    break;
  }
}
year.change = function ()
{
  if (year.selectedIndex > 0)
  {
    _root.myBlogDate.text = "Requesting Data";
    GrabData ();
  }
};
year.addEventListener ("change", year);
```

The change event handler ensures the user hasen't selected the first item in the list (a label that reads "Select a Year"), displays "Requesting Data" in the myBlogDate dynamic text field, and calls GrabData.

The code for the month drop-down works in much the same way.

The remainder of the code deals with fetching and reading the XML data from the server. First, we have the GrabData function that makes the request:

```
function GrabData ()
{
  _root.curMonth = month.value;
  _root.curYear = year.value;
  var xml = new XML ();
  xml.ignoreWhite = true;
  xml.onLoad = showMonthInfo;
  xml.load ('http://www.sitepoint.com/books/flashant1/' +
      'examples/blog.php?month=' + _root.curMonth +
      '&year=' + _root.curYear);
}
```

The function populates two variables in the root of the timeline from the ComboBoxes (curMonth and curYear). We then create a new instance of the XML class, set up an onLoad event handler for it, and load the server-side script, passing the selected month and year in the query string. Aside from the two variables we send with our request, this code is identical to the code we used back in Chapter 5.

When the data is received, the `onLoad` event handler, `showMonthInfo`, is triggered. This is a sizeable chunk of code, so let's consider it in pieces.

We start by setting the `myBlogDate` label to display the month and year we have fetched for display. We also clear the `myBlogContent` text area:

```
function showMonthInfo (success)
{
  _root.myBlogDate.text = _root.curMonth + "/" + _root.curYear;
  _root.myBlogContent.text = "";
```

Next, if the `success` parameter passed to the event handler indicates the request failed, or if the top-level element of the XML data is not a `blog` tag, we report an error and exit the function:

```
if (!success || this.childNodes[0].nodeName != "blog")
{
  _root.numberOfResults.text = "Error retrieving results.";
  return;
}
```

We then count the number of child tags within the `blog` tag, and display it as the number of entries in the `numberOfResults` `Label`:

```
var blog = this.childNodes[0];
_root.numberOfResults.text = blog.childNodes.length +
    " entries this month";
```

Next, we loop through the child tags, double-checking that each is an `entry` before looping through *its* child tags:

```
for (i = 0; i < blog.childNodes.length; i++)
{
  if (blog.childNodes[i].nodeName == "entry")
  {
    var entry = blog.childNodes[i];
    for (j = 0; j < entry.childNodes.length; j++)
    {
```

Depending on the tag name of the child, we output the text within the tag in either normal or bold text (using an HTML b tag), followed by one or two line breaks:

```
        if (entry.childNodes[j].nodeName == "datetime")
        {
          _root.myBlogContent.text +=
```

```
            entry.childNodes[j].firstChild.nodeValue +
                "<br />";
    }
    else if (entry.childNodes[j].nodeName == "title")
    {
      _root.myBlogContent.text += "<b>" +
                entry.childNodes[j].firstChild.nodeValue +
                "</b><br /><br />";
    }
    else if (entry.childNodes[j].nodeName == "content")
    {
      _root.myBlogContent.text +=
                entry.childNodes[j].firstChild.nodeValue +
                "<br /><br />";
    }
```

When all the loops are complete, we'll have output all of the blog entries to the myBlogContent TextArea.

11. Save and preview your work.

Wow! That is one sophisticated application! Have a play with those ComboBoxes. Scrutinize the data that's returned, paying close attention to the information areas above the TextArea when there are no data, and when there is a given number of entries. From here, you can easily modify this application for your own needs.

Storing Preferences with a Local Shared Object

TheLocal Shared Objects rock, period. They make short work of saving user session settings to the client machine, and pulling the data back into the application later. You'll wonder how you ever managed without them!

In this example, we'll save the settings for the month and year ComboBoxes from the previous example, as well as the checked or unchecked status of a checkbox. The modified interface can be seen in Figure 8.6.

Figure 8.6. Store preferences using a Local Shared Object.

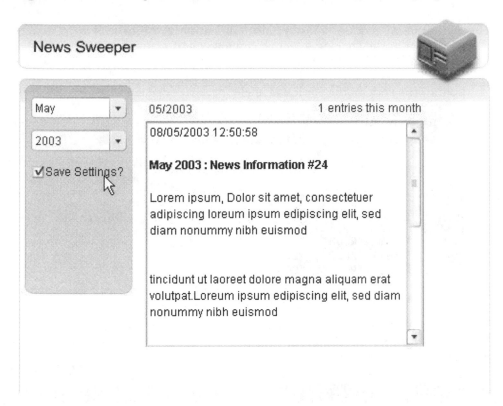

To edit this effect, locate `blog-prefs.fla` in the code archive.

Setting the Scene

1. Open the finished `.fla` from the previous example (`blog.fla`) either from the code archive or your completed version. Select the first frame of the Text layer and drag an instance of the `CheckBox` component from the UI Components section of the Components Panel onto the stage, naming the instance `savesettings`.

2. Change the label parameter of the `CheckBox` to `Save Settings?`

That's all we need to add by way of visible components; the real changes are under the hood, in the ActionScript.

Adding the ActionScript

The ActionScript requires substantial modification in order to save selections made by users in the CheckBox, month ComboBox and year ComboBox.

3. Select the first frame of the Actions layer and make the changes shown in bold to the code in the Actions Panel.

File: **blog-prefs.fla**   Actions : 1

```
var so = SharedObject.getLocal("savedSelection");
this.onLoad = GrabData;
var now = new Date ();

year.addItem ("Select a Year", "0");
year.addItem ("2005", "2005");
year.addItem ("2004", "2004");
year.addItem ("2003", "2003");
year.addItem ("2002", "2002");
year.addItem ("2001", "2001");
var currentYear;
if (so.data.year != undefined)
{
  currentYear = so.data.year;
}
else
{
  currentYear = now.getFullYear ();
}
for (i = 0; i < year.length; i++)
{
  if (year.getItemAt (i).data == currentYear)
  {
    year.setSelectedIndex (i);
    break;
  }
}
year.change = function ()
{
  if (year.selectedIndex > 0)
  {
    _root.myBlogDate.text = "Requesting Data";
    SaveSelection ();
    GrabData ();
  }
};
```

```
year.addEventListener ("change", year);

month.addItem ("Select a Month", "0");
month.addItem ("January", "1");
month.addItem ("February", "2");
month.addItem ("March", "3");
month.addItom ("April", "4");
month.addItem ("May", "5");
month.addItem ("June", "6");
month.addItem ("July", "7");
month.addItem ("August", "8");
month.addItem ("September", "9");
month.addItem ("October", "10");
month.addItem ("November", "11");
month.addItem ("December", "12");
if (so.data.month != undefined)
{
  month.setSelectedIndex(so.data.month);
}
else
{
  month.setSelectedIndex (now.getMonth () + 1);
}
month.change = function ()
{
  if (month.selectedIndex > 0)
  {
    _root.myBlogDate.text = "Requesting Data";
    SaveSelection ();
    GrabData ();
  }
};
month.addEventListener ("change", month);

savesettings.selected = (so.data.year != undefined);
savesettings.click = function ()
{
  SaveSelection();
}
savesettings.addEventListener("click", savesettings);

function SaveSelection()
{
  if (savesettings.selected)
  {
    so.data.month = month.selectedItem.data;
```

```
      so.data.year = year.selectedItem.data;
    }
    else
    {
      so.data.month = undefined;
      so.data.year = undefined;
    }
}

function GrabData ()
{
  _root.curMonth = month.value;
  _root.curYear = year.value;
  var xml = new XML ();
  xml.ignoreWhite = true;
  xml.onLoad = showMonthInfo;
  xml.load ('http://www.sitepoint.com/books/flashant1/' +
      'examples/blog.php?month=' + _root.curMonth +
      '&year=' + _root.curYear);
}
function showMonthInfo (success)
{
  _root.myBlogDate.text = _root.curMonth + "/" + _root.curYear;
  _root.myBlogContent.text = "";
  if (!success || this.childNodes[0].nodeName != "blog")
  {
    _root.numberOfResults.text = "Error retrieving results.";
    return;
  }
  var blog = this.childNodes[0];
  _root.numberOfResults.text = blog.childNodes.length +
      " entries this month";
  for (i = 0; i < blog.childNodes.length; i++)
  {
    if (blog.childNodes[i].nodeName == "entry")
    {
      var entry = blog.childNodes[i];
      for (j = 0; j < entry.childNodes.length; j++)
      {
        if (entry.childNodes[j].nodeName == "datetime")
        {
          _root.myBlogContent.text +=
              entry.childNodes[j].firstChild.nodeValue +
              "<br />";
        }
        else if (entry.childNodes[j].nodeName == "title")
```

```
        {
            _root.myBlogContent.text += "<b>" +
                entry.childNodes[j].firstChild.nodeValue +
                "</b><br /><br />";
        }
        else if (entry.childNodes[j].nodeName == "content")
        {
            _root.myBlogContent.text +=
                entry.childNodes[j].firstChild.nodeValue +
                "<br /><br />";
        }
    }
  }
 }
}
```

The first line of code obtains a `SharedObject` and stores it in a variable named so.

```
var so = SharedObject.getLocal("savedSelection");
```

We'll use this object to store persistently the year and month selected by the user (`so.data.year` and `so.data.month`, respectively).

We then modify the code that controls the initial selection for the year drop-down so that it uses the stored value if this is available:

```
if (so.data.year != undefined)
{
  currentYear = so.data.year;
}
else
{
  currentYear = now.getFullYear ();
}
```

We make a similar change to the code for the month drop-down's initial selection.

We also need to set the initial state of the `savesettings CheckBox`. To do this, we simply check whether or not a stored value exists for the year; if it does, we select the `CheckBox`:

```
savesettings.selected = (so.data.year != undefined);
```

In order to use these stored values, we must first store them! The `SaveSelection` function takes care of this and is called in the change event handlers for the two drop-downs:

```
year.change = function ()
{
  if (year.selectedIndex > 0)
  {
    _root.myBlogDate.text = "Requesting Data";
    SaveSelection ();
    GrabData ();
  }
};
```

We also set up a click event handler for the new `CheckBox` that calls `SaveSelection`:

```
savesettings.click = function ()
{
  SaveSelection();
}
savesettings.addEventListener("click", savesettings);
```

Let's look at the `SaveSelection` function itself:

```
function SaveSelection()
{
  if (savesettings.selected)
  {
    so.data.month = month.selectedItem.data;
    so.data.year = year.selectedItem.data;
  }
  else
  {
    so.data.month = undefined;
    so.data.year = undefined;
  }
}
```

This straightforward code checks whether or not the `savesettings CheckBox` is selected (checked). If it is, the currently selected month and year values are stored in `so`. If not, we erase any values that may previously have been saved. To do this, we set them to `undefined`.

4.   Save and preview your work.

When you preview the movie, check the checkbox, select a date and month, exit the preview, then go back in. Your settings should be remembered. Uncheck the checkbox, exit the application and view it again—the ComboBoxes will be reset to the current month and year.

This is a nifty application of a Local Shared Object. It's a great time-saver and an excellent building block for other applications.

Modifications

There are many uses for Local Shared Objects within your applications. We've investigated a single example that saves the settings of our News Sweeper application, but there are numerous situations in which this object can prove useful. Try experimenting with saved settings in other contexts.

Creating a Note Application Using External Data

This example uses data from a text file to create and populate dynamic Post-It-type notes as in Figure 8.7. It demonstrates a useful concept: the separation of design from content. This approach allows others to update the content of the notes without requiring them to edit the Flash source file directly.

Figure 8.7. Text files can be used for dynamic content.

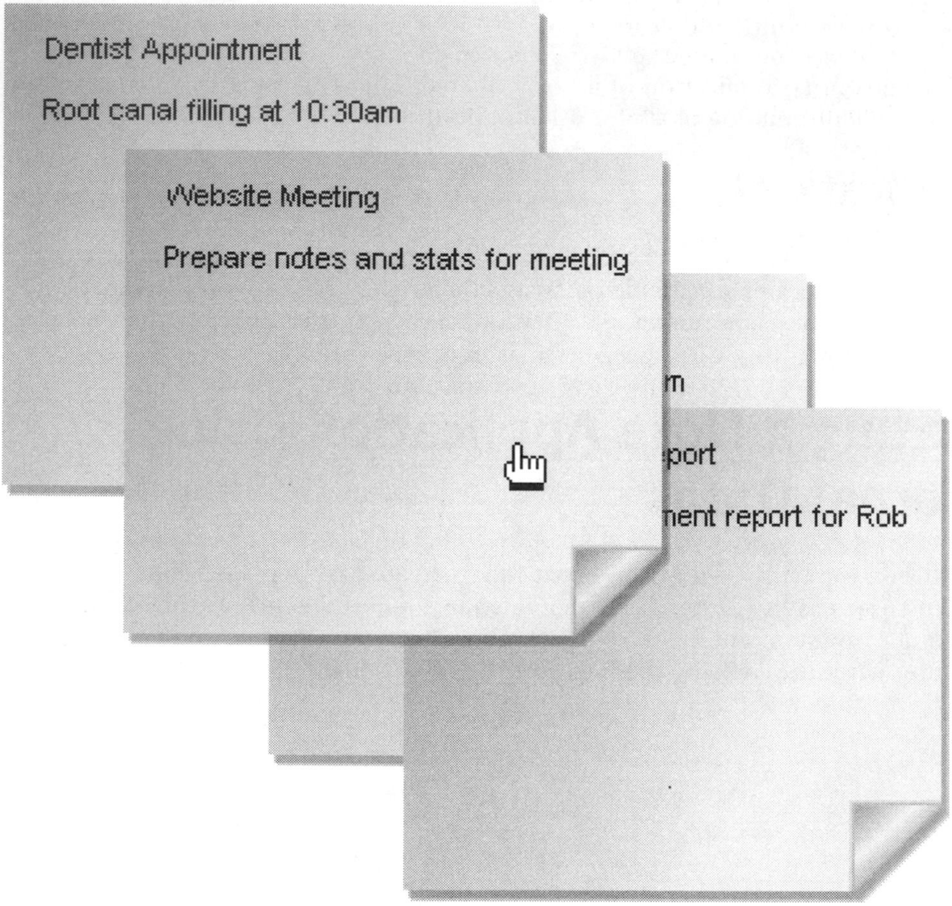

We populate a simple array with data from the text file, and use that dynamically to create the notes and populate the title and content areas with information. Let's get started!

To edit this solution, locate `stickynotes.fla` in the code archive. The file holding the information we'll use to populate the notes, `notes.txt`, can also be found in the code archive.

Setting the Scene

1. Create a new Flash document and accept the default width and height. Change the frame rate to 24 fps and click OK.

2. Rename the default layer as Actions and add below it another layer, named Boxes.

3. Create a new movie clip symbol named infoBox. Rename its default layer Main Interface and add another layer above it, named Text Boxes.

4. Select the first frame of the Main Interface layer and create a 200x180 pixel framing rectangle.

This will act as aframe for two text boxes that we'll add in a moment. You can make the frame as simple or as complicated as you like. In the code archive file, I created a simple rectangle with a smooth gradient changing from orange to yellow, and added a page turn effect at the bottom (see Figure 8.7).

5. Select the first frame of the Text Boxes layer and add two dynamic text fields, each 180 pixels wide. Position the first at the top and name the instance title. Position the other below the title text box and name it content.

6. Select the content text box and, in the Property Inspector, change the line type to Multline.

7. Drag the size handle of the content text box until it's approximately 110 pixels high (see Figure 8.8).

Figure 8.8. Add dynamic text fields to hold the external content.

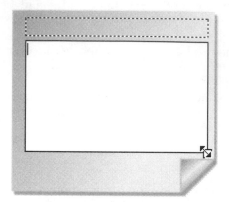

8. Drag an instance of the `infoBox` movie clip from the Library Panel into the first frame of the Boxes layer of the main timeline. Position it off the main stage at (-250, 0) and name it `infoBox`.

Offstage Instance vs. Linkage Identifier

We'll duplicate the clip dynamically and use ActionScript to populate it with data.

Alternately, you can instead give the symbol a linkage identifier in the Library Panel and modify the ActionScript code below to create instances from the library, rather than duplicating an existing instance. The two methods are equivalent; it's simply a matter of preference.

9. Save the movie to a location of your choice.

10. Locate `notes.txt` in the code archive and place it in the same folder as the Flash document.

We're ready to add ActionScript to this effect.

Adding the ActionScript

11. In the main timeline, select the first frame of the Actions layer and add the following code to the Actions Panel:

File: **stickynotes.fla** Actions : 1

```
var infoVars = new LoadVars ();
infoVars.onLoad = function (ok)
{
  if (ok)
  {
    parseInfo ();
  }
};
infoVars.load ("notes.txt");
function parseInfo ()
{
  for (i = 1; infoVars["note" + i] != undefined; i++)
  {
    var note = infoVars["note" + i].split(',');
    var mc = infoBox.duplicateMovieClip ("infoBox" + i, i);
    mc._x = note[0];
    mc._y = note[1];
    mc.title.text = note[2];
    mc.content.text = note[3];

    _root.topNote = mc;
    mc.onPress = function ()
    {
      this.swapDepths (_root.topNote.getDepth () + 1);
      _root.topNote = this;
      startDrag (this);
    };
    mc.onRelease = function ()
    {
      stopDrag ();
    };
  }
}
```

Let's break this down into smaller chunks so we can see what's going on.

First, we create a new LoadVars object called infoVars. We use the onLoad event handler to determine whether or not the load method has been successful, and call the parseInfo function.

```
var infoVars = new LoadVars ();
infoVars.onLoad = function (ok)
{
  if (ok)
```

```
    {
        parseInfo ();
    }
};
infoVars.load ("notes.txt");
```

Before we review how we parse the data, let's look at the contents of notes.txt. The file's structure is simple enough; it contains name/value pairs that define variables—one for each note to be displayed. In the sample provided, the variables are named note1 through note4, and contain four comma-separated values each:

```
note1=50,50,Dentist Appointment,Root canal filling at 10:30am&note
2=100,100,Website Meeting,Prepare notes and stats for meeting&note
3=150,150,Reboot Servers,Reboot Servers before 12pm&note4=200,200,
Prepare Mgmt Report,Prepare management report for Rob
```

Each variable conforms to the following format:

```
noten=xPosition,yPosition,title,content
```

We use the *xPosition* and *yPosition* values to position the note on the stage. The *title* value populates the title text box, while the *content* value populates the content text box.

Now, let's return to the parseInfo function that's called when the text file loads successfully.

```
function parseInfo ()
{
  for (i = 1; infoVars["note" + i] != undefined; i++)
  {
    var note = infoVars["note" + i].split(',');
    var mc = infoBox.duplicateMovieClip ("infoBox" + i, i);
    mc._x = note[0];
    mc._y = note[1];
    mc.title.text = note[2];
    mc.content.text = note[3];
```

We use a for loop to move through the noten variables found in the text file until it hits an undefined variable, which indicates the end of the data.

Within the loop, we split the string of comma-separated values into an array called note. We then create a duplicate of the offstage infoBox movie clip. Using the values in the note array, we set the new movie clip's position, title, and content.

Now, because we use i to set the depth of the new movie clips, the last clip created will sit on top of the stack. We want to allow users to click and drag around the Post-It-type notes, with the last-clicked note rising to the top of the stack. To do this, we keep track of the clip that is on the top of the stack, by setting a variable named topNote:

```
_root.topNote = mc;
```

We then assign "dragging" functions for each of the duplicated instances, using the onPress and onRelease event handlers. The onPress handler obtains the depth of the topmost note (_root.topNote.getDepth ()), adds one to it, and then assigns that as the depth of the clicked movie clip using swapDepths. The topNote variable is then updated to point to the new topmost clip. Finally, we call startDrag to allow the user to drag the note around. The onRelease handler, of course, stops the dragging operation.

```
mc.onPress = function ()
{
  this.swapDepths (_root.topNote.getDepth () + 1);
  _root.topNote = this;
  startDrag (this);
};
mc.onRelease = function ()
{
  stopDrag ();
};
```

12. Save and preview your work.

The data from the text file has successfully been transferred to the dynamic notes, which are arranged on the screen in the order in which they were created. Clicking on any of the nested notes brings it to the front, so that it can clearly be seen, and the notes can be dragged around the screen easily.

Simply adding new entries to the text file can make the application more interesting. There are many other modifications you can make to this effect.

Modifications

Here are a few ideas for extending this example.

Update the text file dynamically when entries are updated

This example is actually a trimmed-down version of an application I use on a daily basis—a pseudo-notice board. In that version, the text file is modified on the fly via ASP and SQL Server interaction when entries are added to the database.

The application allows data to be entered and edited without requiring users to alter the text file directly. It's a rather complex example that's beyond the scope of this book, but it may provide insight into how this example could be extended in a real world scenario.

Store the position of the notes

Using a Local Shared Object, you could save the position of each note by referencing the array instance when the `onRelease` event handler is triggered and storing the _x and _y properties of the duplicated clip.

Use XML

The text file format is simple, but the use of comma-separated values and other simplistic data structures can cause problems. For example, what will happen if a Post-It-type note's text happens to contain a comma? Using the techniques from the blog reader application, you could covert this project to read and parse an XML file containing the notes.

Conclusion

Some of the examples in the chapter are quite complex, requiring some knowledge of server-side coding techniques. Yet, they also demonstrate how powerful Flash can be when connected to external data sources.

We've covered a lot of ground, developed some clever solutions, and written some compact code for data retrieval and presentation.

I hope this chapter has inspired you to create some truly amazing applications!

Debugging

Assuring the best possible quality in your projects with the help of defensive coding techniques and best practices is easier said than done—it requires real vigilance during development. If the inevitable occurs and some sections of your code don't work as expected at testing time, you'll have to do some debugging.

Luckily, a variety of tools are available within Flash MX 2004 for catching errors, finding code that's misbehaving, and monitoring what happens when your code executes.

In this chapter, we'll discuss how you can identify and remove bugs from your applications.

Common Causes of Errors

Most errors that arise during the development of ActionScripted Flash applications can be identified fairly easily. The following list is not exhaustive, but includes most common causes.

Syntax Errors

When you preview a movie within the internal player, "show stopping" bugs will be revealed in the Output Panel as the movie is compiled. These are syntax errors;

they stop the movie from playing and must be fixed before it can be previewed. The good thing about these bugs is that a detailed description is often provided in the Output Panel, complete with the line number on which the error occurred. This makes them relatively easy to track down and fix.

Type Mismatches

ActionScript 2.0, introduced in Flash MX 2004, allows you to declare variable types. Consider the following snippet, in which we create a variable called TextInfo and declare it so that it must contain a String:

```
var TextInfo:String = 5;
```

This code generates the following error in the Output Panel:

```
**Error** Scene=Scene 1, layer=Layer 1, frame=1:Line 1: Type
mismatch in assignment statement: found Number where String is
required.
     var TextInfo:String = 5;

Total ActionScript Errors: 1    Reported Errors: 1
```

When a variable with a declared type is assigned a value of a different type, a type mismatch error is produced. In this example, we assigned a number as the value of a string variable. To correct this, we must either assign a value of the correct type (a text string), or change the declared variable type.

```
var TextInfo:String = "5";
```

```
var NumberInfo:Number = 5;
```

Misspelled Variables

Another common problem (especially when you're copying code from a book!) is misspelled variables. If something isn't working, check to make sure you haven't mistyped a variable name somewhere along the line. This is a particular problem in Flash MX 2004, because ActionScript 2.0 is case-sensitive in regard to variable names.

Unbalanced Brackets

Errors occur when an opening brace, bracket, quote, or parenthesis isn't closed. Take a look at the following example:

```
var NumberInfo:Number = 5;
if (NumberInfo == 5)
{{
  //Do Something Here
  trace ("Equals 5");
}
else
{
  //Do Something Else
  trace ("Not Equal to 5");
}
```

If you preview this code within the internal Flash Player, it fails on line three, due to the presence of an extra brace.

```
**Error** Scene=Scene 1, layer=Layer 1, frame=1:Line 7: 'else'
encountered without matching 'if'
      else

**Error** Scene=Scene 1, layer=Layer 1, frame=1:Line 3: Statement
block must be terminated by '}'
      {{

**Error** Scene=Scene 1, layer=Layer 1, frame=1:Line 12: Syntax
error.

Total ActionScript Errors: 3     Reported Errors: 3
```

Removing the extra brace resolves the problem. Unbalanced identifiers like these are usually the result of mistyping or errant copying and pasting. Fortunately, error-catching routines within the Flash Player make it easy to locate and correct these flaws.

Logic Errors

Problems with the underlying logic that controls the flow of your program usually creep in when you haven't planned your application adequately.

They can be difficult to track down, so it's essential that you plan your applications carefully and thoughtfully, perhaps sketching them out on paper or within a mapping utility before you begin. This way, you can drastically reduce the chances of introducing a logic failure. If errors do occur, you can review the process flow.

Logic errors can be diagnosed using a debugger, as we'll see later in this chapter.

Runtime Errors

Runtime errors can occur at any time during which the code is running, and may not relate directly to syntax. For example, a runtime error might arise within correct code that tries to access a function or variable that doesn't exist, or experiences connection problems when it tries to query a database.

There are many techniques to identify problematic code. Let's discuss some of the more common methods.

Debugging Basics: Using `trace`

In this example, shown in Figure 9.1, we'll look at using `trace`, a handy function that displays information in the Output Panel when you preview a Flash movie. During the development of almost every example in this book, I used the `trace` function to output variables, expressions, and object properties so I could check that everything was working correctly. `trace` proved particularly valuable when I converted data from one type to another.

Figure 9.1. Use the `trace` function to send data to the Output Panel.

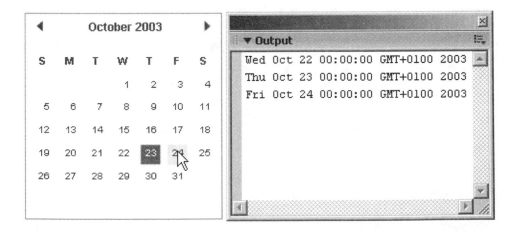

You may already have seen the Output Panel in action when, for example, you wrote ActionScript that had syntax errors or referenced objects that didn't exist. It's a helpful tool and, coupled with the `trace` function, can be extremely useful when you find yourself faced with a tight deadline and some buggy code.

To edit this example, locate `trace.fla` in the code archive.

Setting the Scene

1. Create a new Flash document, and accept the default size and frame rate.

2. Change the name of Layer1 to Actions.

3. Drag an instance of the `DateChooser` component from the UI Components section of the Components Panel onto the stage, naming it `myBlog`.

Adding the ActionScript

Each time users select a date from the `myBlog` `DateChooser`, we want to see the selection appear in the Output Panel. To achieve this, we need to write some simple code, adding an event listener to detect a change event in the component.

4. Add the following code to the first frame of the Actions layer through the Actions Panel:

```
myBlog.change = function (eventObj)
{
  trace (myBlog.selectedDate);
};
myBlog.addEventListener ("change", myBlog);
```

As you can see from this code and Figure 9.1, when users make a selection, we output the `selectedDate` property of the `DateChooser` component to the Output Panel using `trace`. In Figure 9.1, I've clicked on several dates to illustrate this point.

`trace` shows us the data we're working with. Since the date value is extremely lengthy, if we tried to pass this value directly out of Flash to query a database using, say, a `LoadVars` object, we wouldn't get very far. We need to convert the date value into a more useful format.

The date format required by SQL Server is *DD/MM/YYYY*. Let's create a function to convert an ActionScript **Date** object into a string of this format.

5.   Modify the existing code as follows:

```
File: trace.fla                                                    Actions : 1
function FixDate (incomingDate:Date)
{
  var dd = incomingDate.getDate ();
  var mm = incomingDate.getMonth ();
  var yyyy = incomingDate.getFullYear ();
  if (mm < 10)
  {
    mm = "0" + mm;
  }
  if (dd < 10)
  {
    dd = "0" + dd;
  }
  return dd + "/" + mm + "/" + yyyy;
}
myBlog.change = function (eventObj)
{
  trace (FixDate (myBlog.selectedDate));
};
myBlog.addEventListener ("change", myBlog);
```

6.   Save and preview your work.

By passing the variable through the **FixDate** function, we've produced a string in the desired format, as shown in Figure 9.2.

Figure 9.2. Use the `trace` command to verify output from the `FixDate` function.

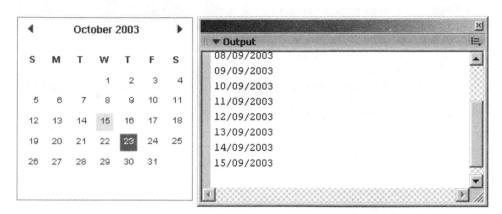

Now that we have the date in the format we require, we know that our SQL query will accept it—life is great! Without the `trace` function, it would be much more difficult and time consuming to trap rogue data.

Using the Error Object

The `Error` class is a new addition to Flash MX 2004. It's a very handy tool for detecting errors or checking conditions within your code.

You can create an `Error` object within a `try` block, then `throw` it. Control (and the `Error` object) is then passed to the `catch` block, where you can handle the error. This is a very useful language feature, so let's look at it in action.

To edit this example, locate `try-catch.fla` in the code archive. It uses the file `notes.txt` (also found in the code archive), which must be placed in the same directory as the movie.

A so-called **try-catch block** is typically coded as follows:

```
try
{
  if (somethingbadhappens)
  {
    throw new Error (errormessage);
  }
```

```
}
catch (theError)
{
  // React to theError
}
```

So, harkening back to our Post-It-type note example in Chapter 8, let's say we expected the external data file to contain at least five notes. We could use this technique to analyze and respond to the situation if this expectation were not met:

1. Create a new Flash document and rename the default layer as Actions.

2. Insert the following code into the first frame of the Actions layer:

File: **try-catch.fla**   Actions : 1

```
var infoVars = new LoadVars ();
infoVars.onLoad = function (ok)
{
  try
  {
    if (!ok)
    {
      throw new Error ("File Not Loaded");
    }
    for (i = 0; this["note" + (i + 1)] != undefined; i++)
    {
      // Handle each note
    }
    if (i < 5)
    {
      throw new Error ("Data Length (" + i + ") Incorrect");
    }
  }
  catch (dataError)
  {
    trace (dataError);
  }
};
infoVars.load ("notes.txt");
```

3. Save your work and preview it in Flash.

An error message will be displayed in the Output Panel because the sample `notes.txt` file contains only four notes.

Within the `onLoad` event handler for the `infoVars` object, we've used a try-catch block in which two `if` statements are set up to detect exceptional circumstances and throw `Error` objects if they occur. The first check determines whether or not the data has been loaded successfully from the external text file. If the check fails—for example, if the text file doesn't exist or, if the file name is wrong—an `Error` object containing the message "File Not Loaded" is thrown.

```
if (!ok)
{
  throw new Error ("File Not Loaded");
}
```

When the error is thrown, control is passed to the `catch` block.

```
catch (dataError)
{
  trace (dataError);
}
```

The `dataError` variable receives the `Error` object. By passing it to the `trace` function, we can send the message it contains to the Output Panel.

The second `if` statement checks to see that the file contains at least five notes by checking the counter variable (`i`) used in the preceding `for` loop.

```
if (i < 5)
{
  throw new Error ("Data Length (" + i + ") Incorrect");
}
```

Using try-catch blocks can help clean up your code, and make building robust applications less of a hassle.

Using the Flash Debugger

There is no better way to find out exactly what your application is doing than with the help of the Flash Debugger. The Debugger Panel is a constantly updated list of the static and dynamic movie clips within the Flash Player. It can be used to view and modify variables at runtime, monitor and modify movie clip properties (during the debugging session only), and monitor the execution of your Action-Script code line by line.

Although the Debugger can be used remotely on the server, the focus here is on local debugging.

To preview a movie in debug mode, press **Ctrl-Shift-Enter** (**Command-Shift-Enter** on Mac), rather than **Ctrl-Enter**, which allows you to preview movies normally. This opens the Debugger Panel and pauses the movie, ready to start debugging. The Debugger is a powerful tool that will save you time by identifying problems in your code, although it can't fix them automatically.

Harnessing the Power of the Debugger

You can debug any Flash document that holds content. A set of tabs appears within the debugger; let's take a little time to understand what each does.

Variables Tab

The Variables tab shows you the names and values of both global and timeline variables. It allows you even to edit the values of variables as the movie runs.

Figure 9.3. View variables within the Debugger Panel's Variables tab.

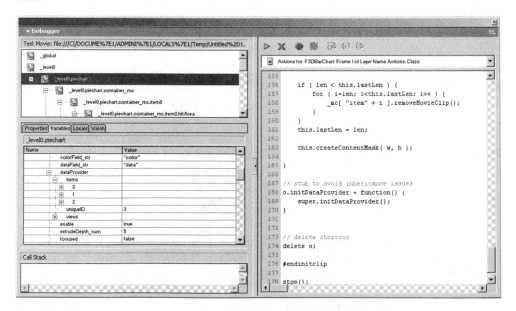

Displaying a given variable value is as simple as selecting the movie clip from the display list, then clicking the Variables tab, as shown in Figure 9.3, to display the clip's variables and their values.

Testing the effect of changing a variable's value is accomplished much more efficiently in the Debugger than in ActionScript. To change the value of a variable, simply double-click it and enter the new value. This affects the movie immediately.

Locals Tab

The Locals tab is a little different. It displays the names of local variables available when a movie is stopped, paused within a function, or stepping in, out, or through a given function. We'll see how the breakpoints, "Step In," "Step Out," and "Step Over" are used within the debugger a little later in this chapter.

Properties Tab

This is used to view the properties of movie clips within an application. It allows you directly to edit any values that aren't read-only and view the results.

Watch Tab

TheWatch tab is valuable when working with large applications that contain many variables, movie clips, and buttons. Watches allow you easily to track variables and their values—even those that exist within the application only briefly. Importantly, Watches let you monitor the states of variables you think may be causing problems.

The Anatomy of the Debugger

Figure 9.4 provides a quick overview of the Debuger Panel's main features.

Figure 9.4. The Debugger offers a number of helpful debugging controls.

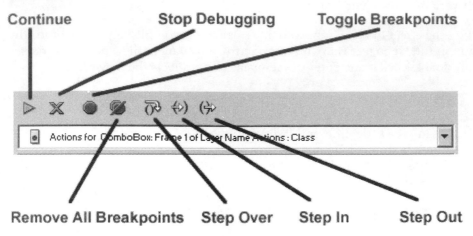

When you play a movie in debug mode and hit a breakpoint, the Debugger Panel displays the section of code in which the breakpoint is located, with a yellow arrow in the left margin indicating its exact location, as shown in Figure 9.5. At that point, the movie is frozen and you can control the code's execution using the buttons at the top of the script pane. Let's look at some of them now.

❑ Clicking the Continue button plays the movie in debug mode until another breakpoint is reached.

❑ Stop Debugging stops the debugging of the current movie, but continues to play it within the Flash Player.

❑ Clicking Step Over advances the execution point past a line of code. Typically, you'd use Step Over to skip a function call. The code within the current line will run normally (including any function calls it contains), and execution will stop at the next line.

❑ Clicking Step In advances the execution point to the next line of code unless the current line contains a function call, in which case the execution point moves to the first line of that function.

❑ Clicking Step Out tells the debugger to finish running the current function call and return to the code that called it, advancing to the next line.

Figure 9.5. A typical view of the debugger window with execution stopped between two breakpoints.

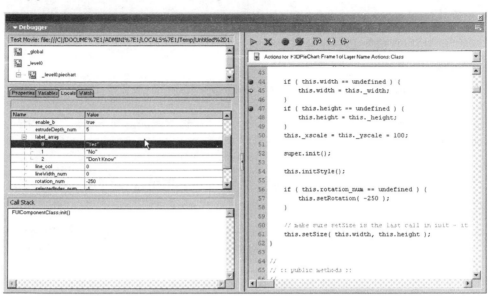

Tiptoe Through the Code

A feature I often use with the Debugger Panel is breakpoints. Breakpoints mark locations at which you may want to stop the movie, providing an excellent opportunity for identifying problems within complex conditional statements. Using breakpoints can prove quicker and easier than scattering `trace` calls throughout your code, especially in complex applications.

The quickest way to add a breakpoint in the Debugger Panel is as follows:

1. Select a section of code from the drop-down list in the right-hand section of the Debugger Panel.

2. Scroll to a line at which you wish to insert a breakpoint.

3. Click in the line's left-hand margin.

You can click the breakpoint again to remove it or, alternatively, use the buttons above the script pane to Set Breakpoint, Remove Breakpoint or Remove All Breakpoints.

You can also add and remove breakpoints in the Actions Panel while you're working on the movie.

Once you've added the breakpoints, press the Continue button above the script pane and the Flash Player will stop at the first breakpoint you defined.

Broken breakpoints

Breakpoints in empty lines of code or within comments will be ignored.

Let's experiment with this a little using the previous example. Locate and open `try-catch.fla` within the code archive. This example also uses `notes.txt`, which is in the code archive. Place it in the same directory as the movie.

1. Preview the movie in Debug Mode (**Ctrl-Shift-Enter** (Win) or **Command-Shift-Enter** (Mac)).

2. In the Debugger Panel, select Actions for Scene 1: Frame 1 of Layer Name Actions from the drop-down list. Add breakpoints at lines six and 14 (the two `if` statements) by clicking in the left-hand margin.

3. Click the Continue button (the green arrow) to start debugging.

Execution stops at the first breakpoint and a yellow arrow appears over its icon, as shown in Figure 9.6.

Figure 9.6. Setting breakpoints within the Debugger Panel is easy.

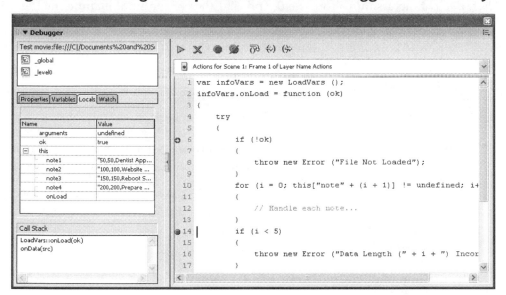

To follow the execution of the code, you can now choose one of the three Step... buttons. As the current line doesn't contain a function call, both Step Over and Step Into will advance execution to the next significant line of code (line ten in this case, assuming the text file was loaded successfully). Step Out would normally allow execution to proceed to the end of the current function (the onLoad event handler), but in this case it will stop at the second breakpoint. The same thing would happen if you resumed execution by clicking the green arrow.

Try the different options available at the two breakpoints to see how you can move through the code. Keep an eye on the location of the yellow arrow pointer that indicates the current position.

Tracking Data in Complex Conditions and Functions

Complex code with lots of data branching can be prone to bugs. A typical scenario is the validation of form fields.

In this example, we'll write some code to ensure that users have entered more than five characters into a form field, and that the content is alphanumeric (i.e., it contains no special characters).

To modify this example, locate `validation.fla` in the code archive.

Setting the Scene

1. Create a new Flash document and accept the default frame rate.

2. Change the name of Layer1 to Actions and add a second layer named Text.

3. Drag an instance of the `TextInput` component from the UI Components section of the Components Panel into the Text layer, naming the instance `inputField`.

Adding the ActionScript

4. Select the first frame of the Actions layer and add the following code to the Actions Panel:

File: **validation.fla**   Actions : 1

```
inputField.change = function ()
{
  if (!checkLength (this.text) || !isAlphaNumeric (this.text))
  {
    trace ("Validation error.");
  }
};
inputField.addEventListener ("change", inputField);
function checkLength (stringToCheck)
{
  return stringToCheck.length >= 5;
}
function isAlphaNumeric (stringToCheck)
{
  for (var i = 0; i < stringToCheck.length; i++)
  {
    if (!isNumber (stringToCheck.charAt (i)) &&
        !isLetter (stringToCheck.charAt (i)))
    {
      return false;
    }
  }
```

```
  return true;
}
function isNumber (character)
{
  return character >= '0' && character <= '9';
}
function isLetter (character)
{
  return character >= 'a' && character <= 'z' ||
     character >= 'A' && character <= 'Z';
}
```

5.   Preview the movie.

By now, the code of this example should be familiar. Whenever the value in the text field is changed, a message is displayed in the Output Panel if the new value is not at least five characters long and entirely alphanumeric.

What's important here is not how the validation code works, but how we can move through it using the debugger.

Using the Debugger to Follow Logical Process Flow

Instead of previewing the movie using the normal method (Control > Test Movie), let's preview it in debug mode.

6.   Select Control > Debug Movie to start the preview.

7.   From the Script Navigation drop-down menu, select Actions for Scene 1: Frame 1 of Layer Name Actions.

The code we added to the Actions layer now appears in the Script Window, ready for debugging.

8.   Add breakpoints at the first line of both validation functions, checkLength and isAlphaNumeric. These are lines 11 and 15 in the example in the code archive, as shown in Figure 9.7.

Figure 9.7. Add breakpoints to code in debug mode.

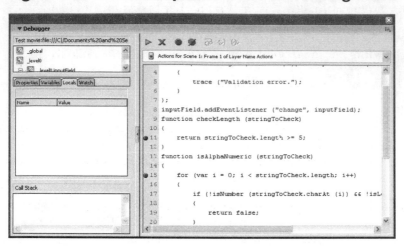

9. Select the `_global` movie and click the Variables tab so you can watch the variables change as the code is processed.

10. Click the Continue button (the green arrow) to start playing the movie.

11. Type an alphanumeric value (e.g., "a") into the input field in the movie.

Every time the value of the content in the input field changes, the `change` event handler is triggered. This calls the `checkLength` function and (if the value is at least five characters long) the `isAlphaNumeric` function.

Notice that a yellow arrow appears at the first breakpoint, in `checkLength`. This line checks the length of the string in the text field and returns true or false. As there's no function call on this line, and because this is the last line in the current function, Step Over, Step In and Step Out all do the same thing.

12. Click the Step In button.

The arrow moves to the line of the `change` event handler that calls `trace` to output the validation error message (line 5). The string in the text field is less than five characters long, so `checkLength` returns false and the `if` statement condition (line 3) is satisfied without even having to call `isAlphaNumeric`. (This is called **short-circuit execution**.)

13. Click the Continue button to resume normal execution.

The message "Validation error." will appear in the Output Panel. The movie is once again running normally, waiting for another breakpoint to be hit.

14. Remove the breakpoint in the `checkLength` function by clicking on the corresponding red breakpoint icon in the margin of the code listing.

15. Type four more alphanumeric characters (e.g. "aaaa") into the text field.

For each of the second, third, and fourth characters, the message "Validation error." will again appear in the Output Panel. When you type the fifth character, however, execution stops at the breakpoint within `isAlphaNumeric` (line 15). For the first time, `checkLength` has returned true, and `isAlphaNumeric` has been called to determine the outcome of the condition for the `if` statement on line 3.

This first line is a `for` loop, with no function calls in it, so Step Over and Step In will do the same thing.

16. Click Step Over or Step In. The yellow arrow will advance to the first line of code within the loop (line 17).

This line contains two function calls: one to `isNumber` and one to `isLetter`.

17. Click the Step In button to step into the function calls on this line. The execution point moves to the first (and only) line of `isNumber`.

18. Click Step Over or Step In again. The execution point moves to the first line of `isLetter`.

19. Click Step Over or Step In again. With the function calls complete, execution returns to `isAlphaNumeric`.

When the first letter of the string is alphanumeric, the condition of the `if` statement on line 17 will be false, and the `for` loop surrounding it will execute again for the second character in the string. The execution point should be back on the `if` statement.

20. Click Step Over to step over any function calls in the current line of code.

The `for` loop loops again, and the execution point again sits on the `if` statement. At a casual glance, however, you might not be sure that anything has actually happened. How can you monitor the progress of the `for` loop?

21. Click on the Locals tab to view variables in the local scope (in this case, the `isAlphaNumeric` function).

On the list of variables, you'll see the `i` variable. If you followed precisely the steps to this point, its value should be 2.

22. Click Continue and normal execution resumes.

Let's try one last thing to see how the Step Out button works:

23. Add a non-alphanumeric character (e.g. "#") to the end of the string currently in the text field.

Execution again ceases at the start of `isAlphaNumeric`. This time, since we have a non-alphanumeric string in the field, we can predict that it will eventually return false. Let's skip ahead to see what happens *after* this function finishes doing its thing.

24. Click the Step Out button to skip to the first line that runs after the current function finishes executing.

The execution point lands on the call to `trace` in the `change` event handler, confirming our prediction that `isAlphaNumeric` returns false.

25. Click Stop Debugging to allow the movie to continue running normally until you're ready to close it.

Debugging Applications with Watches

If you've added components to an application or you have many variables floating around at runtime, you may be overwhelmed by a huge list of variables when you preview the movie in debug mode. Sifting through these variables to find one you want can take a long time, especially if you've forgotten or don't know its name.

If you wish to check only a few variables in a movie, then watches represent a quick means to keep track of them. To add a watch, identify the targeted variable within the debugger's Variables tab, right-click, and select Watch to add it to the Watch tab.

Conclusion

The quickest way to eradicate bugs from your applications is to avoid coding bugs in the first place. But even experienced programmers often introduce at least a bug or two while developing a project.

In this chapter, we covered the nature of syntax errors and how to address them, and discussed how to track down more evasive bugs using the Debugger Panel. We also explored inline methods of revealing error information using `Error` objects and the `trace` function.

When problems in your code reduce or stop the functionality of an application, use the techniques outlined here to address and resolve them.

10 Miscellaneous Effects

Experimentation is the key to discovering exciting new techniques in Flash. Delve into the unknown and, very quickly, you'll find yourself creating startling effects.

This chapter is designed to provide jumping-off points from which you can springboard into some of the lesser-known areas of Flash development. We'll look at using CSS, experience firsthand the awesome power of Flash charting, and finally discuss optimizing a Flash project for search engine placement.

CSS in Flash

Cascading Style Sheets (CSS) in Flash? You think I'm kidding, right? Not at all! While building the latest incarnation of Flash, the development team must really have listened to users, because Flash MX 2004 makes importing and harnessing the power of external CSS files nearly as simple as it is in Dreamweaver MX 2004.

You can format text elements and even use external CSS files to change color, fonts, and layout characteristics efficiently.

In this example, we'll take some HTML text and couple it with externally referenced CSS definitions. The results of this simple yet effective technique are shown in Figure 10.1.

Figure 10.1. CSS can be used in your projects easily and efficiently.

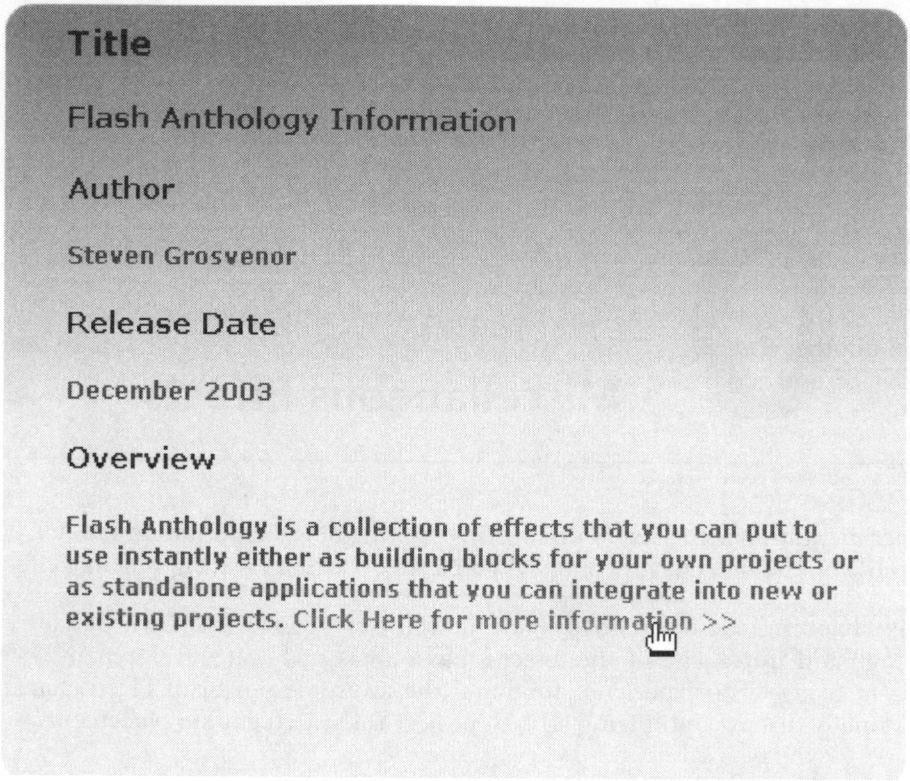

Title

Flash Anthology Information

Author

Steven Grosvenor

Release Date

December 2003

Overview

Flash Anthology is a collection of effects that you can put to use instantly either as building blocks for your own projects or as standalone applications that you can integrate into new or existing projects. Click Here for more information >>

The source files you'll need are `flash.css` and `css.fla`, both of which are in the code archive.

Setting the Scene

1. Create a new Flash document that's 555 pixels wide and 410 pixels high; accept the default frame rate and click OK.

2. Rename the default layer as Actions and, below it, add two layers named Text and Background.

3. In the Text layer, create a new 420 x 370 pixel dynamic text field and position it centrally on the stage. Name the instance cssText.

4. As in previous examples, add a background to frame the text box (see Figure 10.1). A rounded rectangle with a nice gradient will do the trick.

5. Select the `cssText` dynamic text field, use the Property Inspector to change the Line Type to Multiline, and select the Render Text as HTML button.

Don't Embed Font Outlines

Clicking the Character... button in the Property Inspector, and selecting Embed Font Outlines For will render the text invisible. To display CSS-formatted, HTML-generated text, the Flash plug-in must be left free to use the fonts available on the local machine, not embedded font outlines.

Don't bother changing any of the character attributes; we'll create the formatting with CSS and add the content dynamically. Let's now build a CSS file containing some custom styles.

Creating the CSS

You can create CSS files in either a text editor (Notepad for PC and BBEdit for Mac are popular), or in a full-blown CSS editor. I prefer TopStyle 3.0 from Bradbury Software[1], as it offers an excellent range of features and provides great visual feedback.

Let's start assigning CSS styles to the commonly supported HTML tags that will appear within our text field.

6. Open your CSS editor and add the following code:

File: **flash.css**

```
h1 {
  color: #8B0000;
  font-family: Verdana, Geneva, Arial, Helvetica, sans-serif;
  font-weight: bold;
  font-size: 18px;
}
h2 {
  color: #8B0000;
  font-family: Verdana, Geneva, Arial, Helvetica, sans-serif;
  font-weight: bold;
  font-size: 15px;
```

[1] http://www.bradsoft.com/

```
}
p {
  color: #595959;
  font-family: Verdana, Geneva, Arial, Helvetica, sans-serif;
  font-weight: bold;
  font-size: 12px;
}
a:link {
  color: #778899;
  text-decoration: underline;
}
a:hover{
  color: #FF4500;
  text-decoration: none;
}
```

7. Save the file as `flash.css`.

If you're familiar with CSS, there should be nothing surprising here. We start by declaring the properties of the top-level headings and subheadings:

```
h1 {
  color: #8B0000;
  font-family: Verdana, Geneva, Arial, Helvetica, sans-serif;
  font-weight: bold;
  font-size: 18px;
}
h2 {
  color: #8B0000;
  font-family: Verdana, Geneva, Arial, Helvetica, sans-serif;
  font-weight: bold;
  font-size: 15px;
}
```

Limited Support for CSS Syntax

If you're experienced with CSS, you may want to combine the properties common to the h1 and h2 tags into a single rule and then declare their differences separately.

```
h1, h2 {
  color: #8B0000;
  font-family: Verdana, Geneva, Arial, Helvetica,
sans-serif;
  font-weight: bold;
```

```
}
h1 {
   font-size: 18px;
}
h2 {
   font-size: 15px;
}
```

Unfortunately, CSS support in Flash is still in its infancy. The first rule in this code will be ignored, since compound selectors (such as `h1, h2`) are not supported.

Next, we define our standard text style, which we apply to paragraph tags.

```
p {
   color: #595959;
   font-family: Verdana, Geneva, Arial, Helvetica, sans-serif;
   font-weight: bold;
   font-size: 12px;
}
```

Finally, we style our links, using CSS pseudo-classes to alter their appearance when the mouse is over them:

```
a:link {
   color: #778899;
   text-decoration: underline;
}
a:hover {
   color: #FF4500;
   text-decoration: none;
}
```

Let's now import our style sheet into Flash.

Adding the ActionScript

The code for this example is quite straightforward, using the built-in `TextField.StyleSheet` class.

8. Select the first frame of the Actions layer and add the following code to the Actions Panel:

File: **css.fla**   Actions : 1

```
var css = new TextField.StyleSheet ();
var cssFile = "flash.css";
css.onLoad = function (loaded)
{
  if (loaded)
  {
    renderText ();
  }
};
css.load (cssFile);
function renderText ()
{
  cssText.styleSheet = css;
  cssText.text = "<h1>Title</h1>" +
    "<h2>Flash Anthology Information</h2>" +
    "<h2>Author</h2>" +
    "<p>Steven Grosvenor</p>" +
    "<h2>Release Date</h2>" +
    "<p>December 2004</p>" +
    "<h2>Overview</h2>" +
    "<p>Flash Anthology is a collection of effects that " +
    "you can put to use instantly either as building " +
    "blocks for your own projects or as standalone " +
    "applications that you can integrate into new or " +
    "existing projects. " +
    "<a href='http://www.sitepoint.com/books/'>Click " +
    "Here for more information &gt;&gt;</a></p>";
}
```

Let's review how this works. We begin by creating the `css` variable, into which we place an instance of the `Textfield.StyleSheet` class. We then set another variable to store the name of our CSS file (`cssFile`).

```
var css = new TextField.StyleSheet ();
var cssFile = "flash.css";
```

Next, we set up the `onLoad` event handler for the object, which calls `renderText` when the file has loaded successfully, and load the file.

```
css.onLoad = function (loaded)
{
  if (loaded)
  {
    renderText ();
```

```
    }
};
css.load (cssFile);
```

Within the `renderText` function, we apply our style sheet to the `cssText` object and then display the text.

```
function renderText ()
{
  cssText.styleSheet = css;
  cssText.text = "<h1>Title<br /></h1>" +
    "<h2>Flash Anthology Information<br /></h2>" +
    "<h2>Author<br /></h2>" +
    "<p>Steven Grosvenor<br /></p>" +
    "<h2>Release Date<br /></h2>" +
    "<p>December 2004<br /></p>" +
    "<h2>Overview<br /></h2>" +
    "<p>Flash Anthology is a collection of effects that " +
    "you can put to use instantly either as building " +
    "blocks for your own projects or as standalone " +
    "applications that you can integrate into new or " +
    "existing projects. " +
    "<a href='http://www.sitepoint.com/books/'>Click " +
    "here for more information &gt;&gt;</a></p>";
}
```

9. Save the document and preview your work.

Notice how the HTML-generated text appears exactly as specified by our CSS rules. Cool, huh?

Supported Properties

HTML purists may take exception to the liberal use of **br** tags to add spacing between the blocks in the above example. Unfortunately, Flash does not support the margin or padding properties that would be required to add this spacing the correct way.

Flash supports only the following CSS properties:

❑ `text-align`

❑ `font-size`

❑ `text-decoration`

- ❏ `margin-left`

- ❏ `margin-right`

- ❏ `font-style`

- ❏ `font-weight`

- ❏ `text-indent`

- ❏ `font-family`

- ❏ `color`

- ❏ `display`

Charting in Flash

This example shows you how dynamically to assign information to the F3D Pie Chart component found in Flash Charting Components Set 2, which is part of the Macromedia Developer Resource Kit 5, an add-on package available for Flash.

This is not a contrived example: this application is actually produced by the company I work for. As part of a larger project, we're building a digital dashboard of information, fed by SQL Server 2000 and XML within an ASP.NET framework.

The simple nature of the charting component set belies the power of the components it contains. When the component is installed, you need only glance at the reference panel to see the full range of events and properties it places at your fingertips. Several lines of code are all that's required to create the effect shown in Figure 10.2, as Flash again allows you to reference external data sources for information as required.

As this is a commercial set of components, I won't be able to give you a source file for this example. However, you can easily apply the techniques and Action-Script shown here if you purchase it.

Figure 10.2. Use chart components to create charts quickly and easily.

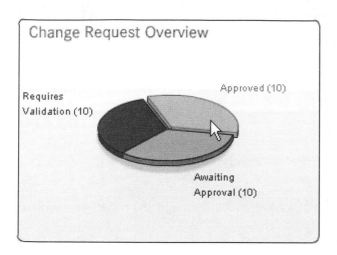

Setting the Scene

1. Create a new Flash document that's 300 pixels wide and 220 pixels high; accept the default frame rate, and click OK.

2. Rename the default layer as Actions and add four layers beneath it, naming them Text, Content, Background, and Frame.

3. Select the first frame of the Frame layer and add a framing rectangle to contain the effect. As before, a simple rounded rectangle with a faint gradient should be all you need.

4. Select the first frame of the Content layer and, having installed the component from the Resource Kit, drag an instance of the `F3DPieChart` component from the Flash Charting Components 2 section of the Components Panel to the stage, positioning it centrally. Name the instance serverLoad.

We don't need to add any data or labels within the Component Inspector; we'll do that with ActionScript.

5. Add a title for the effect in the Text layer.

6. Add any additional decorations you would like to the Background layer.

   In the example shown in Figure 10.2, I added a solid fill ellipse, selected it, then chose Modify > Shape > Soften Fill Edges... to create a subtle shadow under the pie chart.

Now, let's add the ActionScript to get the effect up and running.

Adding the ActionScript

The ActionScript for this effect is straightforward, as most of the hard work is done behind the scenes by the component itself. We just need to supply it with data to display, and provide the labels and colors for the pie chart's slices. Sound simple? It is!

7. Select the first frame of the Actions layer and add the following code to the Actions Panel:

File: **charting.fla**   Actions : 1

```
var intTechValid = 10;
var intNoRequests = 10;
var intAwaitingRequests = 10;
function PopulateChart ()
{
  serverLoad.addItem ({
    data:_root.intTechValid,
    color:0x990000,
    label:"Requires \nValidation (" + _root.intTechValid +
    ")"});
  serverLoad.addItem ({
    data:_root.intNoRequests,
    color:0xFF9900,
    label:"Awaiting \nApproval (" + _root.intNoRequests +
    ")"});
  serverLoad.addItem ({
    data:_root.intAwaitingRequests,
    color:0x6699FF,
    label:"Approved (" + _root.intAwaitingRequests + ")"});
}
var selectListener = new Object ();
selectListener.onSelect = function ()
{
  getURL ("http://www.sitepoint.com/", "_self");
};
```

```
serverLoad.addListener (selectListener);
PopulateChart ();
```

We populate variables with data so we can create the pie chart. In the real world, this data wouldn't be hard-coded, but would instead be retrieved by any number of methods outlined in Chapter 8.

```
var intTechValid = 10;
var intNoRequests = 10;
var intAwaitingRequests = 10;
```

We then add a listener and attach it to the `serverLoad` pie chart component to detect clicks on any of the slices.

```
var selectListener = new Object ();
selectListener.onSelect = function ()
{
  getURL ("http://www.sitepoint.com/", "_self");
};
serverLoad.addListener (selectListener);
```

In this example, we simply send the user off to a URL; in the real world, you would likely move through a series of other actions.

Next, we trigger the `PopulateChart` function to feed the data into the pie chart component.

```
PopulateChart ();
```

Within `PopulateChart` we employ the `addItem` method to populate the label, data, and color properties of the pie chart component.

```
chartInstance.addItem({data:data, label:label, color:color});
```

Here's the completed code for one of the chart slices:

```
serverLoad.addItem ({
   data:_root.intTechValid,
   color:0x990000,
   label:"Requires \nValidation (" + _root.intTechValid + ")"});
```

For the data, we pass the variable as a raw number to control the slice area. We also include this in a descriptive string for the label, and pass a color value for the slice.

This creates the following data label for the slice. Note that , \n forces the start of a new line.

```
Requires
Validation (10)
```

8. Save and preview the document.

I told you the effect was quick! Doesn't it look great? You can add information to the movie as required, to deal with more incoming variables.

Through subtle modification of the code and use of the Reference Panel, you can change the component from a pie chart to a bar chart or any of the other charts in the set. You could even provide users with a drop-down menu, dynamically showing and hiding the different types of charts available based on their selections.

Getting Indexed by Search Engines

While this is not an "effect" as such, it's important to understand the role of search engines when creating content that's destined for the Web.

If you've spent weeks creating a Flash Website with all the bells and whistles, you're losing out if search engines can't see it. There's no point having a killer site if no one knows it exists. Approximately one-third of the traffic to my own sites comes from referring sites (i.e., sites that link to mine), another third from "blind" visits (i.e., with no referrer), and the final third from search engines such as Google and Yahoo!

When developing sites that are embedded in HTML Web pages, you should spend some time creating architecture that will allow search engines easily to retrieve and catalogue your content. There are several ways to achieve this, the most common of which are outlined below.

meta Tags

meta tags, such the as keywords and description tags, allow you to present basic site information to the search engines. They're an important element in obtaining valuable exposure for your Website. Typically, you need to submit your site to search engines; some services are free, but be prepared to pay for submissions.

Each engine uses a different method to rank Web pages, so there's no hard and fast rule for achieving a high ranking. Here are some factors that can positively influence your position:

Wording in page body

Relevant and effectively presented content will help spiders (the automated scripts that crawl sites) to rank your site as a whole, and as individual pages.

`title` tag

While the `title` tag isn't used as extensively as it was a few years ago, it's still valued by some of the major players.

`meta name="keywords"` tag

The importance of this tag in determining rank is in decline. It's actually been dropped by several major search engines due to user abuse.

`meta name="description"` tag

This tag is used to produce a description of your documents for display on search result pages.

Flash content

If your site is predominantly Flash-based, the content within the SWF file(s) will be ignored by spiders. Publishing your movie with File > Publish will automatically create an HTML page in which the SWF file is embedded along with extra information (including text and URLs) above the movie's `object` tag. Of course this will not take into account any external content sources you may reference within the movie.

Links

The more people who link to you, the better. Most search engines assume that a site that attracts links offers valuable content.

If you present predominantly Flash content to the world, be sure to add relevant `title` tags and `keywords` and `description` `meta` tags to the source code of your HTML pages, such as the following:

```
<head>
<title> Add Sharp and To The Point Titles To Your Pages </title>
<meta name="description"
    content="An Interesting and Concise Description" />
<meta name="keywords"
    content="Keywords, relevant to your site, separated, by a
        comma, they can be singular words or phrases" />
</head>
```

```
<body>
Flash Content goes here
</body>
```

As a real world example, here's some of the `meta` information for my site, Phireworx.com.

```
<title>Phireworx :: Sparks the Imagination</title>
<meta name="description" content="Phireworx is the only place to
    come for creative and useful commands for Macromedia
    Fireworks, Flash and Dreamweaver, join our community and
    download the sets!" />
<meta name="keywords" content="Phireworx, Fireworks, Commands,
    Keap, Creative, Plugins, Plug-ins, Juno, Foto, Super Guides,
    Isometric, Axonometric, Dimetric, Projection, Illustration,
    Bitmap Manipulation, Vector, Fireworks MX, Flash MX,
    Dreamweaver MX, Components, Extensions, Extension, Command,
    Commands" />
```

For more on search engine optimization of Flash, check out James Ellis's excellent article, *Accessible Flash*[2].

Macromedia Flash Search Engine Software Development Kit (SDK)

Macromedia has released an SDK that converts Flash text, links, and other information into a HTML format for easy indexing by search engines. The SDK is quite complex, and is designed for advanced developers and software engineers. It can be found here:

http://www.macromedia.com/software/flash/download/search_engine/

Conclusion

Well, that's it. I feel rather sad to be wrapping up. There will be no more lonely nights and weekends with just my PC and a copy of Flash MX 2004 Professional to keep me company! Seriously though, formulating the examples for this book has been a very satisfying experience, and some of the effects are truly amazing. I hope you'll find that every one of them has an important real-world application.

---

[2] http://www.sitepoint.com/article/accessible-flash-parts-1-2

We've covered lots of ground, and now it's time for you to go out and conjure some gret Flash creations. Remember, the key to broadening you understanding and developing successfully in Flash is one simple thing—*experimentation*.

Enjoy the book and enjoy this phenomenal piece of software!

Resource Sites for Flash

Hey, there are some excellent Flash resource sites out there, many of which offer a wealth of other information, too. Many of those listed below represent valuable sources of information for those developing and designing in Flash. Others are purely inspirational!

Community MX

> http://www.communitymx.com/

> The site is loaded with fantastic information and real-world examples—it simply must not be missed. A great site offering articles, tutorials, and extensions.

Phireworx

> http://www.phireworx.com/

> My own site (Phireworx) is a resource site with a difference: not only does it offer interesting articles on Flash, Fireworks, and Dreamweaver, it also offers a series of commercial and non-commercial extensions for Fireworks MX 2004. The site includes many time-saving extensions, ranging from mild to wild to suit your needs, and an extensibility forum for more inquisitive developers.

Oscar Trelles's Flash Blog and Components

> http://www.oscartrelles.com/

> Oscar was the expert reviewer for this book. His site has some great pre-loading components, as well as an extremely well-informed and interesting Flash blog.

Moluv's Picks

> http://www.moluv.com/

> Once you've been to this site, you'll keep coming back! It lists some brilliant and the not-so brilliant Flash sites, and accepts the submission of URLs to sites that users feel are noteworthy.

Flash Kit

http://www.flashkit.com/

One of the granddaddy Flash sites, Flash Kit offers tutorials and source files categorized by area. The site has been going for many years and is an established source of top-notch information.

Joshua Davis Studios

http://www.joshuadavis.com/

An excellent resource site if you're ever wondering what can be accomplished by high-end Flash applications.

Computer Arts

http://www.computerarts.co.uk/

Computer Arts is a UK-based design magazine with excellent tutorials for Flash and other Macromedia products.

Brendan Dawes

http://www.brendandawes.com/headshop/

This excellent resource site rom the author of "Drag Slide Fade" displays many experimental and cutting-edge effects.

Index

F

resizing video clips, scaling alternative, 274
reusability
  advantage of scripted effects, 9
  captured video footage, 251
reverb.mp3 file, 206
rich Internet applications using screens, 312
rollover effects (*see* mouseover effects)
_root keyword, ActionScript, 10
rotating text (*see* circulating text effect)
rotation direction, reversing, 162
rotation speed
  varying with mouse position, 199
  varying, circular menu example, 61
roundNumber function
  mini sound player modification, 217
  random movie loader, 272
  random track overlay effect, 225
rulers, switching on, 37
running tap video simulation, 289
runtime errors, 396

S

SaveSelection function, News Sweeper application, 384
saveSelection function, questionnaire form example, 352
scalability of ActionScript, 21
  scripted animations, 92
ScaleDown method
  zooming text effect, 153–154
ScaleDown method, zooming text effect, 153–154
scaling objects
  according to cursor proximity, 191
  horizontal scaling of jiggling text, 147
  linking to sound volume, 206
  Math.cos function use, 207
  random variation, 100

registration points and, 192
  vertical scaling, 207
  video clips before importing, 274
scaling variable, 3D barrel roll effect, 198
ScheduleTrigger function, zooming text effect, 154
Screen Outline Pane, Flash MX 2004 Professional, 294, 298
ScreenJumper application (*see* form–based navigation)
script navigator pane, 19
script pinning, 19
scripted questionnaire, 341
scripting
  (*see also* ActionScript; server-side scripting)
  function libraries, 92
scrolling navigation systems, 32
Scrubber components, 282
SDK (Software Development Kit) for search engine accessibility, 428
search engines, achieving listing by, 426–428
  Macromedia SDK, 428
secure.php script, login form, 322
secure.swf movie, login form, 314
security model, Flash MX 2004, 4
seek method, NetStream class, 267
send method, LocalConnection class, 366
sendAndLoad method, LoadVars class, 317
  alternatives to, 369
server-side scripting
  breadcrumb.php, 357
  introducing external data with, 355
  online examples, 362, 368, 372
server-side validation
  example, 311
  introduced, 297

Also available from sitepoint.com

Visit http://www.sitepoint.com/books/
for sample chapters or to order!

Build Your Own

Database Driven Website

Using PHP & MySQL

By Kevin Yank

A Practical Step-by-Step Guide

HTML Utopia:

Designing Without Tables

Using CSS

By Dan Shafer

A Practical Step-by-Step Guide

The PHP Anthology

Volume I: Foundations

By Harry Fuecks

Practical Solutions to Common Problems

Covers
MSDE/SQL
and ACCESS!

Build Your Own
ASP.NET Website
Using C# & VB.NET

By Zak Ruvalcaba

A Practical Step-by-Step Guide